CAPTAIN'S DINNER

Also by Adam Cohen

American Pharaoh: Mayor Richard J. Daley: His Battle for Chicago and the Nation

The Perfect Store: Inside eBay

Nothing to Fear: FDR's Inner Circle and the Hundred Days That Created Modern America

Imbeciles: The Supreme Court, American Eugenics, and the Sterilization of Carrie Buck

Supreme Inequality: The Supreme Court's Fifty-Year Battle for a More Unjust America

CAPTAIN'S DINNER

A Shipwreck, an Act of Cannibalism, and a Murder Trial That Changed Legal History

Adam Cohen

Authors Equity
1123 Broadway, Suite 1008
New York, New York 10010

Cover design by John Fontana
Cover art: *Stormy Sea* by Eugene Amus © A. Dagli Orti / © NPL—DeA Picture Library / Bridgeman Images
Book design by Scribe Inc.

We gratefully acknowledge the sources credited beneath images in the insert. Uncredited images are in the public domain.

Most Authors Equity books are available at a discount when purchased in quantity for sales promotions or corporate use. Special editions, which include personalized covers, excerpts, and corporate imprints, can be created when purchased in large quantities. For more information, please email info@authorsequity.com.

Library of Congress Control Number: 2025943279
Print ISBN 9798893310597
Ebook ISBN 9798893310603

Printed in the United States of America
Third printing

www.authorsequity.com

To all of the cabin boys, literal and otherwise

CONTENTS

At his best, man is the noblest of all animals; separated from the law and justice he is the worst.

—Aristotle

INTRODUCTION

On September 6, 1884, a German sailing ship pulled into the harbor in Falmouth, England, and deposited three emaciated men who had been to hell and back. Captain Thomas Dudley, first mate Edwin Stephens, and able seaman Edward Brooks had survived a shipwreck in the South Atlantic and drifted for weeks on the open sea in a flimsy wooden lifeboat. They were eventually rescued, and now that they were safely home, they had a shocking story to tell.

In the lifeboat, the three men—and Richard Parker, their seventeen-year-old cabin boy—had no food or water. They were wasting away, their stomachs empty, their mouths parched, and their tongues turning black. In time, Dudley made a grim decision: They would kill the cabin boy so they could survive on his flesh and blood.

Dudley stabbed Parker to death while Stephens looked on, ready to help. Brooks, the conscientious objector of the group, opposed the killing and refused to participate. Once the deed was done, all three men eagerly drank the cabin boy's blood and feasted on his flesh. This grim food supply kept the three survivors alive for a few crucial days, until the German ship, which happened to be sailing by, stopped and took them onboard.

When Dudley, Stephens, and Brooks arrived back in England, they spoke freely about what they had done. They spared no detail—not even about eating Parker's heart and liver while they were still warm. The men expected to be greeted by their countrymen as returning heroes. They were not worried about being charged with a crime for killing Parker, because they had centuries of tradition and legal history on their side.

Sailors had long been killing other sailors in survival conditions. The practice, which was quaintly called "the custom of the sea," had been written about in literature (Lord Byron included it in his famous poem *Don Juan*) and celebrated in popular song. And it was widely accepted as an enduring fact of the seafaring life. In the long history of British sailing, no Englishman had ever been prosecuted for cannibalism at sea. Indeed, it appeared that no citizen of any country ever had been. Dudley, Stephens, and Brooks were sure they would be able to tell their stories to the authorities and then head back home to their families and friends, putting the whole awful ordeal behind them.

They were wrong. To their great shock, the men were arrested and charged with murder, which in England, at the time, carried the death penalty. The top law enforcement officials in London decided to turn the prosecution into a test case, which would decide whether killing and eating people under survival conditions should be allowed or regarded as a capital crime.

What followed was one of the most controversial criminal trials in English history. Dudley, Stephens, and Brooks's many defenders were outraged that there was a trial at all. They insisted that Parker's killing was justified because it was better for one person to die by stabbing than for four to die of hunger and thirst. They also argued that Dudley and Stephens had simply done what they had to do to stay alive, something that should not be a crime. On the other side, the queen's prosecutors maintained that the killing of the cabin boy was nothing less than murder in cold blood. Murder is an absolute wrong, they insisted, and Parker had the right to his own life, whether or not killing him could help keep others alive. They wanted, in the words of a sea captain weighing in on an earlier cannibalism case, to "bring these maneaters to justice."

Queen v. Dudley and Stephens is one of the most famous cases in Western law. It is a fixture of law schools, where it appears in first-year criminal law textbooks and lectures, and it has made a deep impression on generations of students. To lawyers, its greatest significance is the impact it had on the legal definition of murder. English law had long been unclear about whether someone charged with murder could employ a "necessity defense," the claim that a killing was justified because it ended up saving more lives than the one lost. *Dudley and Stephens* helped clarify the law in England, and its influence crossed the Atlantic Ocean and changed the American law of murder as well.

Dudley and Stephens is even more popular with moral philosophers. It makes a prominent appearance, for example, in a Harvard course called "Justice," which has for decades been one of the university's largest and most esteemed courses. It explores the great issues in moral philosophy from ancient times to the present. Professor Michael Sandel's entire second class—one out of twenty-four class hours—is devoted to *Dudley and Stephens*. That is an extraordinary amount of time for a survey of Western philosophy to devote to just one criminal case, but *Dudley and Stephens* is an extraordinary case.

There are many reasons *Dudley and Stephens* has such an oversized presence, beyond its impact on the law of murder. Some of the fascination is due to its dramatic, even cinematic, story line. It begins with the romance of a small band of sailors heading out on an adventure at sea. It proceeds to a dramatic shipwreck and a desperate struggle to stay alive in a tiny lifeboat, a classic battle of man against nature. And it ends with a high-stakes trial and a landmark court ruling.

Then there is the murder itself. It was a premeditated killing among intimates, in which two men ended the life of a boy they knew well, liked, and had been living with in close quarters. It was the sort of chilling act that raises the uncomfortable prospect that even decent people might have no qualms about slitting a friend's neck if they considered it necessary to survive.

Not least, of course, there is the cannibalism. The law is capacious and includes almost every variety of human experience—but it is hard to think of another major legal case about people calmly deciding that they have the right to kill a friend and survive by feeding off his corpse. This aspect of the case has always given it a special kind of dark allure. As Sigmund Freud observed, people are both repelled by and, on some level, drawn to cannibalism.

People have always liked stories about people eating other people. It features prominently in Greek and Roman myths and literature. In their original versions, many fairy tales involved cannibalism. The witch in *Hansel and Gretel* built her house out of cake and candy to lure children into her oven. Readers and movie audiences are drawn to nonfiction stories of cannibalism, such as *Alive*, the account of the Uruguayan rugby players who resorted to eating the corpses of their dead friends after their plane crashed in the Andes.

Cannibalism is also, it must be said, a subject of dark humor. Monty Python did a whole skit about it, "Lifeboat (Cannibalism)," in which the castaways in a lifeboat debate which of them would be the best to eat, until Michael Palin calls for a waitress, who appears from nowhere and takes an order for "leg of Hodges." With *Dudley and Stephens* on the syllabus, probably no group has joked about cannibalism more than law students. I am in no position to pass judgment. My own initial exposure to the case came not in an academic setting—my criminal law class did not study it—but at a "Come as Your Favorite Case or Legal Doctrine" Halloween party that my great friend Paul Engelmayer and I threw in our first year of law school. Engelmayer, who is now a federal judge in New York, dressed as Captain Dudley, with chicken drumsticks hung around his neck and a spattering of fake blood.

But the main reason that *Dudley and Stephens* has been endlessly discussed and debated for more than a century is that when Dudley and his small crew were floating in their tiny lifeboat, they acted out one of the greatest legal and philosophical thought experiments in history. The choice Dudley and Stephens confronted, to kill or not to kill, is among the most fundamental of all moral quandaries. Murder is a central concern of virtually every major religious and ethical belief system, and it is almost always condemned as wrong. The Ten Commandments that Moses received at Mount Sinai contained the injunction "Thou Shalt Not Kill." The Buddha taught of the karmic consequences of killing humans and animals.

Spiritual and moral traditions, however, also contain an array of circumstances in which taking a life may be permissible. Many religions endorse the death penalty. The Bible sets out a range of crimes, including murder and kidnapping, for which capital punishment may be warranted. Religions also sanction, in some cases, killing during war. In Christianity, according to the "just war theory," killing enemy soldiers in battle can be morally justified. In Hinduism, in the *Bhagavad Gita*, the god Krishna advises a warrior king that it is right to lead his soldiers into battle, though it means killing the enemy. Religions also often condone killing in self-defense. According to Exodus, in the words of a modern translation, "when a burglar is caught breaking in, and is fatally beaten, there shall be no charge of manslaughter" (22:2–3). In Islam, the Qur'an says, "Permission [to fight] is given to those against whom fighting is launched, because they have been wronged" (22:39).

Dudley and Stephens presents an especially challenging variation on the question of when killing is justified: When, if ever, is it acceptable to kill someone who fits none of these categorical exceptions—someone who is not a criminal, or an enemy soldier, or posing a threat—simply because killing them would save lives? Or, to put it another way, is it ever acceptable to sacrifice an innocent person because it is "the lesser of two evils"? Philosophers since ancient times have debated the ethics of taking an innocent life to save other lives. The Greek skeptic Carneades of Cyrene put forth a now famous hypothetical of two sailors who survive a shipwreck and swim toward the same floating plank of wood. One sailor grabs hold of the plank, which can only support one of them, and the other sailor, who is stronger, pushes him off, saving himself but drowning the first sailor. The question is whether the second sailor was justified in pushing off the first one to save his own life or whether doing so was murder. The *Dudley and Stephens* case presents this timeless question of when it is moral to kill—when it is moral to *sacrifice* someone—and it asks the question in a particularly pointed way. What happens if a small, close-knit group of people find themselves in a situation in which they may all be about to die but can save themselves by killing one of their group?

It is an intriguing moral dilemma, but it is also something more. It is an almost perfect representation of one of the major fault lines in modern philosophy. The question of whether to kill the cabin boy is a choice between utilitarianism and rights-based theories of morality.

Dudley's rationale for killing Parker was that it would save the lives of the other three people in the lifeboat. That is a classic statement of the utilitarian position, which holds that the morality of an action should be judged not according to some supposedly inherent nature that makes it a "good" or a "bad" act but rather by asking whether it increases the net sum of well-being. Jeremy Bentham, the founder of modern utilitarianism, believed that people should act in ways that promote "the greatest happiness of the greatest number." To adherents of utilitarianism, morality is a calculation. If there are two bad choices, as there appeared to be in the lifeboat—killing one person or waiting for all four to die—utilitarianism favors calculating which choice produces more total good. In this view, killing the cabin boy to save the other three would not only not be wrong; it would be a moral imperative.

On the other side of the debate are people who believe certain acts are categorically wrong and cannot be excused through a cost-benefit analysis. Immanuel Kant, the German Enlightenment philosopher, said "it is an absolute duty" not to take the life of an innocent person who poses no harm. In this view, killing Parker is simply the murder of an innocent boy, an inherently wrong act that cannot be justified by saying it saved other lives.

In the end, England's High Court of Justice decided the case of *Dudley and Stephens* in an opinion by the lord chief justice. Before it was over, the home secretary, England's highest criminal justice official, would weigh in, and so would Queen Victoria. The lord chief justice's opinion did not merely decide the fate of Dudley and Stephens. It took a strong stand on the profound moral issues at the heart of the case. The *Dudley and Stephens* ruling is one of the most influential statements ever made on the eternal debate between individual rights and ideas about the common good.

A great deal followed from the wreck of a small ship. Dudley and Stephens's decision to kill Parker in that wooden lifeboat and eat his flesh would cause a sensation in England and around the world. Their insistence that sacrificing the cabin boy was ethically and legally justified would divide the nation into opposing camps. And the High Court's ruling would leave an indelible mark on Western law and moral philosophy. But before any of this could happen, a wealthy lawyer in Australia had to buy a yacht in London—and hire Captain Dudley to deliver it to him.

I

The Voyage Begins

By 1883, John Henry Want, a prominent Australian lawyer, had achieved an enviable station in life. Sydney, the city where he lived and practiced law, had gotten its start as a British prison colony, but it had put its ignoble origins behind it and emerged as a bustling colonial port. There was now more than enough commercial activity to keep its lawyers busy and prosperous. Want had risen to the upper echelons of wealth and status in Australia, and he was ready to mark his success with a luxury associated with aristocrats and royalty. He was ready to buy himself a yacht.

In an era when ships were mainly used for joyless commercial transport, yachts were the proudly impractical playthings of rich men. In England, Sir Thomas Lipton, the founder of the tea company, was an avid yachtsman. In America, the Vanderbilt and Morgan families raced yachts. Before long, yachting made its way to Australia, where Want's father, Randolf, a lawyer who had emigrated from England, was an early member of the Royal Sydney Yacht Squadron. John Henry Want had followed in his father's wake and was now a yachtsman himself.

The younger Want traveled from Sydney to London in 1883 to go boat shopping. He could afford a yacht, but he was no Lipton or Vanderbilt. The price mattered, and when the London Yacht Agency showed him new and used yachts, he gravitated toward the used ones, which sold at a sizable discount. After considering the wide range of pleasure boats England had to offer, Want put his money down on a sixteen-year-old yacht called the *Mignonette*.

There were some fine things about Want's new yacht. The *Mignonette* was a smart-looking boat that would impress the yachting crowd when Want sailed it in the waters around Sydney. It was a yawl rig, two masted, with the tall mainmast placed far forward and sails that towered sixty feet above the deck—a classic design that called to mind a sailboat in an oil painting. The *Mignonette* was fifty-two feet long and about twelve feet across the beam—the ship's widest point—and was seven and a half feet deep. It had been built at the Aldous shipyard in Brightlingsea, which had a reputation for producing high-quality boats. More notably, the *Mignonette* was registered with the Royal Albert and New Thames yacht clubs, which would give Want bragging rights in Australia's yachting circles.

The *Mignonette* came with a wooden dinghy that could serve as a lifeboat in case of emergency. The dinghy was a few years older than the yacht, but it was in good condition. Its dimensions—thirteen feet long, about four feet in the beam, and twenty inches deep—were not unusual for a lifeboat on a small yacht, but if anyone actually thought about how it might be used in a shipwreck, they would not be reassured. If the *Mignonette* had more than a couple of passengers needing to abandon ship, seating in the dinghy would be tight and room for supplies practically nonexistent. Its low sides would provide almost no protection against a roiling sea. And since it did not have a mast or sail, the castaways would be compelled to row it. Then there was the fact that it was made out of mahogany only about a quarter of an inch thick, barely more substantial than the sides of a cigar box.

The *Mignonette* had one other possible liability: its age. A sixteen-year-old yacht was not terribly old, but it was also far from new. A well-made yacht of that vintage could be in perfectly fine condition, but it also might not be. There was no way to know for certain what toll sixteen years of briny air, salt water, storms at sea, and even collisions with rocks might have taken on a boat, and if there was damage, it might not be visible.

After Want bought the *Mignonette*, he had to get it home to Sydney. Although it was not particularly large, it would not fit as cargo on a bigger ship. That meant it would have to be sailed from England to Australia, a daunting journey of around sixteen thousand miles. There was no telling what towering waves and violent gales it might encounter along the way, not to mention icebergs. The voyage was a challenging one for any boat, even a rugged clipper, but it would be especially difficult for a diminutive yacht.

Want made clear to the yacht agency that he would not be sailing the *Mignonette* to Sydney himself. That was hardly surprising. The voyage would take months, and then there was the fact that it would be dangerous. Victorian England had many dangerous jobs. There were grimy factories where workers were horribly injured by machinery and dusty coal mines where miners died in explosions. Chimney sweeps got trapped in chimneys and suffocated, and ratcatchers trudged through London sewers and contracted loathsome diseases. What these dangerous jobs had in common was that they were almost invariably done by the poor and nearly poor. Lords of the manor and heirs to industrial fortunes did not mine coal, clean chimneys, or catch rats. And wealthy lawyers did not sail sixteen thousand grueling miles to deliver their own yachts. Want bought the *Mignonette* to frolic in the waters off Sydney. The perilous work of delivering it would be handed off to working-class sailors.

The London Yacht Agency announced that it was seeking a captain to deliver the *Mignonette*. There was, however, no great hurry. The *Mignonette* would be stored in Brightlingsea for the winter and would not set sail until the following spring, when the weather and the prevailing winds would be better. That left plenty of time to find a captain and crew sufficiently adventurous—or perhaps *foolhardy* was the right word—to make the trip.

The yacht agency's search for a captain was occurring at a pivotal moment in sailing history: The Age of Sail was drawing to a close. Steamships had been introduced earlier in the century, and they were quickly taking over, replacing the glorious old-style schooners, clippers, square-riggers, and barks that had long ruled the oceans. Maritime historians have a name for this relatively brief transitional moment: "the dying age of sail."

From England's earliest days, sailing was critical to the national lifeblood. The English themselves were seaborne invaders, Angles and Saxons who braved the North Sea in the 400s from the coast of what is now Germany. Throughout the centuries, sailing ships brought other invaders—the Vikings in the ninth century, the Normans, and a whole new dynasty of kings in the eleventh—but they also brought trade, new technology, and new ideas. As early as King Edgar in the middle of the 900s, English kings recognized that the sovereignty and prosperity of their island nation rested on the decks of their sailing ships.

When Britain's sailing ships ventured farther, they helped build the world's largest empire. Starting with John Cabot in the 1490s, England's explorers traveled to the ends of the earth, establishing colonies and building a global economy. Sailing ships transported raw materials from the New World to the Old, where they fed burgeoning new factories. Alabama cotton was spun into cloth in the mills of Manchester, and West Indies sugar was refined in Liverpool to sweeten afternoon tea in London. All this commercial exchange created enormous wealth for the owners of the ships, the plantations, and the factories—and for Britain itself.

For centuries, sailing offered employment and adventure to the men who worked on those majestic ships. Many young men were drawn to the sailing life because it paid better than mundane land-based jobs. Many more were attracted by the chance to see faraway lands and to spend their days in pursuit of thrills and romance. The number of men who took up the nautical life in the Age of Sail was well into the millions.

Now the Age of Sail was ending for the same reason so many old ways of life were fading: the Industrial Revolution. That great economic upheaval, which began in Britain in the 1700s, had started in manufacturing. The mechanization of textile making made hand looms obsolete. Coal and steam power replaced horsepower. And new factories, with their efficient division of labor, overtook traditional craft methods of production. These changes in manufacturing were pulling England into the modern era. The very landscape of the nation was changing. England had always been a rural nation, full of small towns and villages, but after the Industrial Revolution, it urbanized at a stunning pace. In 1800, about 19 percent of the population lived in cities of five thousand or more. By 1900, more than 67 percent would be city dwellers.

Signs of transformation were everywhere. In the cities, there were factories spewing smoke and fast-growing slums teeming with poor people. In the countryside, stately homes and sprawling estates were being built, financed by the new manufacturing and colonial fortunes. These winds of change reached the maritime world. With the advent of steam power, sails became an archaic technology. Steamships could move goods and passengers faster and more economically than sailing ships. With steam engines, ships were no longer dependent on the vagaries of wind: They did not get blown off course or lie idle in the doldrums. Steam-powered ships could also go places sailboats could not. If the *Mignonette* were a steamboat, it could take a major shortcut to Australia through the Suez Canal. The canal, which opened in 1869, cut thousands of miles off the trip—the whole distance of skirting around Africa—but it was difficult for sailing ships to traverse. The first one that tried shortly after the canal opened, the French bark *Noel*, was wrecked along the way.

The year 1883, when the London Yacht Agency was looking for a captain to deliver the *Mignonette*, was a milestone for steamships. It was the year the total tonnage of Britain's steamers surpassed the tonnage of its sailing fleet. The novelist Joseph Conrad, who deeply loved the sailing life, lamented that the golden age of sailing had passed in "the winking of an eye."

New technologies increase profits for the ownership class, but they do not always help workers. In the dying Age of Sail, sailors suffered what would today be called technological unemployment. Steamships could be built larger than sailing ships, carrying more cargo with fewer sailors, and they were able to offer higher wages and more regular work. Sailing was never enormously lucrative, but now it was becoming increasingly untenable. Thomas Brassey, a member of Parliament and a sailors' advocate, railed in his book *British Seamen* that "it is not creditable to the shipowners that" the men who sailed for them "should be in such abject poverty."

Working conditions on sailing ships declined as the economics of sailing spiraled downward. It was a time, one historian observed, of “rotten gear and patched sails, inadequate food and miserable conditions.” A once-thrilling calling was becoming routinized and depressing. Basil Lubbock, a historian and sailor, regretted that “the calling of the sea is now a dull, monotonous business like any other trade and no longer a romantic profession.” The transition was heartbreaking for the sailors who were caught up in it. Conrad eulogized the old way of life in vivid terms. “The sea of the past was an incomparably beautiful mistress, with inscrutable face, with cruel and promising eyes,” he wrote. “The sea of to-day is a used-up drudge, wrinkled and defaced by the churned-up wakes of brutal propellers, robbed of the enslaving charm of its vastness, stripped of its beauty, of its mystery and of its promise.”

Individual sailors found themselves at a crossroads. Many of the most ambitious “left the sea to go into steam,” as a saying from the time put it. They took jobs on steamships, where pay and conditions were generally better. Some sailors abandoned the sea entirely, taking higher-paying, safer jobs on land. Others simply held on in a dying world. These loyalists were willing to accept low wages and arduous conditions as the price of sticking with a life they loved. Some might even have felt pressed enough by circumstances to sail a tiny yacht across treacherous oceans from England all the way to Australia.

As it happened, the yacht agency had no difficulty finding a captain to deliver the *Mignonette* to Sydney. In November 1883, word of the opening reached Sutton, a lively commercial and transportation hub on the outskirts of London. An experienced sea captain who lived there, Thomas Dudley, was looking for well-paying traditional work, and just as important, he was eager to see Australia. He heard about the assignment and decided to apply.

In some ways, Dudley would be an ideal choice for the assignment. He had sailing in his blood. Dudley was born forty or so miles northeast of London in Tollesbury, which was known as the "village of the plough and sail" for the two main ways its residents earned a living. His family were in the "sail" camp. His father, George Dudley, was a yacht captain, and two older brothers were sailors. Dudley was a yachtsman. When he was a boy, his father had initiated him into the rarefied world of yachting, where conditions and pay were often better than in regular sailing. Dudley had worked on boats like the *Mignonette* for years and won yacht-racing prizes. His reputation as a skilled yacht captain reached as far as the River Clyde in Scotland, where he had sailed and sailed well.

Dudley did not cut an especially dashing figure on the deck of a ship—he was on the short side, a bit stout, and his reddish hair was thinning early—but he had pleasant features that were remarked upon, and he radiated amiability and goodwill. Dudley liked to boast that no man, woman, or child could look him in the eye and say, "Tom Dudley, you have wronged me."

There was one more quality Dudley had that would help with this voyage: fearlessness. Sailing had a way of separating men of courage from those who lacked it. A fierce wind that blew a boat off course, a violent storm that shook a ship to its timbers, a menacing whale or an iceberg—these were terrifying to some, but for a hardy few, they were just part of the adventure. Dudley's unflappable nature would prove useful if the *Mignonette* ran into trouble along its arduous path.

At the same time, there were some aspects of Dudley's record that should have given the yacht agency pause. In his time sailing, Dudley had mainly stayed close to England. He had never crossed the equator, a notable marker of the most well-traveled sailors, much less sailed as far as Australia. And he had certainly never done either in a mere yacht. All this meant he had no first-hand knowledge of the risks that lay ahead or how to prepare for them.

But Dudley wanted the job. For one thing, he needed the money. He had been married for seven years and had two daughters and a son. His wife, Philippa Dudley, had a job of her own as a schoolmistress with the Sutton school system. She liked the work, but her salary did not go far. Dudley had done what he could to increase his earnings. He had studied hard to pass a Board of Trade examination for mates and, overcoming his poor education, succeeded after several attempts. His passing grade certified him for assignments with better working conditions and higher pay than ordinary sailors received. In time, Dudley had worked his way up to captaining ships, but he was struggling with the same tough labor market facing all sailors.

The sailing life was especially brutal for family men. A sailing salary, even for most captains, did not go far in meeting the expenses of a wife and children. Brassey, the reform-minded member of Parliament, observed that children of sailors were being forced into asylums due to the harsh new economics of sailing. Then there was the nature of the job. Sailing required being away from home for weeks or months at a time and sometimes the better part of the year, which was a significant strain on a man with a young family. The work was also physically and mentally demanding for someone heading into middle age.

In fact, Dudley had tried to join the exodus out of sailing. Two years earlier, he thought he had found a promising career on land. He went into partnership with a greengrocer named Smith. But their grocery business failed, and Smith left England. That professional defeat put Dudley back on ships, at least until something better came along. For now, what had come along was the *Mignonette*. The London Yacht Agency was offering appealing terms: £100 in advance and another £100 on delivery of the *Mignonette*. These rates reflected the assignment's unusual challenges. Dudley would have to pay his crew out of the £200, but even so, he would end up well compensated for his efforts.

There was another consideration beyond money that drew Dudley to the *Mignonette*: his hopes for the future. After his grocery had failed, Dudley had come up with a new plan. He had an aunt in Sydney who had offered to let him take over a sailing supply business she was preparing to give up. Dudley wanted to see Australia and his aunt's shop firsthand before deciding whether to move there with his family.

Australia was in the midst of an economic boom. It had been over a century since James Cook sailed along the continent's east coast and claimed it for Great Britain. Australia got off to a rough-and-tumble start as a British penal colony, but after decades of immigration, gold rushes, and outside investments, a new Australia was now emerging. This one was exploding with economic activity, and it had a serious shortage of labor. The combination created some of the highest wages in the world and was earning Australia a reputation as "the working man's paradise." Many Englishmen had already emigrated to Australia—John Henry Want's father among them—and plenty more were considering it. But the voyage was long and costly. Not many working people could afford to relocate, much less to make the sort of exploratory visit Dudley was contemplating. If he was hired to transport the *Mignonette*, he could visit Sydney to look at his aunt's shop and get paid to do it.

Dudley got his wish. On the recommendation of the London Yacht Agency, Want hired him and told him to prepare to set sail the following spring. In early 1884, Dudley spent a few months as captain of the *Myrtle*, a steam yacht that Sir Charles Strickland, a prominent barrister, had taken on a Mediterranean cruise. When his assignment on the *Myrtle* ended in April, Dudley returned to Sutton to spend a little time with his family before heading off on the *Mignonette*.

If Dudley's personal circumstances had been better, and if he had not been so fearless by nature, it might have occurred to him that there were good reasons for him not to take on this assignment. There was the *Mignonette*'s size, which made it ideal for recreational sailing but much less so for the arduous voyage to Australia. There was also Dudley's lack of knowledge about the voyage to Australia. Undeterred, he began to make preparations for the journey with the sort of blithe confidence that good-natured ignorance often bestows.

As the day of departure drew near, Dudley got to work hiring a crew. Recruiting men to go to sea, particularly on long voyages, was not always easy. Many sailors enjoyed life at sea, but it was hard work and often difficult and unpleasant. Signing on with a sailing ship meant, as cultural anthropologist Monique Layton observed, "living in cramped, damp quarters smelling of bilgewater, tar, and unwashed humanity." Disease was rampant on ships. Sailors brought illnesses with them and picked up more at ports of call, and the boats were natural incubators of all the maladies the crew collected. Sailors often came down with "ship fever," a catchall phrase that could refer to yellow fever, typhoid, typhus, dysentery, or malaria. When sailors fell ill, the medical treatments available at sea were primitive and often ineffective, and deaths were common.

Disaster always loomed. Ships were frequently sunk by violent storms or splintered apart by rocks. They got lost and were never heard from again. Proximity to mortality had always been part of sailing. In the seventeenth century, the Puritan minister John Flavel called sailors "a third sort of persons, to be numbered neither with the living nor the dead; their lives hanging continually in suspense before them." That remained true. In 1880, maritime records showed that one in sixty British sailors died violently at sea.

For a captain seeking a crew, sailors were often in short supply. When commercial ships were desperate, they sometimes resorted to paying shady agents known as "crimps" to "shanghai" sailors—drugging them, forging their names on employment contracts, and taking them away by force. The word derived from the notion that the abducted men would often find themselves on the long trip to East Asia, clear out to the port of Shanghai. Similarly, the British navy sometimes relied on "impressment," dragging young men out of taverns or kidnapping them from their beds.

Dudley would not be drugging or kidnapping anyone. He would have to get the word out about the positions and bargain and cajole sailors into accepting. Conditions in the dying Age of Sail would be both a help and a hindrance. Many sailors had by now left sailing, but those who stuck with it were under more pressure than ever to take work when they could find it. As Dudley set out to recruit his crew, there were reasons this particular voyage might be a hard sell. Many sailors would not want to be away from home for the eight months it could take to sail to Australia and back. And many more would be wary of making such a long and difficult trip in a fifty-two-foot yacht.

In early May, Dudley packed for the journey. Along with the usual clothing and supplies he would need for a trip of more than half a year, he was bringing prayer books. Dudley planned to hold religious services on the *Mignonette*. Since he was a devout Anglican and prayer was common onboard ships, this was not so out of the ordinary. But he may also have had a premonition that this unusually challenging voyage would be in particular need of divine intervention.

On May 3, Dudley left home with his wife, Philippa, and their four-year-old daughter, also named Philippa, who were joining him on the short first leg of his journey. He arranged for a friend to sail the *Mignonette* from Brightlingsea, where it was in storage, to Tollesbury. At the same time, Dudley was scouting for crewmen he could hire. He picked up a pair of sailing brothers from Tollesbury, William and Jim Frost. The Frosts agreed to sign on, with the older brother, William, as able seaman and Jim, who was just fourteen, as cabin boy.

While he was in Tollesbury to meet the boat, Dudley received some advice he did not want to hear. His friends and associates urged him not to make the voyage, which they predicted would end in disaster. It would be the first of many such warnings that would be directed to him and his crew. Dudley ignored the naysayers and forged ahead.

The voyage got off to a rocky start. On May 5, when they set sail, "it was blowing a gale of wind," Dudley later recalled. The *Mignonette* made it to Southampton with some difficulty on the morning of May 7. When it docked at Fay's Yard, a shipbuilding and maintenance facility, Philippa Dudley and the younger Philippa got off and returned home, no doubt relieved to be done with an unexpectedly difficult, even frightening, sail. While it was at Fay's Yard, Dudley had the *Mignonette* looked at. If this had just been a routine checkup, it could have been done in Brightlingsea, where the yacht had been stored for the winter. It may have been that Dudley was not satisfied with how the *Mignonette* had held up in the storm on the way down from Tollesbury and he thought it advisable to have it examined and serviced by experts before heading out to sea.

There were also problems of a different kind. The Frost brothers changed their minds about the voyage and backed out. William Frost's wife reportedly objected to him going. The Frost brothers may also have been scared away by the difficult sail they had just experienced as the *Mignonette* made its way from Tollesbury to Southampton. Dudley now had to find replacements. He decided to expand the crew to three. He was persuaded, likely by the troubles he had encountered so far, to add a mate who was skilled in navigation. To fill the position, Dudley signed James Haynes, a sailor from Plymouth. The twenty-nine-year-old Haynes, who had a mate's certificate, had navigation experience, and he had worked aboard schooners, barks, and steamships.

That same day, Dudley signed Edmund Brooks as able seaman. "Ned" Brooks, who was thirty-nine, had been born in Brightlingsea, the town where the *Mignonette* was built, and he worked as a rigger at Fay's Yard, where the *Mignonette* was docked. Brooks was a little taller and bigger than Dudley, with a darker complexion and nearly jet-black hair. He had been born into a sailing family, and he had been a seaman since childhood. When Brooks had heard about the opening on the *Mignonette*, he sought out Dudley, whom he had known for over a decade.

Brooks had some concerns. He asked if the rumors were true that other crew members had already quit. Dudley said they were, but he urged Brooks to set his fears aside and sign on. He offered Brooks the position of able seaman, with a generous salary. The £5 10s. a month was about 30s. more than the job would normally pay. The premium was to compensate, Brooks later said, for the risk of traveling to Australia in such a small boat. In any case, the destination was, for him, a deciding factor. He was considering starting over in Britain's vast southern colony, and like Dudley, he relished the chance to see Australia for free.

Brooks was single, which meant he had no wife to raise objections, but he did have friends who warned that the long journey would be too much for the *Mignonette*. Brooks later told a newspaper reporter that everyone who spoke to him had urged him not to go. But he felt optimistic, and he signed on.

Dudley now had his crew of three in place, but that did not last long. Haynes's wife had objected to the long trip, and almost immediately after signing on, Haynes decided not to go. Haynes was now the third person—after the Frost brothers—to back out. The next day, May 16, Dudley found Haynes's replacement, Edwin Stephens, another navigator. Stephens, who was thirty-six, was well qualified to be mate and navigator, and it helped that he was a little desperate. Like the captain, he had sailing in his blood—in fact, the Stephenses ranked above the Dudleys in the shifting hierarchy of the seafaring world—but he had recently suffered a disastrous setback.

Stephens was born in Southampton, the only son, along with seven daughters, of Richard Stephens, a captain with the Isle of Wight Royal Mail Steam Packet Company. Edwin had followed his father into seafaring. He started out, at fourteen, as a cabin boy on a steamer of the Peninsular and Oriental Line, a prime assignment for a boy hoping to spend his life at sea. Edwin spent his youth on a series of ships, and he stuck with the maritime life even though, when he was twenty, his father drowned in an accident off the Isle of Wight, the large island off the southern coast of England, opposite Southampton. Edwin became a first mate at twenty-three, and he eventually reached the lofty status of first officer on the Union Line's *European*, a 2,272-ton steamer. He was on track to become a captain for the Union Line, a prestigious, well-paying post.

That is when he suffered a crushing reversal. While returning from Cape Town in 1877, the *European* hit a dense fog and crashed into rocks near the English Channel. The 106 passengers and crew survived, but the ship was lost. An official inquiry put responsibility for the accident on the captain, but Stephens, as navigator, did not fully escape blame. The Union Line parted ways with him. Stephens had trouble finding work after that. When he was able to secure a job, it was not at the level of pay or prestige he had formerly enjoyed. He was unemployed when he learned that Dudley was looking for a navigator.

Delivering a used yacht to Australia would be a significant step down from the sort of positions Stephens once held, but he was by now used to that. His bigger concern was the riskiness of the voyage. His father had died in one mishap at sea, and his career as a steamer officer was ended by another. He had more reason than most sailors to be wary of taking on a dangerous assignment.

But Stephens was drawn to the two main enticements Dudley had to offer: generous pay and a free trip to Australia. The pay was certainly appealing. Stephens had a wife and five children and no money coming in. Dudley was offering to pay Stephens £8 a month. That was £1 a month more than Dudley had offered Haynes, which suggested he was now more worried about his ability to recruit and hold on to a crew. Stephens was also interested in traveling to Australia. Like Dudley and Brooks, he was considering emigrating: In Australia, no one would have heard about the wreck of the *European*, and he would finally be free of that black mark on his career. Dudley provided a further incentive when he told Stephens that if he signed on, he might become captain of the *Mignonette* after it was delivered to Jack Want. Taken together, Dudley's inducements and the lack of other options persuaded Stephens to sign on.

There was one more position on the ship, cabin boy, and Dudley filled it the same day he brought on Haynes and Brooks. Dudley hired Richard Parker, an orphan who was seventeen, though he was recorded on the crew list as being eighteen. Like the other three, Parker had been born into a life at sea. He was from Itchen Ferry, a village near Southampton that a contemporary writer described as a "clannish nursery of yacht-sailors and fishermen." True to their hometown's reputation, the Parkers were a sailing family with strong ties to yachting. Parker's father had worked on yachts in the summer and fished in the winter. Richard had a younger sister and three older brothers, two of whom were sailors on yachts. Parker's own love of sailing had started early. He "was always a smart little chap, and knocked about in the boats and got his own living almost as soon as he could crawl," his brother Daniel Parker later said. He was eager to go into the family profession.

Parker had endured a difficult childhood. He lost his mother when he was twelve and his father not long after. He was forced to fend for himself and he had a hard time of it. He "had to live a little bit rough, like the rest of us," Daniel recalled. Parker left school early, before he mastered reading and writing, and Dudley's wife would later say he was "quite ignorant." It was a harsh description of an agreeable young man who had struggled to do his best under challenging circumstances.

Parker's life had improved when John Mathews, an Itchen Ferry yachtsman, and his wife took him in. The Mathews family gave Parker the home he had lost when his parents died. "He was as dear to me and to my husband as if he were our own son," Mrs. Mathews said. Although Parker's nickname was "Little Dickey," he was large for his years. Brooks described him as "a fine, stout boy, almost as stout as I am, and taller than the captain." Parker was popular with his Itchen Ferry neighbors and with the captains he worked for. He had a "reputation of being honest, civil and obliging," a newspaper profile later said, and "his physique gave promise of his becoming a smart man."

For a seventeen-year-old, Parker had impressive boating experience. Along with his yachting skills, he was a talented oarsman. Parker had rowed in the most recent Itchen Ferry Regatta and finished well. He had also sailed, a year earlier, with his adoptive father on a racing cutter called the *Daphne*. The boat's owner, a Mr. Hankinson, was fond of Parker and invited him to return to the *Daphne*, but Parker hungered for bigger challenges. For all his time on the water, he had never been on a real sea voyage.

Parker learned about the opening on the *Mignonette* through the sailing grapevine. Someone from Fay's Yard had brought word to Itchen Ferry that a yacht captain was looking for a cabin boy for a voyage to Australia. Parker came home and told his adoptive parents he wanted to sail on the *Mignonette* if he could get a position on it. The Mathews had the same doubts as Stephens's family and Brooks's friends, insisting the long trip was too dangerous. Mr. Mathews, a yachtsman himself, told Parker he should not go to Australia on such a small boat, and other family members and friends joined in. They spent three or four days "trying hard to persuade him out of going," Mrs. Mathews recalled. But nothing could make Parker rethink his plans. "He would not hear of it," Mrs. Mathews said. Parker insisted that he would be safe. He promised his adoptive parents, "I shan't hurt; the ship's all right."

When Parker met with Dudley, the veteran captain and the eager teenager quickly formed a bond. Dudley offered himself as a father figure to Parker, promising to make a man out of him. Dudley said he would bring elementary school books along so he could teach Parker to read and write. The money Dudley offered was also attractive. Parker would be paid £1 15s. a month. That was a good rate of pay for a cabin boy, and it was more than he had earned on the *Daphne*. And like the other three men, Parker thought Australia might offer more opportunity than his home country. Dudley seized on Parker's interest by telling him that he could continue to work on the *Mignonette* in Sydney, an offer similar to the one he had made to Stephens.

What seemed to win Parker over in the end, more than the money or even the chance to see Australia, was the personal connection he felt with Dudley and the chance he saw to grow into adulthood. He "told us he thought Captain Dudley was a very nice man, and that he intended to teach him everything he could," Mrs. Mathews recalled. "The only words that I remember he kept on saying," Mrs. Mathews told a reporter, "were that he intended to make a man of himself."

Parker went to the Southampton Custom House, the administrative office for maritime matters, to formally accept the job, though he was not literate enough to write his name on the papers and instead signed with a mark. Once it was official and Parker's adoptive parents were resigned to him sailing on the *Mignonette*, they bought him new clothing for the trip. "Well, if you are determined to go I hope everything will be all right," Mrs. Mathews told him, "and that, please God, you will come home again."

Parker's brother Daniel, who was a more experienced sailor, was away at the time. Had he been in Itchen Ferry, he would have joined the chorus of opposition, and he believed he would have succeeded. "If I had seen him before he signed articles," Daniel later said, "I should have persuaded him not to go."

As "master" of the *Mignonette*, as the captain was officially known, Dudley had to file paperwork with the maritime regulators before he was legally permitted to set sail. In the filings, he provided the name of the boat's owner, John Henry Want, and Want's address, which he gave only as "Sydney." Dudley provided the *Mignonette*'s length, weight, and other specifications. And he gave the crew's names, ages, and job titles and their monthly rates of pay. Dudley also had to plan a route. Unlike steamships that could navigate the narrow Suez Canal, the *Mignonette* would have to steer a far longer course, around the southern tip of Africa. The biggest decision Dudley had to make was whether to hug the coast of Africa the whole way south or venture far out into the Atlantic to catch favorable winds. Bigger ships usually chose to swing westward across the open ocean, closer to South America than to Africa, to pick up the "Roaring Forties," strong winds that howl from west to east, between the latitudes of 40° S and 50° S. Those ships had to cover more miles, but the Roaring Forties made for a brisk eastward run. It was a fast route but also a risky one, because there were often rough seas, violent storms, and sometimes deadly icebergs.

Dudley chose what would likely be a calmer but slower path. He would sail along the western coast of Africa, avoiding the worst of the storms and the ice floes to the west and south. His plan was to head from England to Madeira, a Portuguese colonial outpost about three hundred miles off the western coast of Africa. From there, he would proceed to the Cape of Good Hope, close to the tip of the continent. He would stop there for about a week to rest and restock provisions. Then he would head east, across the Indian Ocean, to Australia.

Dudley had chosen the slow route, and he would be sailing it in a slow boat. If he had been captaining a clipper ship, a slim-hulled merchant vessel built for speed, he might have been able to reach Sydney in as little as two months. In the *Mignonette,* it was likely to take twice as long. And even this safer route was hardly without danger. The Cape of Good Hope was famous for treacherous conditions and was once known as the "Cape of Storms." It had a long history of shipwrecks, and many of them had claimed ships larger and sturdier than the *Mignonette.*

Nevertheless, yachts had made it from England to Australia before. The *Vivid,* which was even smaller and lighter than the *Mignonette*, did it in 1864–65, stopping at the Cape of Good Hope along the way. The *Alerte*, which was much larger than the *Mignonette*, had sailed from Falmouth, England, to Sydney in 108 days in 1865 and sailed back home in 115 days. Voyages like these made Dudley and the others believe the *Mignonette* could make it to Sydney safely.

There was one more matter Dudley had to attend to before setting sail: procuring provisions. Captains were responsible for providing their crews with adequate rations for the voyage. While the *Mignonette* was still at Fay's Yard, Dudley had it loaded up with a plentiful supply of tinned beef, sides of bacon, preserved vegetables, fruit, eggs, bread, flour, water, tea, and sugar. Ships usually carried generous stores of rum, ale, and grog, but Dudley was a teetotaler, and he was not bringing any alcohol. Maritime regulations did not require captains to provision their lifeboats, so Dudley did not stow a separate supply of food or water in the *Mignonette*'s dinghy. But captains did have to report to regulators on the overall stock of provisions they would have onboard, and Dudley filled out an "Agreement and Account of Crew" with a weekly food chart. He said he would give the crew bread and meat every day. On Saturday, Sunday, Tuesday, and Thursday, there would be beef, and on the other days, there would be pork. There would also be peas three days out of seven. A note under the list of meats and other foods permitted "substitutes at master's option." It was a phrase that would look very different by the time the voyage was over.

On May 19, the *Mignonette* was about to set sail, and Dudley had to worry until the end about whether he would keep his crew. He had gone back home for a final visit before the departure, and when he returned to Southampton, both Brooks and Stephens were showing signs that they might drop out, as the Frost brothers and Haynes had. Dudley was told that Brooks had decided to take the advice of his friends and abandon the voyage. He spoke with his able seaman and persuaded him to show up when the *Mignonette* set off around 5 p.m. There were also reports that Stephens was wavering, though it is not clear if he was worried about the safety of the trip or the long absence from his family. But in the end, Stephens showed up at the *Mignonette* at the appointed hour.

Parker did not give the captain any such trouble, but that did not mean he was entirely without his own worries. He woke early at the Mathews house and was downstairs by 5 a.m. Parker kissed his adoptive parents goodbye. Mrs. Mathews recalled that he "hung upon both our necks for several minutes." That was when she detected something she had not felt before: a hint that the lad was wavering. "I shall never forget it," she said. "He seemed then sorry that he was going to leave us, and this was the first time that he had shown any sort of regret for the resolve he had taken."

Looming over the day's departure were the warnings all four men had received. Family and friends had told them that the voyage was too dangerous and had urged them not to go. They had all decided in the end to ignore the words of caution and make the trip, but each of the crewmembers had experienced misgivings along the way.

Something else loomed over the *Mignonette*, or rather, three things: the Frost brothers and Haynes. Sailors are a superstitious lot, with a fear of starting voyages on a Friday, whistling into the direction of the wind, and countless other little taboos. Dudley and the *Mignonette* crew had a more tangible bad omen staring right at them on that spring morning: Before the ship ever started its journey, as many sailors had dropped out as had decided to go.

2

The Wreck of the *Mignonette*

Late in the afternoon on May 19, a steam tug towed the *Mignonette* out of Fay's Yard and into the River Itchen. Friends showed up, putting aside any reservations they had, to wish Dudley and the crew Godspeed. The tide was high and the winds were favorable, with a light breeze out of the southeast. Brooks later recalled that "the weather was beautifully fine." The *Mignonette* sailed down the river, and Dudley maneuvered around the Isle of Wight. By midnight, the ship was in the English Channel. The voyage was off to a pleasant start, though not a fast one. Due to light winds, the *Mignonette* was moving at a pace short of what it would need to reach Australia in 120 days.

On the morning of May 21, the *Mignonette* crossed paths with the *Lady Evelyn*, a schooner yacht that was headed for England. There was a nautical tradition of passing ships accepting mail going to the country they were headed to. Although Dudley and the crew had not yet been gone two days, they took advantage of the encounter to send letters home. Around noon, the *Mignonette* reached the Eddystone Lighthouse, whose beacons warned ships away from the treacherous Eddystone Rocks. That soaring structure was so famous as a remote outpost that in *Moby-Dick*, Herman Melville described Nantucket as "more lonely than the Eddystone lighthouse." As the *Mignonette* sailed safely past the Eddystone Rocks, it left the shores of England behind and headed for the open sea. The next morning, it reached Ushant, a small French island at the southwest end of the English Channel. Dudley and the crew could not see the island as they passed by, Dudley recalled, because the sky was so hazy. The *Mignonette* sailed past France, Spain, and Portugal and reached the waters off Morocco.

At midnight on June 1, the *Mignonette*, which was now moving at a brisk pace, reached Madeira, an island off the coast of Africa. Dudley and the crew had no complaints. It had been "fine weather" so far, Dudley would later write. A bustling Portuguese colonial outpost, Madeira had a long history of hosting foreign ships, going back to the 1400s, when it was a major global source of sugar. Dudley replenished the *Mignonette*'s water supply and provisions, and the men took the opportunity to write home again. "All is well," Dudley told his wife in a telegram. Stephens, perhaps moved by the excitement of the voyage, sent his wife a letter aimed at making his Australian dream a reality. He told her he would remain in Sydney at the end of the voyage if she would join him there. In his own letter, Parker assured his adoptive parents that he was "happy and comfortable" and reported that it had been "a fine and pleasant voyage all the way."

The *Mignonette* sailed out of Madeira on June 2, and the good weather continued. The yacht picked up southeast trade winds and headed toward the equator at a nice clip. The blue skies and smooth sailing seemed a rebuke to the doomsayers back home. "The *Mignonette* proved a capital sea boat," Brooks later recalled. Spirits were high, he said, and "we were comfortable together on board." On June 8, San Antonio, the northernmost of the Cape Verde islands, came into sight. The crew spotted an Italian bark the following day, then crossed paths with the *Bride of Lorne*, which sailed out of Liverpool. The *Mignonette*'s men boarded the homebound ship briefly and again took advantage of the encounter to send letters home. The gloomy warnings they had received before their departure were a distant memory. "We all looked forward to a happy termination of a voyage commenced under such happy auspices," Brooks later said.

As the *Mignonette* continued south, it approached an important navigational landmark. It was about to cross the equator, the dividing line between the Northern and Southern Hemispheres, which held special significance in the sailing world. Crossing the equator for the first time was a mark of distinction for sailors. Stephens and Brooks had "crossed the line" before, while the captain and the cabin boy had not.

There were seafaring traditions associated with crossing the line. Sailors who had never done it before were often dunked in the ocean in a "sailor's baptism." Naval ships held elaborate ceremonies, with crewmembers dressing as King Neptune, god of the sea; his wife; and their loyal assistant, Davy Jones. In some of these rituals, the uninitiated, known as pollywogs, were whipped with wet ropes or beaten with planks. These ceremonies could provide relief from the monotony of a long voyage and build esprit de corps, but they were also rooted in superstition, which was plentiful on the open sea. With their baptisms and Roman gods, the playful performances contained both Christian and pre-Christian appeals for protection against storms, sea creatures, and other dangers. They were meant to placate, as one historian notes, "those unseen and often mythical powers that control the potentially tragic fate of sailors."

There does not seem to have been a ceremony on the *Mignonette* when it crossed the equator on June 17. In his account of the journey, Dudley did not mention receiving a sailor's baptism or giving one to Parker. He simply said "all went well," and indeed it had. There still had been no major storms, no towering waves, and no churning seas. As it turned out, though, the men may have made a mistake by not trying to appease the dark forces of the sea. Almost as soon as the *Mignonette* entered the South Atlantic, everything changed. The fair skies that had blanketed the *Mignonette* since it left England suddenly turned menacing. An ominous wind appeared from the south-southeast and steadily gained force. The men's good cheer and confidence abruptly fell away, replaced by concern and then fear.

The real trouble began a few days after crossing the equator, when the *Mignonette* got caught in a heavy cross sea. In a cross sea, waves collide at right angles, creating a grid-like pattern that can be perilous for ships sailing through it. *Patterson's Illustrated Nautical Encyclopedia* describes a cross sea as "a confused, ugly sea, very dangerous for low-sided vessels." Cross seas toss ships from side to side, driving them off course—and sometimes cause them to sink.

As the *Mignonette* rocked violently in the churning waters, the crew knew that the ship was now in danger, and they scrambled to respond. They took down the topmast to lessen the wind's impact on the small boat. The rough weather continued in fits and starts. By June 25, the wind had shifted and was blowing from the northwest. Dudley reduced the sails further, hoping the winds would calm. The northwest wind continued until June 30, when a fierce wind blew to the south-southwest.

Then, as suddenly as the bellowing winds had appeared, they stopped. On July 2 the weather was calm, the breezes were light, and the *Mignonette* was sailing smoothly again. The following day, a hard wind blew again, and the seas were rough, but this outburst did not last long. Finally, the angry gods of the sea appeared to be done raging, and for the first time in about two weeks, the men began to relax. The storms had been jarring, but with the return of calm waters, the men were feeling good again. Their faith in the little yacht had even been buttressed a bit by the recent challenges. "The wind had been hard and shifty," Brooks later recalled, "but she rode out the gale admirably."

Dudley and the crew knew the weather might turn rough again at any moment, and they did their best to prepare. They divided into pairs so they could keep watch around the clock. Dudley and Parker were on one watch and Stephens and Brooks on the other. While one pair tried to sleep below deck, the other looked out for bad weather. It was not long before the next storm came. On July 5, the *Mignonette* was about 1,600 miles northwest of the Cape of Good Hope when conditions once again turned treacherous. "The wind," Dudley later said, was "blowing a fresh gale." He recalled it being "thick with rain." Dudley and Parker kept watch while Stephens and Brooks were down below, wrapped in oilskin clothing, trying to sleep but not succeeding.

Being in a boat on a violent ocean holds a special kind of terror. Stephen Crane described the feeling in "The Open Boat," which he based on his own experience surviving a shipwreck. "A singular disadvantage of the sea," he observed wryly, "lies in the fact that after successfully surmounting one wave you discover that there is another behind it just as important and just as nervously anxious to do something effective in the way of swamping boats." Dudley and the crew were facing just such an onslaught. They knew any wave could deliver a catastrophic blow, and the waves kept coming.

With danger looming, Dudley decided to heave to, or hold the boat in place, until conditions got better, a common technique for protecting ships in rough seas. In heaving to, the sails and the rudder are made to essentially cancel each other out, so the boat almost stands still. Stephens and Brooks came up from below, and all four men did what they could to guard the

Mignonette against a potentially lethal flood of water. Dudley told Stephens to take the helm while he helped Brooks and Parker to reef, or reduce the area of, the squaresail. Dudley decided they should have some tea while they hove to and waited for the gale to blow over, a stubborn act of English tradition amid the chaos of the roiling ocean. As Parker went below to prepare the tea, the other three men went to work securing one of the ship's greatest points of vulnerability, the skylight over the aft cabin. Dudley used a small axe and some tacks to nail canvas over the skylight. Brooks followed Parker below to get lashings that he could use to tie the lifeboat and tackle to the deck.

Just after Parker reemerged from below and moments after Dudley drove the last tack into the skylight cover, a massive wave swelled up from the ocean. It towered halfway up the *Mignonette*'s masthead, and as soon as they saw it, the men knew they were in trouble. Stephens shouted, "Look out!" Dudley glanced up from under the boom "only to see," he later recalled, "a big sea coming right down on the top of us." He was stunned by the wave's sheer size. "It was a roller," he said. "I shall never forget it as long as I live."

Brooks had come up from below just in time to see the enormous wave crash down on the *Mignonette*. The men tried desperately to avoid being thrown out of the boat into the churning sea. Stephens held onto the ropes that he had been using to lash the tiller in place. Brooks grabbed the lines that were securing the ship's lifeboat and wrapped them around his arms. Dudley and Parker gripped the boom tightly while a torrent of water surged over them.

The force of the ocean was overwhelming. Brooks later said that he could not understand how they remained in the boat. While it was happening, he thought they would all be swept overboard. They had managed to cling to the deck, but they could see instantly that the *Mignonette* had suffered crippling damage. The wave's brutal force had torn away the bulwarks, the planking meant to keep the waves from breaking over the deck, and laid the starboard side completely open. Struggling to recover his footing, Stephens saw the sea come rushing in through the mangled planks.

"My God, her side is knocked in!" he shouted. "She is sinking!"

The men looked on in horror as the *Mignonette* filled with seawater. The yacht had suffered a wound no ship could survive. It was going to sink, there was no question, and unless they acted quickly, they would go down with it.

For the next five minutes, there was "nothing but confusion," Stephens later recalled. The men were desperate to escape in the lifeboat, but they had just lashed it down tightly to keep it from washing overboard. While Stephens fought to steer the foundering yacht, the other three men surrounded the dinghy and struggled to get it loose. Dudley was still holding the small axe he had been using to hammer tacks. He used the blade to hack at the cords holding down the stern of the lifeboat, then passed it to Brooks, who cut the cords on the bow. While the *Mignonette* continued to fill with water, the men lowered the dinghy into the sea. It was so light, Brooks said, he was nearly able to throw it into the water himself.

Since there were no provisions in the lifeboat, the men raced to grab whatever supplies they could. Dudley yelled to Parker to bring up a breaker, or cask, of freshwater from below. Parker went down and returned with a breaker, which he threw into the water near the dinghy. The wooden cask would float, and Dudley would be able to pull it from the ocean once he got in the lifeboat.

First, Dudley went on his own retrieval mission. He handed Brooks the painter, the rope holding the dinghy, and rushed into the cabin, which was now filled waist-deep with water. Dudley was looking for food and drinkable water and the sextant to navigate by the sky once they were afloat in the lifeboat. He had trouble finding anything, with the water rising above his waist and gear floating loose in the cabin. And he was running out of time. Stephens, Brooks, and Parker shouted to Dudley to join them before he went down with the ship. He did not come.

Brooks steadied the lifeboat alongside the *Mignonette* so Stephens and Parker could climb in first. Brooks leaped in after them. Dudley was still down in the cabin. He found the sextant and the chronometer. And he pried off the binnacle, the cylindrical container that held the ship's compass. He grabbed six tins of food—preserved meat, he thought.

Water was pouring into the *Mignonette*. Stephens, Brooks, and Parker were yelling from the lifeboat. Dudley came up on deck. He tossed the compass into the lifeboat and threw the sextant and chronometer into the water nearby, mindful not to damage the floor planks of the lifeboat by throwing the heavy gear right in. He tried to toss the food tins into the dinghy, but only one made it in. With the *Mignonette* sinking fast, Dudley finally dropped into the lifeboat. The men hustled to pull their crucial supplies out of the water. They grabbed the sextant and the chronometer, bobbing nearby in their wooden cases, and they managed to retrieve one more of the food tins. The other four were lost in the roiling ocean. They found the wooden stand that went with the breaker of water that Parker had thrown from the yacht, but they could not find the cask itself. They searched for the precious drinking water, but they never found it.

The men had escaped the sinking *Mignonette* with little time to spare. Dudley used the lifeboat's oars to row away from the yacht as it sank into the water before their eyes. "Down she went,"

Dudley later said, "not five minutes from the time the sea struck her."

There is no way of knowing precisely why the *Mignonette* suffered such catastrophic damage from the storm, and there was never an official inquiry. Dudley would later blame the shipwreck, in part, on the age of the *Mignonette*, contending that it was too old for such a long voyage. The yacht may have suffered damage in that time, and there were reports that weaknesses had been spotted when the *Mignonette* was examined at Fay's Yard. One historian conjectured that Dudley, who was known to be careful with money, might not have been willing to pay for all the repair work the *Mignonette* needed. If these accounts are true, Dudley may have borne considerable responsibility for the loss of the *Mignonette* and everything that followed.

The men had not been pulled down with the *Mignonette*, but their ordeal was just beginning. Dudley, Stephens, Brooks, and Parker were crowded into a thirteen-foot-long dinghy that was roughly four feet at its widest. Its sides were only twenty inches high, against the tumbling waves of the ocean, and its thin planks, which were just a quarter-inch thick, seemed terribly fragile. It was strong enough to hold the men afloat, but it was designed for light rowing over short distances, not to stand up against an ocean that had already torn through the far larger and sturdier *Mignonette*.

The men's immediate concern was that the lifeboat was filling up with seawater. They got to work bailing it out, using the bailer and the two halves of the chronometer box, but water was flooding in faster than they could remove it. They took a moment to examine the fragile hull and found that the dinghy had been damaged on its port side when they launched it. A plank was smashed in. Their lifeboat was leaking.

Brooks stopped up the hole with a piece of cotton waste. His quick fix kept much of the water out until the next morning, when Dudley cut some cloth off the bottom of his trousers and shaped a better plug. That helped, but it did not fully solve the problem. "We were always lying in more or less water," Stephens recalled later—a condition that would add nighttime chills and difficulty sleeping to their other miseries.

Fragile and drenched as it was, the lifeboat was all the men had, and their first challenge was to make sure that it could survive in the middle of the South Atlantic. They decided to make a sea anchor, which could be used as a brake and might help in steering the boat. They did not have much to work with, but they cobbled one together from the compass binnacle, the wooden stand from the lost water cask, and some extra boards from the bottom of the lifeboat. Since the dinghy had no rudder, and they did not have the materials to construct one, they would have to steer with just the dinghy's oars and their improvised sea anchor. It was not ideal and, given the rough waters that might appear at any moment, might even prove fatal.

Even if they managed to steer in a direction where they hoped to find a passing ship or an eventual landfall, there was no telling how long that might take, so another crucial problem was their lack of shelter from the elements. The dinghy had no cabin, of course, and no sail to serve as a roof or awning. The men had only their own sodden clothing between themselves and the blistering sun of day, the bracing cold of night, and the occasional driving rain.

But the greatest threat of all was the lack of food and drinkable water. The only food in the lifeboat was in the two one-pound tins Dudley had retrieved from the *Mignonette*—and the men soon got some bad news about them. Dudley had thought the tins contained meat, but when Brooks inspected them, he recognized them as turnip tins. As for drinkable water, there was none. The only water they were able to retrieve from the *Mignonette*, the small breaker that Parker had found, never made it into the lifeboat. As the men continued to bail seawater, the irony of the situation was not lost on them. "Our boat was half full of water, but we had no fresh water," Brooks recalled.

As the excitement of escaping alive from the sinking *Mignonette* faded, the men began to appreciate just how bad things were for them. "We only now had time to realize our position," Stephens later said. Dudley was worried about both the lack of provisions and the menace of the ocean. "No water + only two 1 lb. tins of turnips as our stock of provisions," the captain later wrote in an account of the voyage. The "seas mountain high at times, + the thoughts of our dear ones at home." The men had no idea how they could make their way to safety. The first instinct of anyone lost in a boat at sea is to look around for land, but it is usually of little help. Because of the curvature of the earth, it is not possible to see very far before the sea or land slopes out of sight below the horizon. From the crow's nest of a tall ship, a sailor might be able to see about twelve miles in any direction. Sitting, or even standing, in the dinghy, the men's sightlines were far shorter. Not surprisingly, all they saw was ocean.

The castaways did not know exactly where they were, but they understood that their location was an unfortunate one. The *Mignonette* had sunk in the South Atlantic Ocean at about 27° 10′ south latitude and 9° 50′ west longitude—and that happened to be one of the most remote places on earth. They were almost equidistant between Africa and South America. The Cape of Good Hope was some 1,700 miles to the southeast, and Rio de Janeiro was more than 2,000 miles to the southwest.

It was not only the continents that were impossibly far away. So were the nearest tiny specks of land. St. Helena, the remote island to which Napoleon was exiled after Elba, was about seven hundred miles to the north. Tristan de Cunha, a volcanic island that is roughly six miles at its widest, was about as far to the south. The prevailing winds in the area would not be helpful. They blew from the southeast, which meant the lifeboat would drift toward South America, the farther of the two continents, and away from the nearest islands. Even if the men rowed steadily, their prospects of reaching land in any direction were daunting.

Given their location, a passing ship would be their more likely hope for rescue, but even that was highly unlikely. They were adrift in an enormous expanse of ocean where there was little ship traffic, and the winds were pushing them into ever more desolate waters. And even if a ship passed close by, it was by no means certain the men would be spotted. The crew of a passing ship would not be actively scanning the water looking for lifeboats the way a rescue mission would, and they easily might miss a tiny dinghy bobbing along on the waves. And if the men in the lifeboat saw a ship coming near, they would have no way of signaling their existence. There were no radios, and they did not have flags or flares. All they could do was wave and shout.

Making matters worse, even if a passing ship did spot the men, its crew would be under no obligation to rescue them. International law did not impose a duty to save shipwreck survivors. It would be decades before the international community adopted a global convention establishing the principle that ships must rescue people in distress. English law was also of little help. It encouraged ships to rescue cargo from shipwrecks but not people. There was a legal right to be compensated by the ship's owner for salvaging material goods, but ships that saved passengers and crew could not even count on getting their expenses reimbursed. In the case of the *Zephyrus* in 1842, a court had ruled that people who saved a ship's crew could not sue for compensation. In a decision that sounds perverse to modern ears, the admiralty judge confirmed that rescuers could sue under English law for saving property but said, "I am at a loss to conceive upon what principle the owners can be made answerable for the mere saving of life."

The first night in the dinghy, a new form of terror arrived. At about 11 p.m., as the men sat under the pale light of the moon, they began to hear menacing sounds, and they felt frightening rumblings. They soon realized with horror what was disturbing their peace. "A great shark came knocking its tail against our frail boat," Dudley recalled. The shark, which was almost as large as the boat, rammed the dinghy from below, nearly capsizing it. Just hours after narrowly surviving the storm that wrecked their ship, the men of the *Mignonette* feared they were about to die. Dudley prayed for divine help, and his men beat the shark on the head with an oar. Whether the shark was sent away by God, or scared off by the frantic men, or simply decided there was nothing in the lifeboat of interest, it swam away. There was no damage to the dinghy, but the men took the shark encounter as an ominous sign.

As soon as the shark was gone, the men had to go back to worrying about the weather. Steering with an oar and their makeshift sea anchor, they struggled to keep the lifeboat headed into the wind, to reduce their chances of being swamped or capsized. Even so, there was a constant danger that the churning seawater would flood over the lifeboat's sides, filling it up and sinking it.

The men made it through that first night, and the next, and the one after that. With each passing night, it became clearer that despite the severe deprivations and the dangers that loomed from every direction, it was actually possible for the four of them to survive in the small, fragile dinghy. They developed routines to help them exist in the cramped space that was now their home. Dudley and Brooks stayed mainly in the stern, or rear, the part of a boat traditionally occupied by the captain. Stephens and Parker positioned themselves at midship and in the bow.

Somehow, the men, for the most part, remained stubbornly hopeful. Stephens regularly told the others they were sure to be rescued by a boat soon. Brooks later recalled that hearing this from Stephens, an experienced navigator, gave the others confidence they would eventually be saved. Brooks would later say he himself probably "had the best spirits" of all the men and that he was the most optimistic. "I had been used to small boats in rough weather all my life, and I fully expected we should meet a ship in four or five days at the most," he said. Parker, who was the least knowledgeable about life at sea, was also convinced they would all survive. He kept telling the others they would soon spot land. Only Dudley, the captain, who had begun the voyage with a reputation for fearlessness, was becoming gloomy. He believed they would soon die, but he also thought they had to keep trying to survive and trust in God.

The day after the *Mignonette* sank, Dudley had begun writing a letter to his wife, scrawled on the back of the chronometer's certificate. The letter, which he dated July 6 and addressed "to my dear wife," began with a description of the shipwreck. "*Mignonette* foundered yesterday; weather knocked side in," he wrote. "We had five minutes to get in boat, without food or water." The document, which he would add to over time, revealed his bleak state of mind. Dudley included his home address, "1, Myrtle-road, Sutton, Surrey," so that if anyone found the lifeboat after the men died, an outcome he now considered likely, they could give his wife the handwritten account of his final days.

As the men settled into a routine in the lifeboat and the weather remained mostly calm, they could turn their attention to another sort of threat—or, rather, two threats—hunger and thirst. They were starting to feel both deprivations keenly, but there was no doubt about which one most occupied their thoughts. "We did not feel the hunger so much as the thirst," Brooks recalled. Their focus became how they could lay their hands on something to drink.

The men's instincts were right. Starvation takes time. The early effects of food deprivation can set in quickly—hunger, dizziness, weakness, and then weight loss. But none necessarily means death, or even serious illness, is near. People have fasted for religious, political, and health reasons throughout history, and they have shown it is possible to last days, weeks, even months without food. At the extreme, medical literature records an obese male who fasted under a doctor's supervision for 382 days. But as Dudley and his crew sensed, thirst is different. Water is a key building block of life, integral to just about every crucial bodily function. And human bodies constantly lose water through respiration, urination, and perspiration. The lost liquid must be replenished. When it is not, death follows soon.

The men could live off their own fat, and muscle, for some time as a substitute for the food they were not eating, but they had no way of replacing the lost water. Their bodies could take small compensatory steps for a while, such as sending less water from the kidneys to the bladder to reduce the liquid removed in urination. But if they were not drinking the freshwater they needed—more than three-quarters of a gallon a day—they would suffer symptoms that would quickly progress from bad to serious to fatal. First, the men would experience severe thirst. That had already begun. Then their blood pressure would fall, and they might faint. They would become lightheaded or confused, lethargic or irritable, or all those things by turn. Their hearts would beat too fast. They might be wracked by severe cramps. Further dehydration could damage their kidneys, impairing their ability to remove bodily toxins. Eventually, the lack of water could lead to poor regulation of body temperature, brain swelling, seizures, and death.

There was no way to know how long the men could last. People can die of dehydration in a few days, but they can also survive longer. One study of twentieth-century shipwreck survivors found that the longest any of them had lasted without water was eleven days. Many factors come into play. The men in the lifeboat were healthy adults who began with a good amount of water stored in their bodies. But constant exposure to salt water, harsh wind, and glaring sun was making the water in their bodies evaporate more quickly.

On a boat adrift in the ocean with no drinking water, the obvious source is rain. The lifeboat had already been drenched by furious storms, so it would seem that the men's need for water could be solved by nature. What could be simpler than living off the freshwater that falls from the sky? But it was not that easy. Days went by without any rain, and when rain did fall, it was "squally," with brisk gusts lashing the rain in unpredictable directions. The lifeboat got more wind than water. It seemed as if the rain had a way of passing on both sides without landing in the boat.

The men also lacked good receptacles to catch and save rainwater. The best they could do was hold up their oilskin coats. When it began to rain, the men held their coats up toward the sky. "We waited, with burning throats and stomachs, praying to the Almighty for water until the squall had passed," Stephens said. Even when they did collect some rainwater in their oil-skins, their problems were not over. They had no way to keep out the seawater that splashed and sprayed over the sides of the lifeboat. When too much salt water mixed in, the rainwater became undrinkable. All told, the men managed to drink some rainwater in their first few days adrift, but not much. They usually captured "about a wineglass full," Brooks recalled. "If we caught a little how thankful we were!" Stephens said. "If not, we would hope and pray for the next shower."

There was another source of water too obvious to ignore but too dangerous to drink. People lost at sea often think about drinking seawater, but sailors' folk wisdom has taught since ancient times that its heavy concentration of salt causes nausea, vomiting, madness, and death. Experienced sailors almost always resist the temptation, but it is an endless source of frustration. Samuel Taylor Coleridge spoke for all these thirsty castaways when he wrote, in *The Rime of the Ancient Mariner*, "Water, water every where, nor any drop to drink."

Maritime folk wisdom has been affirmed by modern science. Biologists now know that when a body is dehydrated, it can draw water from its own cells, but those cells are damaged in the process, causing different symptoms generated by different cells in the body. Withdrawing water from the cells of the central nervous system, for instance, can cause a person to decline mentally or even die of paralysis of the respiratory system. Drinking seawater makes the dehydration and the cellular damage worse. Seawater is about 3.5 percent salt, four times the concentration found in the human body. When people drink salt water, their bodies look for water to dilute it, and they pull that water from their bloodstream and their cells. Drinking a mouthful of seawater is harmless, but large amounts can be fatal.

And often it *is* fatal. World War II shipwrecks provided a tragic natural study of the effects of drinking seawater. Some survivors who drank large amounts became delirious, frothed at the mouth, and died. Reviewing wartime shipwreck histories, a lecturer at the Royal College of Physicians in London in 1942 declared that "seawater poisoning must be accounted, after cold, the commonest cause of death in shipwrecked sailors." In 1960, a US Coast Guard study entitled "Dangers of Drinking Sea Water by Shipwrecked Mariners" was emphatic on the point. It concludes, in typography rare for a scientific article, "We cannot stress too much the old rule: ON NO ACCOUNT SHOULD A CASTAWAY DRINK SEA WATER."

Dudley, Stephens, and Brooks were well aware of the old sailors' wisdom. They resolved not to drink seawater no matter how thirsty they became. They explained to Parker, who knew less about such things, that he must not give in to the temptation and that he would regret it if he did.

There was one small source of freshwater in the lifeboat. The two tins Dudley grabbed while evacuating the *Mignonette*—turnips, not meat—contained a little liquid along with the soggy vegetables. After two days in the lifeboat, the men were so thirsty they opened the first tin. It contained five turnips, which the men carefully divided up. They appreciated having something to eat, even if it was not much, but it was the liquid that really lifted their spirits. "That one mouthful," Stephens later said, "seemed so cool to our parched throats."

On the third or fourth day, Stephens calculated the lifeboat's latitude. Using the sextant Dudley had taken from the *Mignonette* and sighting the noon sun, he determined that they were at 24.50° south latitude, which put them roughly in the middle of nowhere.

There was nothing to do but keep going. The lifeboat still leaked, even with the damaged place stopped up, and it kept filling with water. The men bailed, but the water kept coming. At times, the dinghy was half full of water. They knew it would not take much to swamp it and send it to the bottom. After their first tiny meal, the men's entire food supply consisted of a single remaining tin of turnips. Their only drinkable liquid was the water in that tin. There was no nearby land, and the men had not seen another ship since the *Mignonette* went down. There was nothing but open water in every direction.

Dudley and his small crew continued to bob along on the South Atlantic in their little wooden dinghy with just a pair of oars to propel it. They did not give up, but whatever hope they held on to was only of the most general sort. They had no idea where their salvation was coming from—if it was coming at all.

3

The Captain's Proposal

On July 10, the fifth day after the *Mignonette* sank, Brooks spotted something off in the distance. Whatever it was, it appeared to be moving. Brooks was eventually able to make out that it was a sea turtle, and he pointed it out to Dudley. The turtle was windward, and they were about to leave it behind. Brooks, who was steering, pulled the dinghy around to move toward it. When the lifeboat drew close, Stephens was able to grab the sea turtle by the flippers and turn it over. Brooks let go of the oar he was using to steer and helped lift the turtle into the boat. Although it was fairly large, Brooks later recalled that "it came on board as light as a fly."

The capture of the sea turtle was cause for excitement and joy. It would provide the men with the first food they had eaten in five days, other than the canned turnips, and it would be actual meat. Even more important, the turtle would provide them with drinkable liquid. "It gave us all fresh hopes," Dudley said later.

It was a remarkable windfall. Apart from rainwater, sea turtle blood is one of the best sources of life-sustaining liquids available at sea. Fish blood is too rich with protein and salt to ward off dehydration, but sea turtle blood has a different chemistry, and it is a highly effective substitute for freshwater. A forty-five-pound turtle can produce a quart of blood and other fluids. Although the men were focused on their thirst, the sea turtle would also provide pounds of meat. After five days of near starvation, the men's relief and eagerness were overwhelming. The first thing they did was start drinking the sea turtle's blood, which they found enormously refreshing after days of thirst and parched mouths. They planned to save some of the blood for later, but in that they were less successful. They scrambled to catch some blood in the chronometer box, but seawater sprayed in. "We lost the biggest part of the blood through the salt water," Brooks recalled ruefully.

Once their thirst was quenched, Dudley, Brooks, and Parker ate the sea turtle's flesh. Brooks would later speak highly of the taste of the meat. There was "nothing better at sea in the shape of fish than turtle," he said. The men were so pleased by how things were going that they decided to eat the second tin of turnips. While the others ate the sea turtle meat, Stephens refrained. He later said that he did not suffer from hunger the way the others did. "Drink was all I wanted," he recalled. He only began to join in and eat the meat when most of it was already gone.

The relief from the turtle blood did not last. If it had not been contaminated with seawater, Brooks estimated, they would have had a quart or more to drink, which would have lasted them several days. Instead, they were thirsty again almost immediately. Before long, the castaways resorted to something more desperate than drinking turtle blood. Around the eighth day in the lifeboat, they began to drink their own urine. They had held out as long as they could, but from that day on, they consumed urine on a regular basis. Drinking urine was more accepted among sailors than drinking seawater, but it could also be harmful.

Like seawater, urine has high salt levels that can exacerbate dehydration. It also contains waste products and toxins. Urine drinking can also take a psychological toll. As one handbook on emergency medicine warns, drinking urine "will destroy a person's will to survive and hasten their death."

The men improvised other ways of alleviating their thirst. After nine or ten days, Stephens suggested they wet their flannel clothes, wring them out, and put them on again. He and Brooks took off their singlets, dipped them in the sea, and wore them. Stephens later said his idea "certainly relieved us a little, but we felt the cold very much through sitting in our wet shirts." At times, the men even clambered out of the lifeboat and into the water. This was a daunting thing to do on the open ocean—particularly so soon after their encounter with an aggressive shark—and their trepidation was reflected in the care they took. One at a time, Brooks, Stephens, and Parker undressed and went overboard. The man in the water held fast to the boat, while the ones who remained in the dinghy kept watch for sharks. These short dips offered relief from the heat of the blazing sun and, Stephens said, "seemed to slacken our thirst." But they were tiring for the ailing men, and they stopped when they grew too weak to undress and dress again. They knew they might not find the strength to lift themselves back into the lifeboat. At that point, they just sat in the dinghy and dipped their hands in the water.

On the eleventh day, the food from the sea turtle ran out. The turtle had provided about three pounds of meat for each of the men, and they had wanted to stretch it out as long as they could, but there was no way to keep it cool. They tried to preserve some by hanging pieces along the side of the boat to dry, but much of the fat, which was their favorite part, spoiled and had to be thrown overboard. Once the meat was gone, they ate parts that were barely edible. They gnawed on the bones. They spent two days chewing on the skin. They scoured the lifeboat for any scraps they might have dropped. In the end, all that was left was the turtle's shell and its flippers.

The men were back to being constantly hungry and thirsty. Their only encounters with food and drink were now imaginary ones. "If we did get any sleep our dreams would be of eating and drinking," Stephens recalled. The lack of food and water was taking a harsh physical toll. "We were now in our worst straits," Stephens said, "so weak and cramped that we could hardly move." They sat and looked "at each other gradually wasting away—hunger and thirst in each face," he said. "Our lips blackened, and our tongues became very hard," Brooks later recalled. When the men talked, Dudley said, they sounded like wild animals. The grueling conditions were causing the men to develop body sores. Their legs were swollen to the knees and turning black. Brooks, who had boots, was less affected by this particular torment. Stephens was the worst off. "I do not think he could raise himself up," Brooks said.

No time of day in the lifeboat was good, but some were more unbearable than others. At midday, the sun was brutal. Evenings were chilly, and the men had little clothing and no blankets to keep them warm. But nights held the greatest terror. Dudley later looked back on how the men feared "the sky coming dark." Drifting on the black ocean, they had no way of knowing whether a storm, shark, or other peril loomed. "Our nights were the worst time," Stephens said. "They seemed never to end; we dreaded them very much."

There was no indication they were anywhere near land, and they had not seen any sign of a ship since the *Mignonette* went down. Dudley, who had been pessimistic from the beginning, now believed the situation was dire. On July 16 or 17, while Brooks was steering and Stephens was lying down, Dudley made an announcement. It was necessary, he told the others, to kill one of the men in the lifeboat and eat him so the other three could survive. "We shall have to draw lots, my boys," he said.

Dudley was invoking a tradition known as "the custom of the sea." It had long been accepted in the sailing world that when there was not enough food or water to keep everyone alive, lots could be drawn to decide who should be killed and eaten. It was something to be done only in the most extreme circumstances, and Dudley had decided that they had reached that horrible point.

Stephens, Brooks, and Parker would have been familiar with the custom of the sea. It was a part of sailing culture, passed on from sailor to sailor not only through conversations but in stories and songs. There was a whole category of sea shanties, the traditional work songs sung on sailing ships, known as "cannibal ballads." Some of these, such as the "Shipwreck of the *Essex*," recounted instances of lots being drawn to decide who would be sacrificed.

Even many people with no connection to the sea knew of the custom of the sea. It had been written about in leading works of literature. Lord Byron, among the most revered writers of his day, depicted it in one of his most popular epic poems. In *Don Juan*, published between 1819 and 1824, the title character and his tutor, Pedrillo, escape a shipwreck in a lifeboat and run out of food. Desperate, "they spoke of lots for flesh and blood / And who should die to be his fellow's food." Pedrillo lost the drawing and was killed and eaten. In Edgar Allan Poe's only novel, *The Narrative of Arthur Gordon Pym of Nantucket*, sailors draw lots after a shipwreck so "one of us should die to preserve the existence of the others." The men in the *Mignonette* lifeboat were likely not familiar with this American novel, but if they had been, they might have been haunted by an eerie coincidence. In the book, which had been published forty-six years earlier, the sailor who drew the short straw and was eaten was named Richard Parker.

The captain was proposing a fair drawing of lots, in which all four of the men in the lifeboat would have an equal chance of being chosen and an equal chance of living. Still, what he was suggesting was killing—taking a life intentionally and with premeditation. And in invoking the custom of the sea, Dudley was abandoning a central tenet of his faith. He was a religious man, who had brought prayer books on the voyage and frequently importuned God for help. Christianity has clear teachings on the subject. The Ten Commandments include the injunction "Thou shalt not kill," and Jesus taught, "You shall not murder." But Dudley was now prepared to replace the Bible, which instructed him not to kill, with a sailor's tradition that told him he could.

For some sailors, the custom of the sea itself had religious overtones. In the Bible, at some momentous points, men draw lots. When Jesus was nailed to the cross, the Roman soldiers cast lots to see who would keep his clothes. In other parts of the Bible, it is the righteous who cast lots. In Numbers, Moses casts lots to allocate territory to the tribes of Israel. Proverbs describes the divine nature of the act: "The lot is cast into the lap, but its every decision is from the Lord." It could be used on board a ship, similarly, as a way of appealing to God to make a choice too hard to trust to human judgment. When the short lot was drawn, the decision about who should be sacrificed could be thought of as God's will.

But the custom of the sea was above all a solution for a mercilessly practical problem—starvation and impending death—and its ethical balance lands heavily on the side of the pragmatic. In fact, it is no exaggeration to say that the sailors who invented and accepted it developed a workingman's version of utilitarianism, the philosophical theory that holds that the morally right action is the one that produces the greatest good for the greatest number. The custom of the sea replaced the theological absolutes of the Bible and its command against murder with the notion that killing one person could be justified if it meant that more people would survive. Using their own gut intuitions, these sailors had come to conclusions about what is right and good that were similar to the ones that would later be devised by Jeremy Bentham, the founder of utilitarianism, who was educated at Oxford, and John Stuart Mill, who was a philosopher and a member of Parliament.

The custom of the sea had another virtue that some philosophers favored: egalitarianism. Sailing ships were notoriously hierarchical, with captains exercising dictatorial power. But the custom of the sea did not leave it to the captain to decide who should be killed. Nor did it decree that the lowest-ranking person on the ship be sacrificed. It required lots to be drawn on an equal basis so that everyone from the captain to the cabin boy would have the same chance to live.

The custom of the sea did not specify how lots should be drawn. In practice, the drawings ranged widely. Captains or crewmembers sometimes held out straws for people to choose and whoever drew the short straw lost. Sometimes one person drew lots for all present, and as each was drawn, it was announced which person it represented. The mechanics often left something to be desired. People could be told that they had drawn the short straw, or rather that the short straw had been drawn for them, at a drawing they had not been allowed to watch.

The fact that the sailing world embraced the custom of the sea did not mean all the men in the lifeboat had to—and they did not. When Dudley suggested that it was time to draw lots, Stephens and Brooks did not agree. Dudley repeated the idea, but whenever he did, Stephens and Brooks rejected it. "I and Mr. Stephens would not hear of it," Brooks recalled. And it was no small thing for Stephens and Brooks to resist. A captain, the ship's master, had almost unlimited power to decide what happened on board, by both tradition and contract. Stephens, Brooks, and Parker had signed an "Agreement and Account of Crew" that included their consent "to be at all times . . . obedient to the lawful commands of the said Master, or of any person who shall lawfully succeed him." Stephens's and Brooks's refusals were not insubordination, which could be harshly punished, since Dudley was proposing drawing lots rather than commanding it. But it was an indication of the strength of their feelings that they did not defer to their captain's wishes.

It is not clear exactly why each of the men objected, since it does not appear that they gave the captain a reason. They might have believed it was not right to kill anyone under any circumstances. Or they might have believed the situation was not desperate enough yet to take such a drastic measure. Or their motives might have been more self-serving: They may have been focused on the fact that if lots were drawn, there was a one in four chance that they themselves would be the one killed and eaten.

Even less is known about how Parker felt. Dudley did not solicit his opinion on drawing lots. Parker's status as cabin boy apparently put him, in Dudley's eyes, so far below the full crew members that his views should not be taken into account. It was an unjust act of disenfranchisement because if there was a drawing, Parker would be a participant whether he wanted to be or not—and he might end up as food and drink for the other three.

*

After Dudley's proposal was rejected, the men turned their attention to improving their chances of being saved. On their fifteenth day adrift, they set out to convert the dinghy into a sailboat. Sails would give them more control over their direction than their oars and sea anchor did as well as greater speed—and the wind, rather than the exhausted crew, would provide the power to move forward. The men used an oar as a mast and a wooden plank for the yard, the spar on the mast that the sails are attached to. Their shirts became the sails, two shirts on top and one below. Strands from the painter, the rope used to tie the boat to a dock, became the rope for the rigging. Their makeshift sailboat moved over the waves with surprising ease, and they found that they were making progress in moving to the west, where they believed they would have a better chance of meeting another ship. "This seemed to cheer us a bit," Stephens recalled.

Around the time that the sails went up, Parker made a confession. He told the others he was secretly drinking seawater at night, while they were sleeping. He admitted that he had drunk a bailer full of seawater, which was about a quart, and then another half bailerful. Now he had become ill as a result. He had diarrhea, and he was in pain. He had taken to lying down on the bottom of the boat trying to sleep. Brooks was distressed. He knew that seawater would make the boy sicker and could eventually kill him. "I told him he was a very silly young fellow," Brooks recalled. But Parker responded, "I must drink something."

Parker now appeared to be the weakest of the four. Stephens seemed to be the next sickest, with internal pains and legs so swollen he could hardly move. Stephens was not as firm as Brooks in condemning Parker's decision to drink seawater. In fact, he was considering it himself. He quietly asked the cabin boy, out of earshot of the other two, "How does it taste, Dick?"

Parker responded, "Oh, not so bad." Parker said it was "better than what we've been having," a reference to the urine. Before long, Stephens gave in to temptation. He sneaked some seawater in the middle of the night, when Dudley and Brooks could not see him. He later said that the salt water "burnt" his "throat like fire" and that he only drank a few drops and then resolved not to drink any more.

When Parker became sick, Dudley repeated his call for drawing lots. Brooks and Stephens again rejected the idea. While Stephens simply opposed it, Brooks was now more forthcoming about his views. "Let us all die together," he said. "I should not like anyone to kill me," he explained, "and I should not like to kill anyone else."

Brooks's words were revealing. It was now clear that his objections were not about timing. He was not merely saying he did not believe it was necessary to kill someone now, but it might be in the future. Brooks was categorically rejecting the idea that any of them should be killed, at any point. There in the lifeboat, Brooks did not explain why he was resisting in this way, and in later statements about the events, he does not appear to have said any more about how he arrived at his position. It could have been a matter of religious conviction. Brooks was, after all, a man of faith, who prayed throughout the voyage. But the way he worded his objection does not sound particularly religious. He did not explicitly invoke the Bible or Jesus. He did not say it would be a sin to kill, or even that it would be "wrong." He said, "I should not like to," as if he had decided this all on his own. His statement sounded less like Christian dogma than like a personal credo, a statement of conscience.

There is something else striking about Brooks's words: They imply an inherent commitment to equality. His simple dictum did not frame his own life as more valuable than anyone else's.

He was as adamant about not wanting the other men to be killed as he was about not wanting to be killed himself.

It is often said that in survival conditions, no rules apply. Thomas Hobbes, in *Leviathan*, wrote of what he called the battle for existence, which he called the war of "every man, against every man." But Brooks's stand refutes the idea that it has to be every man for himself. Brooks showed that it was possible to hold firmly to moral beliefs even under threat of death.

Brooks's refusal was not the answer Dudley wanted to hear. But in the face of this categorical opposition from his able seaman and his first mate's less-defined objection, Dudley reluctantly backed down. "So let it be," he replied, "but it is hard for four to die, when perhaps one might save the rest."

As the men went back to the hard work of survival, Stephens's health continued to decline. Other than Parker, the first mate "suffered more than any of us," Brooks recalled. With his legs failing him, Stephens now had to crawl if he wanted to move around the boat. The others were worried about him. "One night he was so bad that we thought he was going to die," Brooks said. The men "took hold of his hand, and we prayed together to the Almighty to save us." Parker, meanwhile, showed no signs of improving. He lay at the bottom of the boat for long periods, drifting in and out of sleep. When he was awake, the cabin boy followed what was going on around him and participated in conversations. The castaways prayed out loud at different times of the day but mostly at sunset, because the nights were so difficult, and Parker sometimes prayed with the others. Stephens often asked him, "Have you said your prayers today, Dick?" and the cabin boy always replied, "Yes." Parker never stopped talking of his hope of being rescued, and his older comrades tried to keep his spirits up. They told him he would get better and that, ultimately, they would all be saved. Brooks repeatedly said, "Cheer up, Dickey, it will all come right."

It seemed to Dudley that things were about as bad as they could be. On July 21, in a dark state of mind, he added to the letter he had begun scribbling to his wife on the back of the chronometer certificate the day after the *Mignonette* went down. "We have been here 17 days; have no food," he wrote. "We are all four living, hoping to get passing ship. If not, dear, we must soon die." He told his wife that a certain Mr. Thompson would "put everything right if you go to him." He was sorry that he had undertaken the trip, but he had decided to go believing he "was doing it for our best." He went on to say, "You know, dear, I should so much like to be spared." If he survived, he said, "you would find I should lead a Christian life for the remainder of my days."

But he did not seem to have much faith in their chances for survival. "If ever this note reaches your hands, dear," he wrote, "you know the last of your Tom and loving husband. I am sorry things are gone against us thus far, but hope to meet you and all our dear children in heaven. Do love them for my sake, dear: bless them and you all. I love you all dearly, you know, but it's God's will if I am to part from you, but have hopes of being saved." Dudley signed the letter, "Good-bye and God bless you all, and may He provide for you all.—Your loving husband, Tom Dudley."

On July 23, the situation in the lifeboat was worse than ever. The men had not eaten in eight days, except for the sea turtle skin they had chewed on when the meat was gone. It was the longest they had gone without food. More critically, they had not had freshwater in five days. They caught some rainwater the next day, but the situation remained desperate. Dudley kept raising the subject of drawing lots and said that something would have to be done. Brooks and Stephens did not waver. The men looked at each other, unable to find a path forward. Parker continued to lie in the bottom of the boat, not part of the discussion.

Their most dire need remained the same as ever. "Thirst more than hunger was our trouble," Brooks recalled. But it was not clear what they could do about it. They hoped every day to fill their oilskin coats with rainwater, but rain would not come. As they admitted later, the men could not help thinking of a source of liquid even closer at hand—the blood in Parker's body. The cabin boy might die soon, and when he did, they would be able to drink his blood. The problem was, the men believed that if Parker died of natural causes, the blood would congeal instantly, and it would be undrinkable by the time they realized he was dead.

There were still no passing ships and no sign of land. No rain fell, and no other sea turtle blundered past. The only chance for relief that was within their control was the gruesome one that Dudley proposed. They could decide to kill one of the men in the lifeboat and drink his blood, or they could keep on waiting. As captain, Dudley could have simply drawn straws. After all, a captain's power on a boat had few limits. He may have believed such a momentous decision required support from his crew, or he may have worried he would not be able to carry out the killing if Stephens and Brooks were willing to extend their opposition all the way to physical resistance. Whatever the reason, Dudley kept trying to win over the others. He continued to say something had to be done, but Brooks and Stephens kept objecting, saying, "We shall see a ship tomorrow." A somber mood fell over the lifeboat.

Dudley finally gave up on drawing lots and proposed a new plan. At about three o'clock in the morning, the captain spoke to Stephens. Brooks was steering, and Parker was still lying at the bottom of the boat. They could not hear the captain and the first mate talking.

"What is to be done?" Dudley asked Stephens. "I believe that boy is dying." Then he asked, "How many children have you?"

"Five and a wife," Stephens said.

"I have three and a wife, and would it not be better that we should kill the boy Parker in order that three lives might be saved?" Dudley said.

Dudley did not discuss wives or children with Brooks, who had neither. In making his appeal to Stephens, Dudley argued that Parker was dying anyway. When he described the cabin boy's condition later, in an official report, he would paint a grim picture. Parker "lay gasping for breath and his frail frame was all but lifeless when I insisted that we should put an end to his life + drink the drops of blood if any from his body." But Dudley almost certainly overstated the severity of Parker's illness—to Stephens in the lifeboat and later in the official report. Parker may have been the sickest of the four men, but Brooks and Stephens would later express far more uncertainty about whether Parker was close to death, and they would not mention him "gasping." Stephens might have been reluctant to participate in the murder of Parker, a young man that they all had grown to like very much. But Dudley was trying to persuade him that this would not be much of a murder at all. Parker was going to die anyway, and quite soon, he insisted.

Dudley's new plan also addressed another concern Stephens may have had. The captain had not been able to get Stephens to agree to a drawing in which he himself would have a one in four chance of being selected to be killed and eaten. But now he was offering a plan in which Dudley, Stephens, and Brooks would all be safe. Dudley was stipulating from the start that Parker would be the one to die.

The captain's proposal was a major departure from the custom of the sea, and it lacked some of the classic virtues of that maritime tradition. It did not have the inherent equality of the custom of the sea, which required that everyone on the boat have the same chance of living or dying. And because it did not include the element of chance, there would be no way to believe God—or the fates—had determined the outcome.

Even with the appeal from one husband and father to another and the promise that he would personally be safe, Stephens still hesitated. "If there is no vessel in sight by tomorrow morning, I think we had better kill the lad," Dudley said. Stephens responded that they should "see what daylight brings forth."

Parker, who had been left out of all the previous discussions of drawing lots, was not included in the one about killing *him*, specifically. If he had known what was being planned, he almost certainly would have objected strenuously. At seventeen, Parker had his whole life ahead of him, and he had begun the voyage with an exuberant attitude about life. He wanted to become a man and was considering leaving England for new adventures in Australia. Even with dehydration and starvation taking their toll, he "never said anything to lead us to suppose that his life was a burden to him," Brooks said. Even as he lay on the floor sick and in pain, Parker kept thinking about being rescued. When he slept, he woke up talking about a ship arriving to save them. "A ship was all I ever heard him express a wish about," Brooks said.

When morning broke on July 25, the sky was clear and it was, Brooks recalled, "a very fine day." Dudley and Stephens were sore from sitting, and their legs ached. Brooks, who was in the back steering the lifeboat, was doing a little better. Parker lay at the bottom of the boat, groaning. He had not spoken for hours. Dudley again said something had to be done, though he did not say what. Brooks responded simply, "We shall see a sail to-day." At 6 a.m., Stephens took over the steering. Brooks scanned all around for a ship, but he did not see one.

Once it was clear that the arrival of daylight had not changed anything, Stephens told Dudley that he believed Parker should be killed.

Dudley and his mate now had an agreement, a conspiracy of two. They finalized their plan outside the earshot of Brooks, who would not have agreed, and Parker, who had no idea what lay in store.

It is not clear why Stephens finally gave in. A generous interpretation would be that he believed Dudley's contention that Parker was on the brink of death, so they would merely be speeding up his inevitable death rather than killing him. Stephens might have seen it as essentially an act of efficiency, since it would end Parker's life quickly and let the others drink his blood before it congealed—or even an act of mercy, as Dudley would later suggest. Alternatively, Stephens's change of heart might have been a matter of timing. He may have simply decided that time had run out, and it was the last chance to kill one person to save the other three. But it is also possible that Stephens was motivated purely by self-interest and perhaps had been all along. He had rejected Dudley's proposal to draw lots, which would have meant he had a one in four chance of being killed, but when he was presented with a plan that entailed no chance of dying, only a windfall of food and liquid that could save his life, that was a very different proposition. Stephens's priority throughout may simply have been to optimize his own chances of staying alive.

Whatever the explanation for Stephens's conversion, it gave Dudley all the support he felt he needed. The captain and the first mate had now decided on a course of action. Dudley did not care that his able seaman was opposed or that his cabin boy was never consulted. He grabbed hold of the shrouds, the fragile rigging that held up the improvised mast, and took one final look around. He could not see a ship, or land, or anything else in any direction to change his mind. The decision had now been made. All that remained was to carry it out.

Dudley began by moving Brooks away from Parker. It was not easily done, since the lifeboat was only thirteen feet long and the cabin boy was lying in the middle of it. "You had better go forward and have a sleep," the captain advised Brooks. The able seaman moved to the front of the dinghy and lay down in the bow of the boat, with his feet under a thwart, a part of the dinghy that provided structural support and could be used as a seat. Dudley remained further aft while Stephens steered. Stephens nodded at Parker and then at Brooks. Brooks later said this was the moment he realized what was about to happen. Brooks tried to block everything out. "I had my oilskin coat over my head, trying to sleep," he later recalled. He covered his eyes before he could see any more.

"Hold his feet," Dudley told Stephens. Stephens stood ready to hold Parker down if it was necessary, and he watched as Dudley moved toward the cabin boy. Dudley took out a white-handled penknife. Before he used it, the God-fearing captain had one more matter to attend to. He offered up a prayer for forgiveness so that "our souls might be saved." The cabin boy lay before him in the bottom of the boat, with his arm over his face. Dudley knelt down next to him.

"Now, Dick, your time has come," Dudley said.

Calling Parker "Dick" added a chilling touch of intimacy to the moment. Many people who kill, such as soldiers and executioners, try to depersonalize the individual whose life they are about to end. Dudley did the opposite, addressing Parker affectionately, with his nickname.

"What, me, Sir?" Parker murmured in response.

It was clear from Parker's words that he knew what was about to happen, another unsettling aspect of the scene. Dudley did not strike from behind, ending Parker's life before he could appreciate what was going on. He allowed the cabin boy an awful moment of knowledge of what was about to occur. And there is a particular poignancy to Parker's final word, "Sir." He was speaking with deference to the man who had offered himself, back in May, as a kind of father figure.

"Yes, my boy," Dudley replied.

Dudley pointed his penknife toward the cabin boy's throat. He aimed the blade at the side of the neck that Parker's arm was not covering and plunged it in. Parker remained still, even as the blood started spurting out. The cabin boy's end came quickly. "In a minute all was over," Stephens said. Dudley remembered it as taking just fifteen seconds. Stephens did not have to help. "I know I was expected to hold his feet if he struggled," he said, but Parker did not struggle. Brooks was three feet away when Dudley stabbed the cabin boy. He heard "a little noise" through his oilskin coat, he recalled. When Brooks lifted the coat from his head, he could see Parker had been stabbed to death. Brooks fainted away for a minute or two and woke to see Dudley and Stephens drinking Parker's blood. One drank from the bailer, the other from a turnip tin.

Brooks had not wanted Parker killed, but now that he was dead, the able seaman hoped for some of the blood. "Give me a drop," Brooks asked Dudley. The captain shared what he had, but there was not much drinkable liquid left. Brooks said the blood he received was "quite congealed," but he "sucked it down" as well as he could.

Dudley and Stephens stripped Parker's body, throwing his clothing overboard. When they were done, they sliced open the corpse and removed the internal organs. Dudley, Stephens, and Brooks devoured Parker's heart and liver while they were still warm. Then they tore flesh from Parker's body and immediately began eating it.

The men dug into their meal enthusiastically. It did not deter them that the meat and blood were human—or, more particularly, that it came from a shipmate and friend. Brooks later said that they fully enjoyed the food and drink that had suddenly appeared before them. "I can say that we partook of it with quite as much relish as ordinary food," he said.

It was the most they had eaten since the sinking of the *Mignonette* nearly three weeks earlier. Parker's flesh and blood reenergized the other three. They all agreed that they were "different men" as a result of it. Brooks later said, thinking back on the moment he drank Parker's blood, "I felt quite strong after that."

4

The Cannibalism Taboo

When they ate Parker's lifeless body and drank his blood, Dudley, Stephens, and Brooks crossed a line. They became cannibals. The boundary is a profound one. The taboo against eating human flesh and blood is not a product of a particular culture or religious tradition or historical era. It seems to stem from more primitive feelings. Cannibalism evokes not just shame and guilt but a more visceral, even primordial, reaction: disgust. When they ate Parker, Dudley, Stephens, and Brooks became part of a long, complex, and dark tradition of people eating people.

The natural history of cannibalism is rich and variegated. It has always been a fixture of the animal world, and scientists have documented it in countless species, from polar bears to mollusks. The phrase "pecking order" derives from the bird world, where dominant chickens may peck subordinate ones, who are sometimes pecked to death and eaten. Female praying mantises eat males while they are having sex. Among the springbok mantis, who are avid practitioners of "sexual cannibalism," 60 percent of sexual encounters end with the female biting off the male's head.

In the human evolutionary line, cannibalism is far older than the human race. In what is now Kenya, there is fossil evidence suggesting that evolutionary relatives of humans sometimes butchered and ate each other 1.45 million years ago. That is more than 1 million years before modern humans emerged. The discovery of fossils with revealing cut marks from 800,000 years ago, discovered in a cave in Burgos, Spain, also suggests the existence of "caveman cannibalism" among a not-so-distant prehuman cousin.

Many archaeologists and historians now believe that cannibalism has existed whenever and wherever human beings have lived. In the British Isles, cannibalism long predates Britain. In one instance, modern humans who lived in what is now Somerset fifteen thousand years ago cut off the heads of two adults and a three-year-old child, stripped the bodies of their meat, and crushed the bones to get at the marrow. Archaeologists there found severed skulls that had been chiseled to create cups that could be drunk out of. In more recent eras, cannibalism in Mesoamerica in the fifteenth and sixteenth centuries stands out for the sheer number of victims. The Aztecs engaged in elaborate human sacrifices where victims reportedly numbered in the tens of thousands, often ending with ritualized cannibalism. At the dedication of the main pyramid in Tenochtitlan in 1487, by some estimates, as many as twenty thousand victims or more may have been sacrificed. In modern times, European explorers in the South Pacific recorded extensive accounts of cannibalism. Foreign observers reported that the Maori and Fijians ate their enemies in war. According to one report, Fijians drank the blood of their victims immediately and then cooked their body parts in underground ovens.

While Western discussions of cannibalism often focus on non-Western locations, framing cannibalism as a savage, exotic custom of non-Christian, nonwhite peoples, Europe has its own long history of it. During the famine of 1315 to 1317, eating human flesh was widespread and took many forms. Contemporary chroniclers told of prisoners who, not being regularly fed, attacked newly arriving inmates and ate them while they were still half alive. Not all European cannibalism was prompted by hunger. From the fourteenth to the eighteenth centuries, Europeans ate human body parts and drank blood for their purported medical value. Across the continent, "mummy shops" sprang up, selling human flesh as a panacea. Poor people who could not afford to buy flesh went to public executions and stood under the scaffold with a cup to capture the condemned man's blood as it fell to the ground.

Famously, there were also cases of cannibalism by deranged criminals. In Germany in the 1500s, farmer Peter Stumpp, "the Werewolf of Bedburg," was said to have killed and eaten fourteen children and two pregnant women. The infamous French cannibal Antoine Léger grabbed a young woman in the forest, raped and killed her, and drank her blood and ate her corpse. He was executed by guillotine in 1824.

In its own shorter history, the United States has a deep vein of cannibalism. At the first English settlement, in Jamestown, Virginia, the colonists ate people in the Starving Time of 1609–10, a harsh winter in which about 80 percent of the villagers died. There is archaeological evidence, including the skull of a fourteen-year-old English girl with marks indicating that whoever ate her was, as one account has it, "clearly interested in cheek meat, muscles of the face, tongue, and brain." After the colonies became the United States, Americans had their own notorious cannibals. Among the best known were the survivors of the Donner Party, eighty-seven pioneers who headed west by wagon and were met with freezing weather, illness, and starvation in the winter of 1846–47. Forty-two members of the group died on the trek, and the survivors got by mainly by eating those who had died of natural causes. At first, they were reluctant to eat corpses, but in time their inhibitions fell away. "They stripped the flesh from the bodies, roasted what they needed to eat, and dried the rest for carrying with them," according to *Ordeal by Hunger*, an account of the ill-fated trek. When the corpses ran out, the Donner Party killed and ate two Native Americans who were accompanying them.

There were many more such acts on the American frontier. In February 1874, Alfred Packer, a gold prospector, fed on his five fellow gold-seekers when they were trapped in the snow-packed San Juan Mountains in Colorado. A *Harper's Weekly* writer found a campsite full of corpses, some with chunks hacked out of the chests and thighs. Packer, who confessed and then recanted, fueled public interest in cannibalism when it was reported, perhaps apocryphally, that he had declared that "the breasts of the men" were "the sweetest meat I ever tasted."

The history of cannibalism reveals two things: that there has been a strong taboo against cannibalism in many places and times and that there has also been a great deal of it over the years. Sigmund Freud explained this odd contradiction—the condemnation of cannibalism and the extensive presence of it—by theorizing that mankind is on some level strongly attracted to cannibalism. He regarded it as one of humanity's three great prohibited "instinctual wishes," along with incest and the lust to kill. He believed mankind's innate aggressiveness gives people a repressed desire to eat other people. Civilization had to develop strong taboos against cannibalism, he argued, not because people find it so distasteful but because deep down they have a drive to engage in it.

Freud's observation that people are on some level drawn to cannibalism is supported by the prominent role it has played in Western culture. Cannibalism features in the Bible as the culmination of a litany of fearful punishments that God would unleash on the Israelites if they failed to carry out the Lord's commandments. "You shall eat the offspring of your own body," God warned, through Moses, "the flesh of your sons and daughters, whom the Lord your God has given you." Ancient Greek mythology shows an even greater fascination with stories of people eating people, often their own family members. In the myth of the House of Atreus, Atreus had a grievance against his brother, Thyestes. Atreus served Thyestes a banquet that included the flesh of Thyestes's own children. This grim story is the origin of the phrase "Thyestean banquet" for a meal in which human flesh is served. Cannibalism also plays a central role in the Christian liturgy, which includes, in the Eucharist, the ritual consumption of the body and blood of Christ.

If the stories a society tells its children are another window into its deepest values and tensions, classic fairy tales provide further support for Freud's analysis. The original versions of many fairy tales involved eating young people. In the Brothers Grimm's "Snow White," the evil stepmother wanted to eat Snow White's lungs and liver. In "Hansel and Gretel," the witch kept Hansel in an iron cage, fattening him up to eat. Charles Perrault, a seventeenth-century writer who wrote traditional French versions of "Cinderella," "Little Red Riding Hood," and "Sleeping Beauty," almost always included humans eating humans. One scholar who scoured his works found that "only four stories . . . do not feature cannibalism as such."

Victorian literature, which reflects the cultural values that prevailed at the time of the *Mignonette* disaster, shows a similar fascination. Daniel Defoe's *Robinson Crusoe* was published in 1719, but it was a huge international bestseller throughout the Age of Sail, and perhaps more than any other work of popular literature, it reflected the psyche of the era. At the center of its plot, along with its famous shipwreck and Crusoe's epic struggle for survival, is cannibalism. The anthropologist Shirley

Lindenbaum says the novel "portrays the cannibal as a nexus of ambiguous desire." Crusoe, she argues, "is attracted to the idea of eating human flesh and to being eaten." As elsewhere in the Western literary canon, the attitude toward cannibalism is not complete condemnation. There are elements of an ambivalence that literary scholar David Gill called, borrowing a phrase from Joseph Conrad, "the fascination of the abomination."

Academics who study cannibalism have developed a set of classifications to cover all the varieties that have emerged over the millennia. These "typologies of cannibalism" are based on who is doing the eating, who is being eaten, and why it is occurring. The category an act of cannibalism falls into is often an indicator of how society will respond to it—whether it is regarded as sacred or profane, moral or evil, legal or criminal.

One major distinction is between nutritional and cultural cannibalism. Nutritional cannibalism, a disturbingly anodyne term, refers to eating human flesh to meet dietary needs. This sort of cannibalism is not freighted with any larger meaning, religious or otherwise—it is just about eating. Nutritional cannibalism is common in extreme circumstances, like shipwrecks—but it has also, some anthropologists believe, existed in more mundane circumstances. One study of cannibalism among a particular tribe in New Guinea noted the protein value of human flesh and concluded that people were being eaten as a way for the "marginally well-nourished" population to "essentially resolve its protein insufficiencies."

Cultural cannibalism, or cannibalism not primarily motivated by nutritional need, takes many forms. It can be religiously inspired, like the large-scale human sacrifice practiced by the Aztecs. It can be an instrument of war, used to celebrate a victory in battle or to terrify an enemy. The Ngarigo, an Aboriginal

Australian people, were said to eat the hands and feet of their enemies to acquire some of their courage. Cannibalism can be used as punishment. The Battas of Sumatra were reported to have punished certain crimes with cannibalism, allowing the victims and their family and friends to eat the corpse of an executed wrongdoer.

Most notoriously, there is yet another form of cannibalism: psychopathic cannibalism, driven by obsession, sadism, or sexual perversion. Western legal annals are filled with cases of people eating other people because of their own dark drives, like Peter Stumpp and Antoine Léger. A recent American example is Jeffrey Dahmer, who killed people after he had sex with them in a pattern *The New York Times* described as "the same routine: sex, drugs in a drink, death and dismemberment."

There is even tenderhearted cannibalism. The anthropologist Beth Conklin, who did field research among the Wari of Brazil, described their "compassionate cannibalism." She interviewed a father whose two-year-old son had died, who looked back wistfully to the traditions of his tribe decades earlier. He preferred the time when the Wari roasted and ate the flesh and internal organs of their dead loved ones. "It's cold in the earth," the grieving father said. "It was better in the old days, when the others ate the body. Then we did not think about our child's body much. We did not remember our child as much, and we were not so sad."

In medieval China, young people occasionally engaged in "filial cannibalism," which combined the Confucian virtue of respect for elders with the eating of human flesh. As Key Ray Chong relates in *Cannibalism in China*, "children would cut off parts of their body and make them into soup to please family members, particularly their parents." *Gegu*, or "filial slicing," could be done to express reverence in the abstract, but it often had the more specific purpose of trying to cure a sick relative. The curative form of filial cannibalism was celebrated in the late Ming dynasty story "A Slice of Liver for Grandma."

The cannibalism of Dudley, Stephens, and Brooks was nutritional cannibalism of a specific sort—a subcategory known as survival cannibalism. In extreme conditions, when no other food source is available, humans will consume human flesh to stay alive. Driven by the primal will to survive in extraordinary circumstances such as famines, military sieges, shipwrecks, and arduous journeys, people can take desperate measures. "It is as though," University of California evolutionary psychologist Lewis Petrinovich explains, "the outer coverings of society have been peeled away to reveal the basic core of human nature." The Donner Party, Alfred Packer, and the residents of Europe during the famine of 1315 to 1317 all turned to survival cannibalism. In each of these instances, there was a crisis that made food scarce, and the answer starving people came up with was eating human flesh.

Survival cannibalism is often associated with shipwrecks. In the Age of Sail, when sailing traffic was at its height, shipwrecks were common, and more than a few of them ended in people eating other people to survive. One historian who examined survival at sea in that era concluded that anyone who believed cannibalism was rare "did not bother to look very carefully." It happened often enough that cannibalism featured in the British Parliament's discussion of sailing safety. When the House of Commons debated an Unseaworthy Ships bill in 1875, the bill's sponsor, Samuel Plimsoll, invoked several shipwrecks that ended in cannibalism to argue that more had to be done to protect sailors and passengers. Plimsoll provided graphic descriptions, including of a shipwreck in which four bodies were "found under the maintop, all dead, with part of one of their comrades hung up, as if in a butcher's shop."

Within the nutritional cannibalism subcategory of survival cannibalism, the eating of Parker on the *Mignonette* belongs to an even more particular subcategory: survival cannibalism at sea. But the typologies of cannibalism do not end there. There is still one more classification it falls into, and for the three survivors of the *Mignonette*, this final distinction was destined to become the most important one of all.

The most fundamental dichotomy in cannibalism is whether the person who was eaten was alive or dead. Russia, whose famines and wartime sieges offer an extensive history of cannibalism, has different words for the two distinct acts: *Trupoyedstvo* is "corpse-eating," and *lyudoyedstvo* is "person-eating." The distinction is critical, since killing to eat is not only cannibalism but murder, which brings it to a whole other level.

There are obvious moral and legal differences between these two kinds of cannibalism. The crash of Uruguayan Air Force Flight 571 in the Andes, the incident made famous by the book and movie *Alive*, was an example of corpse-eating. The survivors, who are some of the best-known cannibals of all time, ate the dead bodies of their fellow passengers. No one was killed to be eaten. Jeffrey Dahmer, who is also the subject of books and movies, was a person eater.

Many people regard corpse-eating with disgust, but people are rarely seriously condemned or punished for eating a dead body in survival conditions. It is widely accepted that the drive to stay alive should outweigh the taboo against eating human flesh. In the *Alive* incident, a priest told the survivors that the Catholic Church did not regard it as a sin to engage, "in extremis," in cannibalism of dead bodies. In a case of killing someone to eat, the ethical and legal considerations are more complex.

Murder is both a grave moral offense in almost every religious and moral tradition and the most serious of crimes. If the men in the *Mignonette* lifeboat survived, they would be notorious as cannibals for eating Parker's flesh, but it would be the killing of Parker rather than the eating of him that would be the far weightier transgression—and the one that would have the most fateful consequences for them.

At the time of the *Mignonette*'s voyage, there was already a long history of survival cannibalism at sea. The actions of Dudley, Stephens, and Brooks would inevitably be judged in the context of what had come before, but among past incidents, the particulars varied considerably. Sometimes people survived by eating the already dead; in other cases they killed people to eat. Sometimes the custom of the sea was followed and lots were drawn; other times it was not.

When the shipmates chosen for consumption were already dead, the survivors were likely to come out looking sympathetic. One such case unfolded in 1710, after the wreck of the *Nottingham Galley*, a British cargo ship sailing from London to the American colonies with a crew of fourteen. It was lost in a gale off the coast of Maine. The captain and crew were stranded on Boon Island, a collection of jagged rocks without vegetation that a poet called "the forelornest place that can be imagined." After two and a half weeks in freezing December weather, the ship's carpenter died of starvation and hypothermia. The thought of eating him was "most grievous and shocking," the captain recalled, but the men's views changed as they became hungrier. Finally, they threw away the head, hands, and feet—the parts that looked the most disturbingly human—washed the rest of the flesh, and wrapped it in seaweed to make sandwiches. In January, a ship appeared and the men were rescued without having had to kill anyone to survive.

The *Francis Mary* was carrying twenty-one people and a cargo of lumber from New Brunswick to Liverpool in 1826 when it was damaged in a gale. Food and water ran out, and people began dying of starvation and other causes. As they did, the survivors sliced up the corpses, washed them in seawater, dried them in the sun, and ate them. After a month, a ship appeared and rescued the six survivors. One of the rescuers was impressed by the array of food he saw laid out on the deck, exclaiming, "You have yet, I perceive, fresh meat!" But his demeanor changed when he realized the meat was human.

When the general public learned what occurred after the wrecks of the *Nottingham Galley* and the *Francis Mary* and other shipwrecks that ended in the eating of corpses, they reacted with shock and horror. But they also accepted that cannibalism of the already dead should not be punished. No serious efforts were made to bring criminal charges against any of the survivors.

In other disasters at sea, there were no dead bodies available for eating. The crews and passengers were confronted with the same dire choice the men in the *Mignonette* lifeboat faced. In many of these wrecks, a decision was made to select someone to be killed and eaten. Often, though not always, it was done by drawing lots.

Perhaps the earliest recorded instance of cannibalism on a British ship comes from an account written in 1641 about a voyage in the West Indies. The ship left St. Kitts for a one-night voyage with seven English sailors onboard, but a storm drove it out to sea. Unable to reach land, the men ran out of food and feared they would starve. One sailor proposed following the custom of the sea, and lots were drawn. The sailor who made the suggestion lost, and there was a second drawing to decide who would kill him. The sailor who lost the first drawing was killed by the sailor who lost the second, and the other men ate his flesh and drank his blood. They lived off his body until the boat came ashore on St. Martin seventeen days later.

Another British ship, the *Dolphin*, resorted to the custom of the sea in 1759. It was damaged in a storm while traveling from the Canary Islands to New York and drifted for months, with provisions running down. After the men on board ate all the food and the ship's dog and cat, they decided to draw lots. A Spanish passenger, Anthony Galatea, lost and was shot in the head and eaten. The captain and seven crewmembers were eventually rescued by another ship.

Six years later, the crew of an American ship, the *Peggy*, also sacrificed someone. The *Peggy* sailed from the Azores to New York, carrying a cargo of wine and brandy and a captain and eight crewmembers, including an enslaved Black man. It hit a series of gales that damaged the ship and left it drifting aimlessly. As food ran out, the men ate whatever they could find, including a cat, two pigeons, and barnacles scraped off the sides of the ship. The crew decided someone had to be killed and eaten. They told the captain they had drawn straws and the enslaved man lost. The captain later said he did not approve but felt powerless to stop it. The crew killed the enslaved man and feasted on his corpse. One ripped out the liver and ate it raw, and the men cooked the meat on an open fire. About two weeks later, when it was all gone, the crew drew lots a second time, but before another person was killed, a rescue ship arrived.

One of the most famous cases of cannibalism by lot occurred after the wreck that inspired *Moby-Dick*. The *Essex*, a whaling ship that sailed out of Nantucket, was sailing between the Galapagos Islands and Hawaii in 1820 when an eighty-five-foot sperm whale rammed into it. As it sank, the crew of twenty escaped in three whaleboats. There was cannibalism on the whaleboats, most of it the consumption of the already dead. But on the boat commanded by the captain, George Pollard, there were no corpses to eat. The crew drew lots, and an eighteen-year-old named Owen Coffin lost and was eaten. Pollard's boat eventually crossed paths with the whaling ship *Dauphin* off the coast of South America. When the *Dauphin*'s crew pulled the battered boat alongside, they found two living men—Pollard and one crewmember—and a number of human bones.

Finally, a particularly dramatic drawing of lots occurred in 1835. While hauling timber from Newfoundland, the *Francis Spaight* was wrecked in a storm, leaving just fifteen survivors. After about sixteen days, when food and water ran out, the captain decided to draw lots. He limited the drawing to the four boys onboard, because they had no wives or children. One of the boys, fourteen-year-old Patrick O'Brien, objected loudly. He only stopped when he was told that if the boys did not draw lots, he would be the one killed.

The lots were drawn in an unusual way. O'Brien was told to kneel and was blindfolded. A sailor drew sticks, and after each one, O'Brien was asked to call out the name of one of the four boys. When he said his own name, he was told the short stick had been drawn, though he could not see it for himself. O'Brien was bitter about how he was chosen and vowed to come back after death and haunt whoever killed him. The captain ordered the cook, who was responsible for feeding the crew, to slit O'Brien's throat. When he did, a crewmember caught the boy's blood in a tureen. The men started eating his corpse, and they hung his limbs over the stern to preserve them. In the next few days, the cook went mad, and when he became violent, the men cut his neck and drank his blood, and another of the boys was bled to death. Soon afterward, the crew spotted an American ship and, in a ghoulish maneuver, caught its attention by waving O'Brien's severed hands and feet.

Clearly, there was much room for things to be done badly when a lethal decision was made by drawing lots. There were instances, though, in which the captain or crewmembers simply decided who should die, the way Dudley chose Parker. In some cases, they insisted they had objective reasons for choosing the person they did, the way Dudley said he chose Parker because he was so sick and had no wife or children. The second killing on the *Francis Spaight* was one of these. The cook was chosen to be killed and eaten because he had gone mad—or so the survivors said. A similar thing occurred in 1878, when the *Sallie M. Steelman* was damaged in a gale twenty miles east of Cape Hatteras, North Carolina. After forty-three days, the crew later recounted, a Black sailor, George Seaman, "was driven crazy by his sufferings" and threatened to kill one of the sailors. They had no choice, they said, but to kill Seaman to protect the captain. The crew severed his head and threw it overboard, then stripped off his flesh and fried it in a pan. A passing schooner eventually spotted the ship and rescued the captain and five remaining crewmembers.

A disturbing pattern emerges from these cases of men drawing lots at sea. The custom of the sea decreed that decisions about who should be killed should be made through a random process; ideally, it treated everyone on the ship as an equal who deserved the same chance of living or dying as anyone else. But that was not how it worked in practice. The losers in cannibalism drawings were, very disproportionately, outsiders or people at the bottom of the various hierarchies on the ship. On the *Dolphin*, the one Spaniard on an English crew was said to have drawn the short straw. On the *Peggy*, the only enslaved man was said to have lost. On the *Essex* whaleboat, an eighteen-year-old was selected by the older men, and on the *Francis Spaight*, a fourteen-year-old was chosen in a drawing that included only the boys.

All these declared outcomes are suspect. In the case of the *Dolphin*, one historian expressed doubt about how the short straw managed to fall "on the obvious victim." It seems likely that the English sailors conspired to rig the drawing against the only Spaniard, or even that there was no drawing at all. The crew of the *Francis Spaight* abandoned all pretense of fairness when they limited the drawing to just the boys. Patrick O'Brien, the troublemaker of the group who was chosen for death, was another "obvious victim." As for the *Peggy*, the claim that the one enslaved man on the ship lost an honest drawing of lots was never credible. Even the captain later said he doubted the crew had acted fairly.

No less an authority than *The Times*, one of England's most respected newspapers, declared in the year of the *Mignonette* voyage that when lots were drawn at sea, the "choice of victim" was not "made with perfect impartiality." *The Times* observed that the victims usually had something in common. "The weakest will generally be singled out for death," the paper said, and "even if lots be cast, somehow the fate will not fall on the strong man able to defend himself, but on one who is helpless." A similar pattern prevailed when lots were not drawn at all and the captain or crew chose who should be sacrificed. The reasons given for selecting the person who was killed were not necessarily true. The surviving crew of the *Sallie M. Steelman* claimed that the Black sailor who was killed and eaten had become crazy and violent. But there was no way to independently confirm that claim, and the survivors had good reason to say Seaman posed a threat, whether he did or not.

It is not surprising that this pattern emerged. Social scientists have observed that in a wide range of contexts, people in power are inclined to select members of their own group for favored outcomes. This sort of bias is especially common in difficult situations. As the title of one social science study put it, "In-Group Favoritism Overrides Fairness When Resources Are Limited." In-group favoritism has been observed in cannibalism specifically. "It is not advantageous," evolutionary psychologist Lewis Petrinovich observes dryly, "to be a member of . . . a different race, or even to be a stranger when people are driven by starvation." The tendency to eat outsiders first, Petrinovich says, is tied to basic human instincts, such as a reluctance to eat direct kin and the power of a social contract to unite a community against outsiders.

Another explanation is the hierarchical nature of the sailing world. There were clearly delineated lines of authority, with captains at the top and cabin boys at the bottom. When there was something unpleasant to be done, from swabbing the deck to being killed and eaten, there was a natural tendency to look to the lowliest member—often the cabin boy. There was also a pragmatic reason for choosing outsiders and weak people. When singling out a person to be killed and eaten, there was always a chance the person who was selected would fight back. A strong victim or one with friends and allies on the ship might end up killing the intended killer. It was easier, as *The Times* observed, to choose the "helpless" person. One historian noted that cabin boys were particularly likely to be chosen because they were generally "young and small" and "easily subdued."

Given these patterns, the selection of Parker was likely, perhaps even inevitable. Parker was at the bottom of every hierarchy in the *Mignonette* lifeboat. He was the lowest ranking, least paid, youngest, most inexperienced, least capable, last hired, and sickest. Even if Stephens and Brooks had agreed to draw straws, it is not hard to imagine that Dudley would have been inclined to arrange, as captains and crews had been doing for centuries, for the lowliest member of the group to lose the drawing—and that was Parker.

When cannibalism at sea involves killing the victim, a fundamental question arises: Should it be prosecuted as murder? From a legal standpoint, these cases have all the elements of homicide: Each one involved an intentional killing of an innocent person that could not be justified as an act of self-defense against someone who was posing a threat. Yet even though these killings meet the legal criteria for murder, there were aspects of them that argued against bringing charges against the cannibals. One was the strong tradition of deference to captains. For much of the Age of Sail, the law barely extended to ships, which were regarded almost as sovereign states. Captains had what the law called "absolute discretion" in many areas. Their dominion was inherent in the title "master," commonly used for captains, which was short for the full legal title "master under God." It was widely accepted that captains were free to do what they wanted to their crews, almost without limit. Sailors could be flogged, and often were, with a diabolical device known as a cat o' nine tails, which could rip flesh off their backs. They could be keelhauled, or dragged under the keel of the ship, an agonizing near-drowning experience. A series of maritime laws were enacted in the mid-nineteenth century to formally bar captains from abusing their crews, but in practice, land-bound police, prosecutors, and judges did not often intervene over captains' actions on their own ships.

Another factor was the "custom of the sea." The sailing world had long ago decided that when people were in danger of starving, it was acceptable to kill and eat someone. Even though it was only tradition, not a legal doctrine, the criminal justice system had been inclined to condone it. After all, the custom of the sea was undergirded by a certain pragmatic logic: the idea that a killing was justified if it saved more lives. Prosecutors were used to bringing charges against people who killed out of malice or greed. Shipwreck survivors who killed someone to eat them could insist that they were motivated by the benign goal of saving a larger number of lives. Prosecutors were reluctant to accuse someone of murder if their actions could legitimately be seen as choosing the lesser of two evils. Over the centuries in which sailors had been killing and eating people in survival situations, no one had ever been prosecuted for it in a British court, much less convicted of a crime.

The seven English sailors in the 1641 St. Kitts shipwreck did not suffer any legal consequences. When their ship arrived in St. Martin, they were taken back to St. Kitts, where a British prosecutor initially charged them with homicide, but another legal officer soon dismissed the charges on the grounds that the murder and cannibalism were done out of necessity. The crewmembers of the *Dolphin*, who killed and ate the Spanish passenger, also went free. The crew of the *Peggy*, who killed the enslaved Black man on board, were not punished either. Nor was anyone prosecuted for the deaths on the whaleboats after the sinking of the Essex. When the *Sallie M. Steelman* arrived in New York, *The New York Times* reported that there would be an investigation of George Seaman's death. According to the paper, the crew was reluctant to answer questions "and continually inquired if any punishment was liable to be inflicted upon them for their act of cannibalism." They need not have worried. No one was prosecuted. Things worked out even better for the survivors of the *Francis Spaight*, who had killed fourteen-year-old Patrick O'Brien. When they were brought to Falmouth, England, they made no attempt to hide their cannibalism, and no charges were filed against them. When they returned to Limerick, Ireland, they were welcomed as brave victims of circumstance. A fund drive was launched to help them recover from their ordeal.

In their lifeboat, the men of the *Mignonette* had more immediate threats to worry about than the legality of what they had just done. Even with their newfound supply of food and drink, they were still adrift in a deserted expanse of ocean, with no nearby land in any direction. They remained at the mercy of the elements, which could send another storm their way at any time—and of the ocean, which could send another shark. If the men gave any thought to whether they might get in trouble for what they had just done, they would have quickly rejected the possibility. Even though they had not drawn lots, the killing of Parker had saved three lives as they saw it. No Englishman had ever been prosecuted for cannibalism at sea, and they had no reason to believe they would be the first. In fact, if the men in the lifeboat knew the story of the *Francis Spaight*, they might even have harbored hopes of being welcomed home the way those cannibals had been earlier in the century—as heroes.

5

A Difficult Homecoming

While Dudley, Stephens, and Brooks sat in the lifeboat digesting Parker's body, they had time to reflect on what they had just done. As unpleasant as the whole matter had been for all three of the survivors, Dudley had no regrets about taking the cabin boy's life, then drinking his blood and feeding off his corpse. He was convinced that it was better than the alternative of allowing all four of them to die of thirst or hunger. "The act was absolutely necessary to sustain the existence of those remaining," he said later. Still, his conviction that he had done the right thing was mixed with an element of disgust. The events in the lifeboat that morning would leave an indelible mark on him. Dudley would later say that he could "never forget the sight of my two unfortunate companions over that ghastly meal" at which they all were "like mad wolfs."

Brooks was more disturbed by what happened. He had never wavered in his opposition to killing anyone and had refused to participate. He shared in the blood and flesh once Parker was dead, but he was torn—willing to survive on Parker's flesh but continuing to believe the cabin boy should not have been killed. Looking back on it, Brooks found the whole series of events soul crushing. Until Parker was killed, Brooks had eagerly hoped to be rescued, but afterward, he said, "My heart was cold." He would later find these dark feelings impossible to put behind him. "When I am by myself I think about it a good deal," he said, "and my thoughts then of what I have seen and what we went through are very dreadful."

The men tore into their new supply of meat eagerly, despite its grim provenance. Dudley and Brooks ate the most rapidly and consumed the greatest quantity. Stephens, who was the sickest, ate less than the others—because he was the least hungry, not because he was the most squeamish. In the future, when they thought back on what occurred on the lifeboat, none of them would complain that they found the meat at all unpleasant to eat. On the contrary, their assessment of the meat matches what many people have said after engaging in cannibalism—that it actually tasted quite good. There are many such testimonials, including Alfred Packer reportedly saying that men's chests yielded the sweetest meat he had ever tasted and a crewmember on the *Sallie M. Steelman* declaring that the meat from the sailor who was killed was as good as any beefsteak he ever ate. According to those who have studied the matter, human meat is not all that different from meats that people are used to eating. It looks a lot like beef, with a similarly rich, red appearance. But people who have eaten human flesh compare the taste not to beef or chicken but to pork. There were reports in Germany in the 1910s and 1920s of two separate serial killers who sold their victims' flesh on the black market as pork.

The men in the lifeboat ate heartily from their new bounty. The biggest problem with their harvest of human flesh was a practical one. With the hot sun beating down, it was not easy to keep it from spoiling. The men appreciated how valuable the meat was and did their best to preserve it. They washed it with salt water and kept it covered. They kept "cutting out the bad," as Dudley put it, and tossed the rotten parts overboard. In the four days following the killing, they consumed about half of Parker's flesh. They were grateful for the sustenance it provided. "We all said many times it and it alone kept life in our bodies," Dudley said.

The day after Parker was killed, it rained, and as Dudley recalled, "we caught a nice drink of water." They drank a good amount, and they were even able to store some rainwater for later. The timing of the rain raised a troubling question: Had it really been necessary to sacrifice Parker after all? If Dudley had not killed Parker and the cabin boy had managed to hold on for just one more day, all four of them would have had their thirsts quenched in a far more conventional way.

On July 29, at about 6:30 a.m., Brooks was, he later said, "sitting thinking to myself and praying to the Almighty to rescue us from death." It was breakfast time, Dudley recalled, "just as we were having our feast," and Brooks, who was steering, saw a glint on the water four or five miles away. It took a moment to make it out, but he could see that it was a mast and a sail.

"Sail, oh!" Brooks cried out. "Oh, my God, here's a ship coming straight for us."

Dudley and Stephens stopped eating breakfast and exploded with unrestrained joy. In this moment, the men were "like a lot of lunatics," Stephens said later. Brooks recalled that "we all prayed together out loud that she would not miss us, all promising to lead a different life than we had done, if the Almighty would only give us strength to reach the vessel." The men tried frantically to make sure the passing ship saw them. Realizing that the wind was blowing them away from their potential rescuers, they raced to take down their improvised sails, made of the men's shirts, and Dudley and Brooks rowed windward with all their might. Stephens waved his shirt to get the passing ship's attention, but he was too exhausted to hold it up for long. They were in "dreadful suspense," Brooks later said, as they waited to find out if the ship would rescue them.

When it was clear that the bark was headed toward them, the men could hardly contain their happiness. "Hold on for a little while longer," Stephens urged Dudley and Brooks, "for they are keeping away from the wind and are coming down on us." The ship forged ahead and kept getting closer. The men "very much rejoiced and all thanked God for His mercy," Brooks recalled.

The ship coming toward them was the *Moctezuma*, a 442-ton, three-masted German bark sailing out of Hamburg. It was returning home from South America with a cargo of fustic, a tropical wood used to make dye. The captain, P. H. Simonsen, had been looking through his telescope when he spotted a speck in the distance. At first, Simonsen had trouble making out what he was seeing. When he realized it was a small boat, he ordered his crew to change course and head toward it.

An hour and a half after Brooks had first spotted its sails, the *Moctezuma* pulled alongside the dinghy. A sailor on the German boat tossed out a rope. Dudley grabbed it and wrapped it around a seat in the lifeboat. Stephens, who was seated in the aft, or rear, of the lifeboat, called out, "Oh, captain, for God's sake help us! We have been twenty-four days and have had nothing to eat or drink; help us on board!" Two *Moctezuma* crewmembers, Julius Erich Martin Wiese and Christopher Drewe, climbed down to the lifeboat and secured it to their ship. In the lifeboat, they saw three weather-beaten, emaciated men, who were looking up at them with expressions of excitement and relief. The German crewmembers noticed something else on the lifeboat that they had trouble identifying. Wiese later recalled seeing "some small pieces of flesh and one little piece of a rib." He could not tell what sort of flesh and bone they were, he later said, and "we were too excited to ascertain."

Maneuvering from the small lifeboat into the much-larger *Moctezuma* was a challenge. Dudley and Stephens were too weak to climb up, so the German sailors put ropes around them to hoist them up. Even though Brooks had badly swollen legs and was not in much better condition than the others, he was able to grab onto the *Moctezuma*'s hull and make his way up on his own.

The survivors told the German captain "our sad tale," as Dudley called it, not withholding any important details. This would later turn out to be a pivotal moment. It was when the men first told the outside world what had happened in the lifeboat. Once they did, they would forever be known as killers and cannibals.

It would not have been hard for Dudley, Stephens, and Brooks to tell a different story, and they would not have had to change the facts much. They could have said that Parker had died from drinking seawater and that they had only begun to eat his corpse when he was already dead. In that telling, the men would have been corpse eaters, not people eaters—cannibals but not murderers.

There is no way of knowing why they told their rescuers the truth. They might not even have thought about whether to engage in a cover-up. Up until they were saved, the men had been focused on not dying. Then when they found themselves safely on the German boat, they may have simply blurted it all out. Or they may have been proud of the strength and resourcefulness they had mustered in order to survive. Alternatively, there might have been disagreement among the men about how honest to be, and there is some reason to believe there was. Dudley's wife would later suggest in a letter that one of the men did not believe they should reveal to the world what they had done, while her husband insisted that they should.

Dudley made a request that showed that he, at least, was not interested in putting the events on the lifeboat behind him. He asked Simonsen if they could bring what was left of Parker's corpse back to England. The German captain refused Dudley's request. He ordered his sailors to remove the remnants from the lifeboat. Wiese later recalled that the crew "threw the flesh and bone overboard." Since Wiese said he saw only some small pieces of flesh and a little piece of a rib, one of the men may have tossed most of Parker's remains overboard by the time they were about to be rescued. Dudley also asked to bring the lifeboat back as a grim souvenir of everything that had happened. Simonsen agreed to this, and his men carried the wooden dinghy onto the *Moctezuma*. Dudley also kept his chronometer, sextant, and compass.

The *Moctezuma* had picked the men up in a remote part of the South Atlantic, some one thousand miles northeast of Rio de Janeiro. They had been marooned in the dinghy for nearly twenty-four days, from the afternoon of July 5 to the morning of July 29. They had drifted west, roughly along the Tropic of Capricorn, about nine hundred miles. The German crew was shocked by the survivors' ragged appearance. Wiese helped Stephens out of his clothes and gave him new ones. He noticed, he said, that "there did not appear to be much flesh upon his bones." The men's feet were very swollen, he later said, and "during the first two or three days they could not lie and could not walk." The crew gave the men water, starting with just a half glass to avoid shocking their systems. Brooks later recalled how refreshing those first sips were. After half an hour, the crew served the men brandy, tea, and some food.

With three very unwell Englishmen onboard, Simonsen decided the ship would make a stop at Falmouth, on the southern coast of England, on the way back to Germany. Sailing at the bark's rapid clip, it would still take more than a month to get there. The survivors' spirits were high from the rescue, but they remained physically depleted, painfully sore, and unable to walk. Stephens later said that while they were on the German boat, their "extremities seemed to have entirely lost life." The captain and crew of the *Moctezuma* worked hard to nurse their guests back to health. Simonsen's wife had come along for the journey and did a great deal to look after all three of the new passengers. The next day, Dudley added to his injuries. He sat on a chamber pot and broke it, lacerating his backside. Simonsen helped attend to the wounds, which Dudley later described as "not a very pleasant task for him to perform." In his weakened state, Dudley's new injuries were slow to heal. Throughout his time on the boat, it would be too painful for him to sit, forcing him to stand or lie down.

During the long crossing to Falmouth, Dudley began writing a report on the events of the last three months. He was as forthcoming in it as he was in his discussions with his rescuers. He admitted without equivocation that he had killed Parker. "I offered up a prayer for the poor boy's soul," Dudley wrote, and then it was over with "not a moment's work." Even though Dudley did not hold back about how the cabin boy had died, his account was less than accurate in other respects.

His deviations from the truth made him look better than the real story would have, and some of the misstatements were substantial. In his written account, Dudley said that on the eighteenth day, "We arranged if nothing was in sight at sunrise + no rain came to put the poor lad Parker out of his misery by killing him." Dudley's use of "we" suggested that all three men had agreed to kill Parker—which was emphatically not the case—omitting that it was Dudley's idea, that Stephens had initially resisted it, and that Brooks had remained opposed until the end. Dudley also wrote that the next morning he, Stephens, and Brooks had "made signs between ourselves we had better do it," another false suggestion that all three men supported the killing.

Dudley's claim that the killing was done to "put the poor lad Parker out of his misery" was also misleading. That suggested that Dudley had acted out of mercy when the captain had actually made it very clear in his discussions with Stephens and Brooks leading up to the killing that his motive was to provide food and drink for them to consume. Dudley's contention was also at odds with Parker's own words and actions in the lifeboat. Parker had repeatedly said that he expected a rescue ship to appear on the horizon, and as Brooks observed, Parker had never suggested to the others "that his life was a burden to him." Dudley claimed in his account that Parker was "all but lifeless" at the time of the killing. Brooks would later contradict this in sworn testimony, saying that it was not clear to him which of the four men in the boat would be the first to die. Parker's final words, "What, me, Sir?" also belied Dudley's account. They showed that the cabin boy was aware enough of his surroundings and rational enough to understand what was happening up until the very end—and was surprised that he had been chosen to die.

Dudley was not lying to avoid criminal liability, since he did not consider that to be a possibility. But his account did make him come off as more sympathetic—the noble captain, objective and high minded—than he actually had been. In his first documented telling of the killing, he was acting on behalf of the entire crew, he was putting Parker out of his misery, and he was merely speeding up the death of someone who was already nearly dead. It sounded a lot better than the truth.

When Dudley, Stephens, and Brooks arrived in Falmouth on the morning of Saturday, September 6, their awful ordeal at sea finally came to an end. Falmouth's harbor pilot, Gustavus Collins, met the *Moctezuma* and led it into port. Collins was the first Englishman the survivors told about the sinking of the *Mignonette* and everything that happened afterward. When they stepped ashore, it was their first time setting foot on English soil since May. They had spent thirty-eight days convalescing on the German ship, and they were doing better, but they were still far from well. All three men still had difficulty walking.

Shortly after they landed, at nine o'clock in the morning, Dudley sent a telegram to his wife to let her know what had happened and to tell her he was back in England. "*Mignonette* foundered, July 5, 1,200 miles from Cape," he wrote. "In boat twenty-four days; sufferings fearful. All well now." His wife had not heard from him since his telegraph from Madeira in early June.

The first stop Dudley, Stephens, and Brooks made was at the Royal Cornwall Sailors' Home. A welcome feature of port life that emerged in the Victorian era, sailors' homes provided cheap lodging, basic medical care, and a ready-made social life for sailors who were far from home. When the men arrived at Falmouth's sailors' home, just a short walk from the harbor, the superintendent, Captain Jose, personally attended to them. He served them a meal that they said, not surprisingly, was the finest they had eaten in some time. When they finished eating, they were taken to the Falmouth Custom House to meet with Robert Gandy Cheesman, the collector of customs and receiver of wrecks for West Cornwall. Cheesman would lead an investigation of the wreck of the *Mignonette*. Dudley told Stephens and Brooks to cooperate fully. The men arrived at the Custom House at 11 a.m., and Dudley announced, "We have come to make our statements with reference to the loss of our vessel, the *Mignonette*."

Cheesman had his clerk, Samuel Tresidder, take depositions from all three men, using printed forms designed for the purpose. Tresidder asked how the *Mignonette* was lost, how the men survived, and how they made it back to England. He questioned each one separately, out of earshot of the others. The men offered up all the grim details. They described the killing and eating of Parker fully and without apology. Dudley did not hold back about the cannibalism. All three of the men "subsisted on the flesh until the twenty-fourth day," he said, "when the German Barque *Moctezuma* bore down and picked up the survivors."

Dudley stuck closer to the facts than he had in the report he wrote on the *Moctezuma*. This time, he did not suggest that Parker had been killed to "put an end to his sufferings." He emphasized, rather, that it was done "to sustain existence of those remaining." He did not say the cabin boy was "all but lifeless." He described him only as "very weak." He also accepted a greater role in instigating the killing. He did not tell Tresidder that he and Stephens and Brooks were all in on the plan. Dudley now said he had done it "with the assistance of the mate Edwin Stephens."

Dudley was now hewing closer to the truth in describing what had happened on the lifeboat. One reason for the increased honesty may have been that he was now talking to official investigators, who were hearing from all three of the survivors. When Dudley wrote his report, he may have believed he would have the final word on what had happened in the lifeboat; now he knew that Stephens's and Brooks's versions would be part of the official record, and if he misstated what had occurred, there would be other accounts to contradict him. Nevertheless, the captain still misstated what happened in one critical respect. He continued to suggest that all three men supported the killing. They "all agreed," Dudley said, "that the act was absolutely necessary." He failed to acknowledge that Brooks had consistently opposed killing anyone.

In his own statement, Stephens also described the killing and freely admitted his role in it. He said he agreed with Dudley "that it was absolutely necessary one should be sacrificed to save the rest," and he pointed out that Dudley "selected . . . Richard Parker . . . as being the weakest." Stephens said he "agreed on this and the master accordingly killed the lad." Unlike Dudley, Stephens did not suggest that Brooks had supported the killing. Stephens was candid about their cannibalism, using the same kind of direct language Dudley did. "The whole subsisted on the body until 29 July when they were picked up at about 10 a.m. by the German barque 'Moctezuma' and brought to Falmouth," he said.

Brooks's statement has been lost to history. Based on what he would later say, it is likely that he was as forthcoming as the other two men, but he would almost certainly have said, as he consistently did later, that he never wanted anyone killed.

When they were finished, Cheesman asked each man, "Is that a true statement of the circumstances attending the loss of the vessel?" Each affirmed that it was, and Cheesman cosigned the statements to be sent to London for the Board of Trade to use in its investigation of the wreck.

After Dudley finished his official statement, he talked one-on-one with Cheesman in the Custom House's long room, adding more details about the killing and the cannibalism. He told Cheesman he had proposed drawing lots but that Stephens and

Brooks would not agree to it. He explained that he then spoke to Stephens about killing Parker without drawing lots. Dudley also told Cheesman that when it seemed to him that Stephens and Brooks did not have the heart to do the killing, he realized he would have to do it himself. He said Parker was lying at the bottom of the boat with his hand over his face, and he showed Cheesman the position of the cabin boy's arm.

While Cheesman listened intently, Dudley continued his account. "I took out my knife first offering a prayer to God to forgive us for what we were about to do," Dudley said. He repeated his brief exchange with Parker, in which he had said that the cabin boy's time had come and that Parker had responded, "What, me, Sir?" In a dramatic flourish, Dudley acted out the killing for Cheesman. "I then put my knife in there," he said, referring to the side of Parker's neck. Dudley took the knife out of his pocket and demonstrated on his own neck where he had stabbed the cabin boy. Dudley said Parker's legs never moved and that it was over in about fifteen seconds.

Finally, Dudley provided Cheesman with some more details about the cannibalism that had occurred. He said that "the blood spurted out and we caught it" and that they drank it while it was still warm. Dudley recalled that they felt refreshed afterward. He recounted stripping Parker's body, cutting it open, taking out the heart and liver, and eating them while they were still warm.

While the two men talked, James Laverty, a Falmouth harbor police sergeant who had been keeping an eye on the three survivors, listened in. When Dudley acted out cutting Parker's throat, the sharp-eyed Laverty saw possible evidence. He asked Dudley to give him the knife. Dudley handed it over, but he said he wished to eventually get it back, the sergeant recalled, to have it as a "keepsake." It was another indication that Dudley seemed eager for souvenirs of the events in the lifeboat, much like his taking the dinghy and his navigational instruments back with him. Laverty told Dudley he would return the knife when it was no longer needed as evidence.

It was not clear what Laverty wanted the evidence for. He may have been thinking only of the Board of Trade's shipwreck investigation and collecting a full record of the loss of the *Mignonette*. But Dudley's knife did not have any direct bearing on the shipwreck. If Dudley had been more cautious, he might have wondered why the Falmouth police wanted his knife and whether it meant they had an interest in the killing of Parker. If that was the case, it was now too late for Dudley to avoid incriminating himself. He had already admitted everything that had happened and given a sworn statement.

But Dudley was not thinking that way. None of the men were. They had fully cooperated with the official shipwreck investigation, and they believed that everything was settled and they would now be free to go home. Dudley's confidence was reflected in a second telegram he sent his wife. At noon, he wrote, "Am here, as well as can be expected; hope to be enabled to finish work and leave for home tonight."

The officials in Falmouth saw things differently. It was true that people who engaged in survival cannibalism at sea had never been prosecuted in an English court, but the legal landscape was changing in ways that may have escaped the notice of everyday seafarers like Dudley, Stephens, and Brooks.

The change was being driven by wide-ranging reforms at the national level. Old ways of doing things were breaking down, including the long tradition of allowing captains to operate with near-total autonomy outside of the reach of English law. In recent decades, reformers had succeeded in extending the rule of law to the world of sailing in important ways. For one, major new legislation now covered fatalities at sea. The Merchant Shipping Act of 1854 said in section 269, "Whenever any case of Death happens on board any Foreign-going Ship, the Shipping Master shall on the Arrival of such Ship at the Port where the Crew is discharged inquire into the Cause of such Death." The law required the Custom House to make serious inquiries when seamen like Dudley, Stephens, and Brooks returned from a voyage on which someone had died. Furthermore, it stipulated if an inquiry suggested that a death had "been caused by Violence or other improper Means," the shipping master "shall either report the Matter to the Board of Trade, or, if the Emergency of the Case so requires, shall take immediate Steps for bringing the Offender or Offenders to Justice." When Dudley expected that he and the other men would be able to leave Falmouth after answering Cheesman's questions, he was apparently not thinking about section 269 of the Merchant Shipping Act.

But the Falmouth authorities were. If Cheesman had regarded his inquiry as just a shipwreck investigation, he would have thanked Dudley, Stephens, and Brooks for their testimony and sent them on their way. Instead, when the men's statements were complete, at about 2:50 p.m., Cheesman telegraphed the Board of Trade to ask how he should proceed. He wanted to know whether the men should be detained, an indication that he considered them possible "offenders" under section 269. Within a half hour, the Board of Trade responded that Cheesman should hold all three men. The board now had its own decision to make about whether the *Mignonette* survivors should be charged with a crime. Rather than take a position itself, the board forwarded the matter to the Home Office, the government department that was responsible for prosecuting crimes. But the Home Office was closed because it was Saturday, and it did not respond.

Sergeant Laverty was also treating Parker's killing as a possible crime, something that was evident from the moment he took possession of Dudley's knife. He went to find the mayor of Falmouth, Henry Liddicoat. Laverty explained what he had seen and heard concerning the three men who had arrived by boat in Falmouth that morning. Liddicoat signed arrest warrants for Dudley, Stephens, and Brooks.

In ordering the arrests, Liddicoat may merely have been following the directions of the Board of Trade, which had told Cheesman to detain the men. But it is also possible that the mayor, who had a judicial office as the head of the town's magistrates, was relying on his own reading of the Merchant Shipping Act. Based on what Laverty had observed in the Custom House, it seemed clear that section 269 was triggered. A "death" had occurred "on board" a "foreign-going ship," and it had been caused "by violence." The law said that "if the Emergency of the Case so requires," steps must be taken immediately "for bringing the Offenders to Justice." The mayor appeared to be taking those steps. Laverty brought the warrants back with him to the Custom House, and that afternoon he placed Dudley, Stephens, and Brooks under arrest on a charge of murder. He took the men to the jail in the Falmouth police station and locked them up.

Dudley, Stephens, and Brooks were shocked. They had already made plans to leave for home that evening, and they certainly had not expected to be jailed. "If people could only imagine for a moment what our sufferings were in the boat, such a charge as that made against us would be about the last thing that would be thought of," Brooks said. For Brooks in particular, that reaction is easy to understand: He had argued against killing Parker and had covered his head to avoid watching it, but he was now in the same jail cell as Dudley, who had stabbed Parker in the neck, and Stephens, who had looked on, ready to hold down the cabin boy's legs.

Suddenly, everything had changed for the men. "Shall not be able to come home to-night, until things are settled here," Dudley wrote to his wife in his third telegram of the day. The men were scheduled to appear at a preliminary hearing before the Falmouth magistrates on Monday morning. At the hearing, everything would become clearer. The magistrates could decide that Dudley, Stephens, and Brooks should be released and sent home to their families and friends after the agonies of the past two months. Or they could put the men on trial for murder.

6

A Bad Time to Be a Cannibal

The prosecution would have a straightforward case to make to the magistrates on Monday morning. Dudley had taken a knife and stabbed Parker to death. It was an intentional and premeditated act. And there could be no claim of self-defense, because Parker did not pose a danger to anyone. All the elements of the crime of murder were present. The prosecutors also had all the evidence they needed. Dudley, Stephens, and Brooks had given sworn statements attesting to the facts, and those would very likely be admissible at the hearing. The authorities even had the murder weapon in their possession.

The defense would have a much harder time. It was true that no Englishman had ever been prosecuted for cannibalism at sea. But that was a historical observation, not a legal argument. The lack of prosecutions reflected a belief among police and prosecutors that survival cannibalism was not a crime, but there was no law saying so, and no court had ever ruled that it was legal.

The defense's main argument would have to be a doctrine known as the "necessity defense." Dudley said it was necessary to kill Parker "to sustain the existence of those remaining." That is, without taking one life, four would have been lost. The necessity defense is based on a simple premise: In extremely difficult circumstances, people should be free to take the action that minimizes harm. As Glanville Williams, a Cambridge University scholar, explains the concept, "Some acts that would otherwise be wrong are rendered rightful by a good purpose, or by the necessity of choosing the lesser of two evils." The necessity defense has deep roots in Western law and philosophy. One legal scholar described it in a classic criminal law treatise as "anciently woven into the fabric of our culture." An old Latin maxim, with origins in Christian canon law, holds that *necessitas legem non habet*, or "necessity knows no law."

But for the men who had survived by taking Parker's life, there was a big problem: It was not clear that English law recognized a necessity defense in homicide prosecutions. The necessity defense had been used occasionally, in scattered cases going back centuries, but none of them bore a close resemblance to what happened on the *Mignonette*, where an innocent person was killed so that others could stay alive. The strongest precedent the men could invoke was an American case, *United States v. Holmes*. It involved a homicide, and that homicide was on a ship in distress. The defendant was, like the *Mignonette* defendants, a seafarer who believed that killing someone on the boat would ultimately save more lives.

Holmes arose out of the wreck of the *William Brown*, an American cargo ship that sailed from Liverpool to Philadelphia in 1841. The ship, which had a crew of seventeen and sixty-five Irish and Scottish immigrants as passengers, struck an iceberg off Newfoundland. More than one-third of the people on the *William Brown* died in the immediate aftermath of the collision, while the rest evacuated on two lifeboats. The lifeboats were not equally seaworthy. The captain, the second mate, seven crewmembers, and one passenger escaped on the jollyboat, the sturdier and safer of the two. The first mate Francis Rhodes, eight crewmembers, and thirty-two passengers ended up in the longboat, whose problems were evident right away. It leaked badly, and there were too many people crammed onto it. But the captain would not let anyone from the longboat switch over to the jollyboat.

It began to rain, and the sea got rough. The longboat's crew and passengers bailed water as fast as they could but still seemed to be on the verge of sinking. The crew decided that the only way to keep the longboat afloat was to reduce the number of people onboard. Led by a twenty-six-year-old Finnish sailor named Alexander William Holmes, the crew began throwing people overboard. They made the self-serving decision that only passengers would be sacrificed, and they chose who would be tossed over without consulting with the passengers. Some passengers pled for their lives or physically resisted, but Holmes and the other crewmembers were not deterred. They eventually threw fourteen of the seventeen male passengers overboard, along with two of the women.

A few hours after the last passenger was tossed out, an American ship, the *Crescent*, spotted the longboat and rescued everyone. The timing of the rescue called the crew's decisions into question. If they had waited a little longer before throwing passengers overboard, most or all of them would likely have lived. The *Crescent* delivered the *William Brown* survivors to Le Havre, France. The British and American consuls there were sympathetic to the crewmembers' predicament and the hard choice they had faced. They decided not to charge anyone from the longboat with a crime. But back in America, people viewed the deaths differently. Crusading newspapers called for the crewmembers to be prosecuted. "Let a court decide," the *Public Ledger of Philadelphia* implored, "how far imperious circumstances warranted or extenuated their conduct." The paper insisted the charge should be murder. Catholic immigrant communities also spoke out, troubled by reports that most of the people who died on the *William Brown* were Irish Catholics, while Protestant Scots largely survived.

The Philadelphia district attorney decided to prosecute. He kept the case simple by charging only Holmes, the leader, just for manslaughter for killing a single passenger, Francis Askins. At that time, US Supreme Court justices still "rode circuit," serving as trial judges in federal courts across the country, and a sitting Supreme Court justice, Henry Baldwin, presided over Holmes's trial. The prosecution contended that Holmes had committed homicide when he threw Askins overboard. Several survivors testified about what Holmes did. The prosecutors also argued that as a crewmember, Holmes had an affirmative duty to protect the passengers.

Holmes put forth a necessity defense, which did have established precedents in American law. In one well-known case, a court had ruled for a ship owner whose captain and crew had violated a United States trade embargo by sailing into a port in the West Indies and selling its goods. The ship owner argued that the captain entered the port to get away from a deadly storm, and once he was there, the authorities forced him to sell the cargo. A federal court in New York ruled that "the necessity which is proved to have existed excused the party from all guilt."

In the *William Brown* case, Holmes's lawyers argued that when he threw the passengers overboard, Holmes had chosen the lesser of two evils. If he had not done so, there was a significant chance the longboat would have sunk, his lawyers said. Killing some passengers was preferable to allowing everyone to die. But it was a problem for the defense that Holmes had not drawn lots to choose who to throw overboard. Holmes and the other crewmembers had decided who should die. Holmes's lawyers said the conditions were not right for drawing lots. "Lots, in cases of famine, where means of subsistence are wanting for all the crew, is what the history of maritime disaster records," they said, "but who has ever told of casting lots at midnight, in a sinking boat, in the midst of darkness, of rain, of terror, and of confusion?"

Justice Baldwin gave instructions to the jury, setting out the law of necessity as he saw it. He said American law recognized a necessity defense even against a charge of homicide—but he put strict conditions on how it could be used. First, he said, the person taking a life "must be under no obligation to make his own safety secondary to the safety of others." Holmes did not meet this condition because crews have a special duty to passengers, he said. They must "undergo whatever hazard is necessary to preserve the boat and the passengers." Crewmembers who were needed to operate the ship should be spared, Justice Baldwin said, but any unnecessary members should be sacrificed before any passengers were.

The other condition, according to Justice Baldwin, was that the people thrown overboard had to be chosen in a way that gave everyone an "equal chance for their life." Drawing lots, he said, was "the fairest mode, and, in some sort, an appeal to God, for selection of the victim." No other method was "so consonant both to humanity and to justice," and it would require "peculiar" circumstances to "dispense with its exercise." With this condition, Justice Baldwin was effectively giving a legal imprimatur to the custom of the sea.

Justice Baldwin was clearly pushing the jury toward a conviction with his instructions, but he also believed Holmes should be dealt with leniently. There should be "some punishment," in cases like this one, he said, but the law "yet looks with a benignant eye, through the thing done, to the mind and to the heart." Following his lead, the jury found Holmes guilty, with a recommendation of mercy. Justice Baldwin could have imposed a punishment of three years and a $1,000 fine, but he sentenced Holmes to six months and a fine of $20. In response to a plea for clemency, President John Tyler kept the prison sentence but removed the fine.

If Dudley, Stephens, and Brooks wanted to use a necessity defense, the *Holmes* case could be helpful. A US Supreme Court justice had declared that American law, at least, recognized such a defense, even to a charge of homicide. Under the right circumstances, Justice Baldwin had ruled, it could be legal to kill a person to save other lives. The facts were also remarkably close to what happened on the *Mignonette* lifeboat—it was a case of trying to save lives in extreme conditions at sea. The *Mignonette* defendants could also take heart from the lenient sentence Holmes had received.

But there were also important ways that *Holmes* was not helpful at all. Justice Baldwin said the necessity defense to a charge of sacrificing someone at sea required, with few exceptions, lots to be drawn so everyone had an "equal chance" to live. Dudley had not drawn lots, and there was a good chance that Justice Baldwin would have advised a jury to convict the *Mignonette* defendants. Another problem with the *Holmes* ruling was that it came from an American court. An English court might be interested in the case's reasoning but had no duty to follow it.

Although the defense lawyers for Dudley, Stephens, and Brooks would not have a strong legal precedent to rely on, there were some prominent legal commentators who supported a necessity defense, even to a homicide charge. One was Francis Bacon, a leading lawyer, member of Parliament, and philosopher of the early modern era. In 1639, Bacon wrote about the classic hypothetical circumstance, first put forth by the Greek skeptic Carneades of Cyrene, in which two sailors survive a shipwreck and grab hold of a plank of wood. Seeing that the plank can only support one of them, one sailor shoves the other one away, saving his own life by drowning the other. Bacon said pushing a rival off was "justifiable." In *The Elements of the Common Laws of England*, he invoked the maxim *necessitas inducit privilegium quoad jura privata*, or "necessity carrieth a privilege in itself." Bacon had an expansive view of the necessity doctrine beyond sailors and planks of wood. He also believed that if a hungry man stole food, necessity should be a defense to a charge of theft.

William Blackstone, the single most respected commentator on English law, had also endorsed the necessity defense. Blackstone, a justice of the Court of King's Bench and a member of Parliament, wrote the four-volume *Commentaries on the Laws of England* starting in 1765. It was a highly influential treatise, which was taught in law schools and cited in court decisions. In it, Blackstone took up the plank hypothetical, and he agreed with Bacon that it was not a crime for one sailor to shove the other one off. Someone who "preserves his own life at the expense of another man's is excusable through unavoidable necessity," he wrote.

As respected as Blackstone and Bacon were, their writings were not court rulings. Judges did not have to follow them, and on some issues, their views were at variance with actual British law. Bacon may have believed that hungry men who stole food were not committing a crime, but the courts of England certainly did not agree.

There were other influential commentators who opposed the necessity defense on principle and considered it a dangerous doctrine. They insisted that an inherently bad act, such as murder or theft, cannot be excused by an individual's subjective assessment of what is best or necessary in an extreme situation. Mathew Hale, an important seventeenth-century judge and legal scholar, said that a hungry man who steals food and pleads necessity must be found guilty. If the court accepted his necessity defense, Lord Hale wrote, "men's properties would be under a strange insecurity, being laid open to other men's necessities, whereof no man can possibly judge but the party himself."

Even if Dudley, Stephens, and Brooks persuaded a court that English law permitted the necessity defense to a charge of homicide, they would still have to show that it applied in their case. They would have to demonstrate that killing Parker was the lesser of two evils. That might not be easy. Dudley had felt that the calculation was straightforward: It was better to sacrifice Parker than for all four men to die. But a court might hold that if Parker had not been killed, all four men might have survived to be rescued. If the men could have held on a bit longer without killing anyone, the defendants had actually chosen the greater of two evils.

For Dudley, Stephens, and Brooks, the problem was not only that English law provided no precedent that supported killing Parker. It was also that English society was changing rapidly, and the law was evolving along with it. Both society and the law seemed to be moving away from a placid acceptance of cannibalism at sea. The England that the *Mignonette* survivors returned to was not the same country that it had been in 1641, when the cannibal sailors were freed in St. Kitts, or even in 1835, when the *Francis Spaight* survivors were welcomed home as heroes.

As the Industrial Revolution transformed England, a new Victorian mindset was emerging. The Victorian era, which had begun decades earlier, in 1837, when Queen Victoria ascended the throne, is often associated with conservative values and sanctimony, and there is some truth to that image. Many Victorians were swept up in religious fervor, donating generously to missionary work overseas. Victorian moralists even inspected the great classics of English literature for lewdness and "bowdlerized" them, as their heavy-handed editing was called, after Thomas Bowdler, a physician who published a sanitized version of Shakespeare. In 1885, the year after the *Mignonette* sank, England criminalized homosexual acts it characterized as "gross indecency," and a decade later, Oscar Wilde would be imprisoned under the new law. The era was not far in the past when *Webster's* defined "Victorian" as "prudish, strict, old-fashioned, dated." But that was only a partial picture. Judged by the standard of lasting impact on the world, the Victorian was, to a far greater extent, an age of ambitious reform.

The Victorians were on a mission to examine every aspect of society and devise ways of improving it. The most prominent thinkers spoke passionately about this drive. The philosopher John Stuart Mill said his "object in life" was "to be a reformer of the world." Thomas Babington Macaulay, a leading Whig politician and historian, promoted what came to be known as "Whig history," the idea that society moved inexorably from misery and oppression to better times. "The history of our country during the last one hundred and sixty years," Macaulay wrote in 1848, "is eminently the history of physical, of moral, and of intellectual improvement."

A major theme of Victorian literature was the belief that society was a problem to be solved. There was a proliferation of "condition of England" novels, which focused on the plight of the dispossessed. Charles Dickens, the great English novelist of the age, introduced middle-class readers to the workhouse in *Oliver Twist* and pilloried harsh industrial capitalism in *Hard Times*. In *A Christmas Carol*, Joseph Marley's ghost exclaimed to Scrooge, "Mankind was my business. The common welfare was my business; charity, mercy, forbearance and benevolence, were, all, my business." One of the most popular children's books was Charles Kingsley's *The Water-Babies*, which shined a light on the horrors of slum poverty and child labor. The book, whose young protagonist was a chimney sweep, helped pass the Chimney Sweepers Act of 1864, which barred hiring young children as chimney sweeps.

Crusading nonfiction reported on the conditions faced by people struggling on society's lower rungs. Andrew Mearns's *The Bitter Cry of Outcast London: An Inquiry into the Condition of the Abject Poor* revealed the dire state of London's slums and called for major housing reforms. Journalist William T. Stead's newspaper series "The Maiden Tribute of Modern Babylon" exposed child prostitution in London as a "veritable slave trade." Stead's articles helped pass the Criminal Law Amendment Act of 1885, known as "Stead's Act," which raised the age of consent to sixteen.

There were also people making more fundamental critiques of society. *The Communist Manifesto* was partly conceived in Victorian England, in the collaboration of Karl Marx and Friedrich Engels, whose family owned textile mills in Manchester. In 1884, the same year the *Mignonette* set sail, socialist intellectuals in London formed the Fabian Society and began writing pamphlets and books promoting trade unions and the public ownership of land and industry. There was an explosion of voluntary organizations dedicated to societal improvement. Wealthy donors backed the Working Men's Club movement, which established clubs with lounges, game rooms, and libraries in working-class neighborhoods to promote healthy recreation and discourage drinking and vice. Florence Nightingale returned from nursing British soldiers in the Crimean War to campaign for improved health care. William Booth founded the Salvation Army, which adopted military trappings for its mission of turning around the lives of what it called "thieves, prostitutes, gamblers, and drunkards."

Meanwhile, reformers in Parliament enacted laws that dramatically transformed British society. Britain had already largely abolished slavery throughout the empire by the start of the Victorian era, with landmark laws enacted in 1807 and 1833, but there was still a great deal of societal uplift to be done through legislation. In 1846, the repeal of the Corn Laws, which had imposed large tariffs on grain and other imports, ushered in a new age of free trade, lowering food prices for the poor and working classes. The Second Reform Act of 1867 extended the right to vote to significant parts of the working class, and the Third Reform Act of 1884–85 granted the franchise to men working in agriculture, expanding the electorate even further. A major women's suffrage movement began in the Victorian era, ultimately culminating in laws extending the vote to women in 1918 and 1928. With these dramatic changes, a new social order was emerging.

Many of the new laws focused on protecting the most vulnerable members of society. High on this list were laborers, whose working conditions had declined with the rise of mass production. Laws like the Factory Act of 1878 reined in some of the most abusive practices of modern industrial capitalism. Slowly but surely, the country was putting limits on the ability of wealthy employers to overwork and otherwise exploit their workers. The reformers also championed women and children. Parliament enacted laws to help women who had been driven into prostitution. One of these, the Criminal Law Amendment Act of 1885, made it easier to prosecute brothel keepers. In 1889, the Prevention of Cruelty to, and Protection of, Children Act recognized, for the first time, the crime of mistreating a child.

This Victorian impulse for improvement reached into virtually every corner of British society. One unglamorous but important cause was "sanitary reform," aimed at converting the nation's infrastructure from cesspools to sewage systems. It was part of a general war on uncleanliness in an era when, as Sabine Schülting notes in *Dirt in Victorian Literature and Culture*, people often conflated "moral and physical filthiness." But this crusade went well beyond symbolism. It played a crucial role in fighting the spread of serious diseases.

This reform ethos, which stretched from the festering cesspools of the London slums to the well-upholstered halls of the House of Lords, eventually reached the seafaring world. In 1835, the first sailors' home opened in London. Reformers wanted to bring a civilizing influence to Britain's port districts, where sailors were surrounded by an array of dangers. In his autobiographical novel *Redburn*, Herman Melville recalled the turpitude he had seen in 1839 down by the Liverpool docks. When a sailor arrived in this netherworld, Melville wrote, "landlords, barkeepers, clothiers, crimps, and boarding-house loungers" were waiting to "devour him, limb by limb." Sailors' homes offered a refuge. They provided safe, clean accommodations where gambling, alcohol, and prostitution were prohibited. They often had dining and medical facilities. The sailors' home movement drew support from reformers for both the material aid and the moral guidance they gave to vulnerable sailors far from home. After the London Sailors' Home, many more opened. Among these, in 1852, was the Royal Cornwall Sailors' Home in Falmouth, which would later take in Dudley, Stephens, and Brooks.

In the waning days of sail, the British government also took an active interest in reforms for sailors. In 1836, just before the start of Queen Victoria's reign, the House of Commons' Select Committee on Shipwrecks issued an influential report, which was followed by a steady stream of additional reports on shipwreck safety from select committees and royal commissions. Parliament soon enacted a series of laws regulating the maritime world, including the Seamen's Protection Act of 1845, the Mercantile Marine Act of 1850, and the Merchant Shipping Act of 1854. This flurry of major laws officially extended British law and the British courts to the maritime world. Among other things, the sweeping new rules supplanted much of the authority ship captains had traditionally wielded.

These laws also, for the first time, gave the government responsibility for investigating shipwrecks. They placed authority for investigations with the Board of Trade and authorized the chief customs officer near where the loss occurred or where witnesses had landed to conduct an inquiry on the board's behalf. These were the laws that authorized Robert Gandy Cheesman to investigate the *Mignonette* wreck, questioning the survivors and reporting to the Board of Trade in London. Dudley, Stephens, and Brooks thus found themselves squarely in the sights of a major reform movement that was transforming how crime at sea was handled. The new laws ended the tradition of quasisovereignty that had allowed British ships to operate, in the words of one historian, as "a harsh and barbarous world of their own." The legal system, not ship captains, would now have the final word on what was legal onboard a ship.

The Victorian mindset and the maritime laws it brought into existence were directly in conflict with survival cannibalism at sea. Under the new rules, all violent acts that occurred on a ship were to be investigated as possible crimes. The Board of Trade and Custom House officials, not captains, would be in charge of the investigations and would decide whether to refer the individuals involved for criminal prosecution. People who killed someone on a ship to engage in survival cannibalism could no longer count on the authorities to look the other way.

There were other changes afoot in Victorian England, beyond the reforms to maritime law, that could also present serious problems for Dudley, Stephens, and Brooks. There was a far-reaching turn away from violence. Murder was going out of fashion, part of a centuries-long shift that saw homicide rates plummet. In the Middle Ages, there had been an estimated twenty homicides per one hundred thousand in England, falling to about ten per one hundred thousand in 1600, and that would drop to just one per one hundred thousand by the twentieth century. In 1835, the United Kingdom adopted the Cruelty to Animals Act, which banned dogfighting, cockfighting, and bearbaiting. In 1868, it ended public executions. In the discussion leading up to that decision, John Parry, a leading opponent of capital punishment, had declared that anyone who would watch a public execution should be "considered to belong to a degraded class of persons who like to witness horrible and repulsive sights."

This growing discomfort with violence was part of what the German Jewish sociologist Norbert Elias called "the civilizing process" in a famous book by that name. Elias observed that in Europe over the centuries, behavior changed on relatively small matters, such as blowing one's nose on one's sleeve, at the same time as it evolved on larger ones, such as the use of violence to resolve disputes. Elias believed that as modern countries became more powerful, they aspired to enforce standards of civilized conduct of all kinds. He wrote about an "expanding threshold of repugnance" that changed attitudes toward violent behavior.

As its "threshold of repugnance" expanded in the 1800s, England was becoming less likely to accept a cabin boy being stabbed to death and eaten. Dudley, Stephens, and Brooks might have been welcomed home as heroes in an earlier era, but now a growing number of their countrymen might be inclined to regard them as barbarians.

Dudley's choice of victim, once in line with the norms of the custom of the sea, was another factor that might now weigh against the men. Even as child labor continued widely, a growing current in Victorian culture idealized children as delightful, innocent creatures—a national obsession that came to be known as the "cult of the child." Lewis Carroll's *Alice's Adventures in Wonderland* romanticized the purity of children, and Charles Dickens centered intelligent children as protagonists who were often more ethical than his adult characters. Reformers known as "child-savers" devoted themselves to protecting vulnerable children. The Society for the Prevention of Cruelty to Children, founded in 1883, took action against parents who abused their children. This newfound public esteem and concern for children would likely not be a favorable backdrop for Dudley, who had looked at the one young person in the lifeboat and seen not a child deserving special protection but an easy meal for saving the lives of three adults.

Yet another Victorian intellectual current might lend support to the prosecution of Dudley, Stephens, and Brooks. It was a sudden national discussion that had broken out over something that, at least on the surface, seemed completely unrelated to survival cannibalism at sea. But this change—in how Britain began to think about its empire and imperialism more generally—could shape how English people judged Englishmen who were admitted cannibals.

The year before Dudley, Stephens, and Brooks were arrested, 1883, Sir John Robert Seeley, a professor of modern history at Cambridge University, ventured one of the most famous statements ever made about the British Empire. Britain, he remarked, had "conquered and peopled half the world in a fit of absence of mind." Seeley's dubious assertion—conquest and empire certainly require more intentionality than he allowed—challenged the English people to think more consciously about the purposes and goals of British colonialism.

Seeley's declaration, made in his book *The Expansion of England*, set off a national conversation about the purpose of the British Empire. It was largely a jingoistic and racist discussion focused on British civilization's purported superiority and the importance of sharing it with, or imposing it on, what British imperialists saw as "less civilized" people. Sixteen years later, Rudyard Kipling would express these views unabashedly in his now-infamous poem "The White Man's Burden," which called on white colonial powers to send "the best ye breed" to civilize "new-caught sullen peoples, Half devil and half child." There was a lot of talk about the great gifts Britain decided it had to offer the world—its culture, its religion, its exemplary way of life.

All this arguably made 1884 the worst year in history to be an English cannibal. Cannibalism was connected in the national mind with all of the things England was convinced it was not. Cannibalism had long been seen as "the prime symbol or signifier of 'barbarism,'" as anthropologist Shirley Lindenbaum has observed. For Victorians, cannibalism was "the absolute nadir of human behavior," Patrick Brantlinger notes in *Taming Cannibals: Race and the Victorians*. Englishmen of the era believed that it was "practiced by black or brown savages but not by white Christians, who are horrified by it."

The Victorian view of cannibalism was shaped by the reports that English explorers and missionaries brought back from their travels. These colorful, often apocryphal accounts were designed to accentuate the exoticism of the regions Britain had conquered and to make English people feel pride in their self-proclaimed superiority to the natives of remote islands and Africa. Cannibalism stories spread widely through popular books with titles like *Five Years with the Congo Cannibals*. As the historians Dorothy Hammond and Alta Jablow observed in their book *The Africa That Never Was: Four Centuries of British Writing About Africa*, European writers "were far more addicted to tales of cannibalism than . . . Africans ever were to cannibalism."

Cannibalism dispatches reached a peak in the decades before the *Mignonette* set sail. Britain's colonization of the South Pacific made cannibalism a subject of national fascination. Fevered reports of cannibalism among the local tribesmen were used to justify Britain's blood-drenched foreign incursions half a world away. They were given a respectful audience by institutions like the Royal Society, the scientific academy that operated with a royal charter. Naturally, a dichotomy contrasting "civilized" Englishmen with "savage" cannibals required that Englishmen must not be cannibals. Despite the documented instances of English cannibalism in cases like the wreck of the *Dolphin* and the *Francis Spaight*, some influential voices insisted that cannibalism was simply not the sort of thing Englishmen engaged in. In an 1841 letter to the editor of *The Times*, a respected voice of the English mainstream, a reader congratulated his "fellow-countrymen" that cannibalism "has never been heard of, and I trust never will, on board an English ship."

Yet here were Dudley, Stephens, and Brooks openly presenting themselves as cannibals, with an implicit belief that they had the right to eat another human being. Their legal defense was asking the English courts to declare, for the first time, that cannibalism was acceptable for Englishmen in difficult circumstances. Given the discussion of empire going on around them, their timing could hardly have been worse.

In fact, there were already indications by 1884 that the English legal system's tacit acceptance of cannibalism at sea had begun to erode. The strongest evidence had come a decade earlier, when there was another in the long line of English shipwrecks in which the crew resorted to cannibalism. If history was any guide, the legal system should have ignored it—but this time, things went a bit differently.

The *Euxine*, a Liverpool-based sailing ship, went down in the South Atlantic in 1874 when its cargo of coal spontaneously combusted and set it on fire. The crew divided into three boats. One boat, carrying second mate James Archer and seven other crewmembers, got separated from the others, and despite his best efforts, Archer could not find land. After nineteen days, food ran out, and the men resorted to the custom of the sea. Twenty-year-old Francis Gioffous was declared to have drawn the short straw. Gioffous was not the only foreigner in the boat, but he was a dark-skinned Italian who spoke little English—which made him the sort of outsider who usually lost these drawings.

One of the sailors cut Gioffous's throat with a knife and severed his head. The sailors drank his blood and ate his heart and liver. Hours after the gruesome meal, a Dutch bark appeared and rescued the men in the lifeboat. The survivors were brought to the British colony of Singapore, where they told the authorities their story. While the British colonial authorities considered bringing murder charges, members of the public spoke out. A sea captain named G. H. Harrington insisted in a letter to the *Singapore Daily Times* that "however great the sufferings may be, seamen are not allowed to sacrifice one of their number that one may live." He called for steps to "be taken to bring these maneaters to justice."

After the British attorney general in Singapore set the men free, officials at the Board of Trade in London seriously considered bringing a murder prosecution. But the officials worried that a jury might acquit, sending a message that people on ships could be killed and eaten without any consequences. There were also political considerations, since the *Euxine* was owned by an influential member of Parliament who might be blamed for the fire on his ship. Besides, one official argued, "the details are too disgusting to take to court."

In the end, the investigation was dropped. Even so, the crew had briefly been treated as possible criminal defendants. It is unlikely the *Mignonette* survivors knew of the case. There was little coverage of it in English papers, and the articles that were written presented the *Euxine* survivors as unfortunate victims rather than suspects. But if Dudley, Stephens, and Brooks had known how close the *Euxine* case had come to a prosecution, they would no doubt have been more worried.

In the ten years since the *Euxine* disaster, the Victorian reformers had been scoring more victories, and the Board of Trade might be inclined to act more boldly now. There had still not been a single instance in which sailors who engaged in cannibalism at sea had been charged with a crime, but it was possible, as the men awaited their fate in the Falmouth jail, that England might be poised to end that long tradition and make an effort, in Captain Harrington's words, to "bring these maneaters to justice."

7

From Sailors to Criminal Defendants

When Dudley, Stephens, and Brooks were arrested and thrown in jail, they were stunned to find themselves there. From the moment they first considered killing someone to survive in the lifeboat, they had been secure in the knowledge that England did not prosecute people for cannibalism at sea. But now they found themselves arrested for murder, which carried the death penalty. In almost no time, they had gone from thinking they were on their way home to their families and friends to contemplating the real possibility that they would be hanged.

While they sat in jail, the news of the *Mignonette*'s ordeal captivated Britain. The story of three obscure seafarers arriving in an English port town with a shocking story of survival made newspaper headlines from the biggest cities to the smallest towns. The headlines trumpeted the news: "Terrible Sufferings," "Frightful Privations," and "Terrible Tale of the Sea."

It was big news overseas too. The day after the men arrived in Falmouth, *The New York Sun* ran a dispatch from London on its front page, under the headline "Cannibalism at Sea." *The Sydney Evening News*, the paper the men would have been reading if the *Mignonette* had completed its journey, reported on this

"Horrible Tale of the Sea"—and seized on the local angle, with the subheadline "Mr. J. H. Want's Yacht Abandoned."

It was little wonder that the public found the *Mignonette* saga so fascinating. It was a shipwreck, and people loved to read about disasters at sea. It was also a murder story, and Victorians were wildly obsessed with murder. The same moralism that led them to examine society's ills drew them to its darkest moments—and gruesome killings were a favorite. One scholar notes that in 1801 only 67 articles in *The Times* mentioned murder, but by the 1880s, an average of 1,003 articles a year did. A popular Victorian pastime was "murder sightseeing." People showed up at crime scenes and "traipsed through the gore-spattered rooms, peering not only at the blood splashes and other grisly reminders of the atrocity, but also at the bodies themselves." Larger audiences flocked to see well-crafted replicas of murder scenes and murderers. When Madame Tussaud's wax museum set up shop in London, the Tussaud family noticed that the English public was most drawn to the infamous "Chamber of Horrors," with its assortment of killers and psychopaths. But the *Mignonette* story had a macabre frisson that few murder tales could match: It ended in cannibalism.

As reports of their exploits spread, Dudley, Stephens, and Brooks received a stream of visitors at the Falmouth jail. A doctor arrived every day to treat Dudley's chamber pot injury. Mayor Liddicoat visited the prisoners to offer support, despite the fact that he was the one who had signed the arrest warrants that landed them there. Members of the general public also filed in, an early indication of the strong sympathy Dudley, Stephens, and Brooks had from ordinary citizens, even as the authorities were weighing whether to bring capital charges. Some came bearing gifts. A group of women presented the prisoners with a Bible and a half-crown contribution toward their defense. The people of Falmouth were "very kind," Stephens said, "and I cannot too strongly express my appreciation of all that was done for us there."

One citizen expressed his solidarity more forcefully. Mayor Liddicoat received a letter postmarked in Sheffield that contained, as the London *Standard* reported, "little but a tissue of bad language towards the mayor for his having issued warrants for the apprehension of the three men." The letter writer said he would be coming to Falmouth the following week to shoot Liddicoat.

It was clear from these earliest days that there was a sharp divergence in the reaction to the men's case. Many high government officials, newspaper writers, and other well-placed members of society were inclined to see cannibalism at sea as a problem in need of solving and the *Mignonette* cannibals as criminals. To Victorian reformers, in particular, cannibalism at sea represented a part of the old order that they were trying to revamp. At the same time, much of the general public—especially the working class—was on the survivors' side. They were less inclined to see the killing of Parker as a crime and more apt to view it as an understandable act of desperate men. In seafaring communities like Falmouth, people had respect for the long-standing traditions of the sailing world, including the custom of the sea. They saw the men as heroes who had found a way of surviving in dire circumstances. The first of these grassroots supporters were now visiting the Falmouth jail, but many more would show up for the men in different ways in the days ahead.

While Dudley, Stephens, and Brooks waited, in their jail cell, the Falmouth authorities were working to put together a legal case. Likely on instruction from James Laverty, the harbor police sergeant, a boatman named Richard Hodge met with the captain of the *Moctezuma* and took possession of the lifeboat, along with the chronometer and sextant that Dudley had rescued from the *Mignonette*, a pair of oars, a bundle of underclothing and papers, and a pair of crutches. Talking with the German sailors who had rescued the men from the lifeboat, Hodge secured two witnesses, Julius Erich Martin Wiese and Christopher Drewe, to testify before the magistrates.

Hodge delivered the physical items to Laverty at about 8 p.m. on Sunday, September 7, the day after the men arrived in Falmouth. The smaller items were held at the Custom House for use as evidence. Laverty moved the lifeboat to a warehouse, where it was locked up to safeguard it from the prying eyes and groping hands of the public. The battered dinghy was a crime scene now, and Custom House officials came to the warehouse to inspect it as part of the investigation.

The authorities eventually decided that the only items they needed to hold on to were the lifeboat and Dudley's knife. Laverty went to the jail that same Sunday night to present Dudley with a list of all the other things the police had from the *Moctezuma*. He asked the captain what he wanted done with them. Dudley asked for them to be delivered to John Burton, the proprietor of Falmouth's Old Curiosity Shop. The shop, which advertised itself as "a large and valuable collection of curiosities from every region under the sun," stocked wares ranging from ancient musketry to bottled snakes and monkey heads. Dudley was hoping Burton could sell the *Mignonette* items to curiosity seekers to raise money for the men's defense.

After the authorities completed their inspection of the lifeboat, they returned it to Dudley. Seeing another chance to raise funds, he arranged to have it put on display. Quite a few seamen were among the crowds that paid to see the infamous dinghy. They expressed "the greatest surprise," the *Nottingham*

Evening Post reported, "that so frail a craft could have lived at all in such weather as Captain Dudley and his companions experienced." Later, the lifeboat went on display at a special exhibition at the Royal Polytechnic Hall, with the proceeds going only to Stephens and Brooks, who were in the direst financial situation.

Supporters of the men launched fundraising drives for their defense. Two yacht clubs made an appeal in a letter in the *Exeter and Plymouth Gazette*, declaring that Dudley, Stephens, and Brooks had "lost their all" and "literally" had "no adequate funds to defend their lives with," and they implored readers to give "some assistance for these men," who had "passed through frightful sufferings." The sum of £38 2s. 6d. had already been collected, the yachtsmen noted with gratitude. Local newspapers gave the fundraisers free publicity and encouraged their readers to be generous. "Go and see" the lifeboat of the "Yacht *Mignonette* at Buckingham's, and leave some coppers for the men," the *Falmouth News Slip* urged. The *Newcastle Courant* kept its readers' expectations in check by advising them that "there are no marks in it of blood that can easily be seen."

On Monday morning, September 8, a crowd was waiting outside the jail to see the survivors of the *Mignonette* led out to appear before the magistrates for an inquiry to determine whether there was enough evidence of a crime to warrant a full trial before a judge and jury. The public showed up in large numbers at Falmouth's Town Hall to see the famous cannibals with their own eyes. The case had produced "great excitement in Falmouth," *The Freeman's Journal* reported, and *The Cornishman* noted that the courtroom was "densely crowded." Mayor Liddicoat presided, flanked by six other magistrates. The proceeding began with a reading of the charges against Dudley,

Stephens, and Brooks. The men stood accused of murder, which put the prosecution on a high-stakes trajectory.

The magistrates had no real choice about the charges. English law had only one degree of murder; there was no second or third degree. Nor could the men be prosecuted for manslaughter, which applied only to killings that were either provoked or unintentional. In this case, Parker had clearly done nothing to provoke his own death, and there was no doubt that the act was intentional. There was no separate charge of cannibalism. As one contemporary legal scholar explained, there did not appear to be any precedents for charging people for eating another person. A criminal charge of this kind generally required a showing of harm to the public, he noted, and "it is difficult to see how the eating of a dead body can affect the public at large, when no one is there to see it done except those who participate in the act." So Dudley, Stephens, and Brooks would face a straightforward charge of murder.

The main evidence against them would be the sworn statements that they had given voluntarily at the Custom House. The magistrates also had the account that Dudley had written on the *Moctezuma* and the white penknife he had used to kill Parker. The German sailors who had helped rescue the men, Wiese and Drewe, were also in the courtroom and available to testify.

There was little that Dudley, Stephens, and Brooks could offer in response. In England at the time, odd as it seems by modern standards, criminal defendants were barred from giving sworn testimony at their own trials. It was thought to be a conflict of interest. As William Blackstone explained in the 1700s, all witnesses could be called "except such as are *infamous* or such as are *interested* in the event of the cause." In both civil and criminal cases, witnesses who had a stake in the outcome were considered likely to perjure themselves. In a criminal case, that meant defendants had to watch in silence as the charges against them were advanced and refuted by the sworn testimony of others.

The prisoners would have to speak in court through the reading of their Custom House statements. It was a poor substitute for testifying. When the men gave their statements, they were helping with a shipwreck investigation, not defending themselves against a capital murder charge. Limiting them to testifying only through their written statements also denied them the advantages that would have come from speaking in their own voices about the awful circumstances they found themselves in when they decided to kill Parker.

Dudley, Stephens, and Brooks had retained Harry Tilly, a Falmouth solicitor, to represent them. Tilly, a partner in the local firm of Fox & Tilly, was a respected lawyer who was more than capable of mounting a strong defense.

The magistrates heard testimony from Laverty, the harbor police sergeant, who told them what he had seen in the past two days. He recalled being at the Custom House when the men gave their statements. Most notably, he recounted hearing Dudley describe to Robert Gandy Cheesman precisely how he killed Parker. The police sergeant testified that Dudley had said he had offered up a prayer asking God to forgive him for what he was about to do and had told Parker, "Your time has come." Laverty then described Dudley taking a small knife from his pocket and demonstrating on his own neck where he had stuck the knife into Parker's neck. The sergeant showed the magistrates the knife he took from Dudley.

On cross-examination, Tilly got Laverty to say that he had not heard Cheesman warn Dudley that his answers could be used to charge him with a crime. Tilly was less successful in his questions about Parker's condition. Laverty said he did not hear

Dudley say that Parker was "nearly dead." He did hear Dudley say that the cabin boy was "very weak."

When Tilly was done, the court clerk had a request. The government had standardized the handling of death penalty cases, putting officials in London, rather than local ones, in charge of prosecutions. High-ranking justice officials in London had started to deliberate over what should be done in the case. Acting as an intermediary between the London officials and the Falmouth court, the court clerk asked the magistrates to adjourn the hearing until the Treasury Solicitor's office could give its view to the court on whether the case should move forward.

To spectators not familiar with the intricacies of the government, the clerk's proposal would have sounded confusing, but despite its name, the Treasury Solicitor's office was in charge of the government's legal work, not its finances. The Treasury Solicitor represented many governmental departments, including the Home Office, the department in charge of criminal justice. In that capacity, the Treasury Solicitor took the lead on major prosecutions across the country—which now included the case against Dudley, Stephens, and Brooks.

The magistrates agreed to the delay that the clerk and Treasury asked for. Mayor Liddicoat adjourned the hearing until Thursday, September 11, when Treasury would be prepared to give its views. That left a final question, whether the prisoners should be freed on bail until then. Tilly urged the magistrates to let his clients out on bond. Bail was almost never granted in murder cases, but Tilly emphasized the unusual circumstances under which Parker was killed. He also pointed to an admission he had extracted from Laverty on cross-examination: that his clients had been truthful about what happened and had volunteered the evidence that was being used against them.

The mayor asked if the defendants were prepared to produce bail. Tilly said Dudley had told him that they would meet any reasonable bail. While Tilly made his plea for bail, Dudley, who still had not seen his wife or children since he had set sail on the *Mignonette*, wept in open court.

The magistrates talked in private. When they were done, the mayor told Tilly they regretted that, given the nature of the case, they could not grant bail. It was, like the arrests, an indication that the government was taking the killing of Parker seriously. Dudley, Stephens, and Brooks were remanded to the Falmouth jail, where they would remain while Treasury considered how to proceed.

The following night, Parker's brother Daniel came to Falmouth. Daniel was working on the yacht *Marguerite*, which was berthed at Torquay, about seventy miles away along England's southwest coast. He had heard a report of his brother's death on Sunday, but he had not believed it. The next morning, the skipper had read a newspaper story about it to the whole crew, and Daniel took a leave to travel to Falmouth. He went in solidarity with Richard, he told a newspaper reporter, "my object being to let the people know there that someone owned him."

When he arrived in Falmouth, Daniel went to the police station. While he was talking to the Inspector of Police, Dudley, who was in the police jail, heard him and had an eerie sensation. "Why, that's little Dick's voice," Dudley exclaimed.

Daniel presented himself to Dudley. Meeting his brother's former shipmates for the first time, he spoke with all three and shook their hands, starting with Dudley. Daniel later said he was "very glad" he had come to Falmouth, because it "set my mind at rest."

On the same day, Philippa Dudley, who was still in Sutton, received a letter from her husband. He asked her not to come to

Falmouth for the legal proceedings. "Don't think about coming down," he told her. "It would only make you ill—the journey and seeing me here." Dudley noted ruefully that his legal troubles all stemmed from his own honesty. "They say it was my statement that caused the enquiry," he wrote. "I have told the truth. If I had told a lie I should be sharing the comforts of home instead of being here."

As bad as things looked now, Dudley assured his wife it would all work out. "No harm can come to me or any of us, dear," he wrote. He urged her, "Trust in God to give you the strength to bear the horrid lies that are in the papers." He did not specify what the lies were, and in fact, the most unsettling things the papers were saying were true.

Philippa Dudley was still working as a schoolmistress and caring for the Dudley children, but she found time to speak out on her husband's behalf to the reporters who had descended on Sutton. "I believe my husband has told everything as it happened," she told one reporter. "He was always candid. I don't think he means to contradict the main incident, but I cannot believe they were in their right minds; their sufferings must have reduced them to a state of frenzy."

Mrs. Dudley, not surprisingly, told the story in a way that reflected well on her husband. "Put yourself in his place," she continued. "Any man with a wife and children in the same position would have acted similarly."

Stephens's wife, Ann, who lived in Southampton, was not speaking to the press nearly as much as Philippa Dudley, but she did tell a reporter that Stephens was the kindest and noblest of husbands, who would not hurt a living creature willingly. The news from Falmouth was taking a toll on the Stephens family. Ann Stephens was said to be "in a state of extreme mental distress" and being cared for by neighbors. She "bursts into tears at the mere mention of the troubles of her husband," according to a news story. Even the Stephens's five children, it was reported, "seemed frightened, as if understanding the heavy afflictions so suddenly come upon their home."

While Falmouth authorities put the proceedings on hold, officials in London were discussing whether Dudley, Stephens, and Brooks should face murder charges. The Treasury Solicitor would carry out any prosecution, but the actual decision was up to the home secretary, William Harcourt, the powerful cabinet official who headed the Home Office. Harcourt would have the final word on how the prosecution proceeded.

When the first reports about the killing of Parker reached the Home Office, their gruesome subject matter caused a stir. Harcourt's son Lewis, who served as his father's private secretary, wrote with some alarm in his journal, "We have received a hideous account of cannibalism by the crew of a yacht called the *Mignonette* which was lost near Cape Town and the 3 survivors were picked up after they had eaten nearly the whole of a boy they had killed."

Far from the bustling, workaday port town of Falmouth, the Home Office was housed in a stately complex of government offices in a posh part of London not far from Buckingham Palace, in one of the world's great centers of wealth and power. William Vernon Harcourt was very much a part of this rarefied world. Both the Harcourt and Vernon families had arrived in England with William the Conqueror, and his Harcourt ancestors could trace their lineage in Oxfordshire back to the twelfth century. Harcourt's youth had been awash in privilege. He was educated by a Swiss governess and at private schools, where he was steeped in both the classics and the social graces. Even in the exalted confines of Trinity College, Cambridge, he stood out. Tall and handsome, young Harcourt "knew more of literature and politics than any of us," a fellow Cambridge student recalled. "He was witty and full of anecdotes of distinguished men who were only names to me."

Harcourt was elected president of the Cambridge Union, the prestigious debate and speech society. Before long he began to express and refine his liberal views, which were at odds with the conservative politics of his family. He argued for positions such as expanding the right to vote that he would later bring with him into government. After graduating, he wrote for the highly regarded *Saturday Review*, studied law, and quickly moved up in the profession. He became a member of the bar and, in 1868, a Liberal member of Parliament from Oxford.

Harcourt married a woman he adored. "Every day," he once said, he found "more and more to love in my sweet wife, and she seems to me nothing less than an angel." But tragedy arrived in two awful strikes. His first son died in infancy, and then his wife died three years into their marriage after giving birth to their second son. That son, Lewis, whom his doting father dubbed "Loulou," became the center of Harcourt's world.

In Parliament, Harcourt was known for strong views and a pugnacious style, which earned him the nickname "the Great Gladiator." He and the Liberal Party leader, William Gladstone, were often at odds, but when Gladstone became prime minister in 1880, he made Harcourt his home secretary. Gladstone said he needed "men of the greatest vigour and capacity to fill the weightiest offices of state."

As home secretary, Harcourt embodied the Victorian ethos of progressive reform. On the issues he cared most about, which included the rights of the accused, he was an influential force for discarding the old pieties and adopting more compassionate policies. Harcourt was particularly concerned about the treatment of prison inmates. "He was a man of singularly generous heart, and the Home Office was never administered by any one who had more sympathy with the prisoner and the captive," recalled Sir Evelyn Ruggles-Brise, a noted prison reformer who worked for Harcourt.

Harcourt had a special concern for juveniles caught up in the criminal justice system, a sentiment aligned with the Victorian "cult of the child." He believed prison was almost invariably a bad place for young people. On one occasion, he wrote a letter to Queen Victoria about the six thousand youth, aged twelve to sixteen, who were sent to prison each year, many for "trifling offenses, as, for instance, a boy of nine years old for throwing stones, several boys of eleven and twelve years for damaging grass by running about in the fields." His letter was meant as a plea. "Sir William humbly begs leave to represent to Your Majesty that protracted imprisonment in such cases has an injurious effect both upon the physical and moral nature of children of tender years," he wrote. The queen's private secretary, Sir Henry Ponsonby, responded that the entreaty had made a positive impression on the queen. Her true feelings were considerably less progressive: "She would like to whip them," Ponsonby wrote to Harcourt in a private letter, "but it seems that that cannot be done."

Harcourt's concern for the disadvantaged extended to matters large and small. He once wrote a letter explaining why he did not oppose the "itinerant shows" that were proliferating in working-class London neighborhoods. While his government was doing what it could "for the improvement of the houses and homes of the poor for their health and their education," according to Harcourt, he felt it was also important to support things that brought them happiness. "I rejoice," he said, "when I see an accidental space occupied by the yellow caravan or the booth of the showman which offers a precarious entertainment to those who find too little joy between the gutter and the grave."

Harcourt's instinctive sympathy for those caught in difficult life circumstances and his advocacy for accused prisoners might suggest that he would take the side of the survivors of the *Mignonette*, as they faced the harshest punishment for a crime arguably forced on them by circumstances. But there were other considerations that might have led him to view their case more harshly. Harcourt was not a man of the people with working-class roots or a port-towner's respect for seafaring ways like the custom of the sea. Nor was he a conservative who reflexively respected the captain's authority over his ship and crew, nor a legal traditionalist who might be inclined to defer to the centuries-old history of not prosecuting sailors who engaged in survival cannibalism.

Harcourt was, in fact, the opposite of all of these things. He was a progressive reformer, inclined to approach the question from the perspective of the underdog, the young and sick cabin boy who wanted to keep living. As for survival cannibalism, the ancient practice at the heart of the case, he was apt to view it the way progressive reformers looked at almost everything they disapproved of: as a social problem that needed fixing.

When the urgent request for guidance came in from Falmouth, it was rushed to the Home Office and brought to Harcourt personally. Harcourt asked the opinion of the attorney general, Sir Henry James, the 1st Baron James of Hereford, who replied with wry, but unambiguous, advice. "The *Mignonette* people ought to be properly prosecuted," he wrote back. If they were not, he said, "I shall decline in the future to sit near any man with a large appetite." Still, James was not without sympathy for Dudley, Stephens, and Brooks. He went on to say that "when convicted you can let them off."

Harcourt's own reaction to the case was not as lighthearted. On September 8, two days after the *Mignonette* survivors landed in Falmouth and gave their statements at the Custom House, the Home Office received a notification about the case with the title "R. Parker of the '*Mignonette*.'" Harcourt wrote on it, that day or soon after, "This is a very dreadful case. The law must decide what is the character of this terrible act."

Harcourt said he "should like the Public Prosecutor to take charge of the case so that it may be properly dealt with." Acting on these instructions, Sir Adolphus Liddell, the permanent undersecretary of state, sent letters to the director of public prosecutions and the Board of Trade telling them that the prosecution should proceed. It appeared that the government did not intend to treat this case with the indifference officials had shown to other survival cannibalism cases throughout history.

When the instructions from London reached Falmouth, the local authorities moved quickly. On Thursday, September 11, Dudley, Stephens, and Brooks were taken out of their jail cell and brought back to court. The court clerk told the magistrates he had received word that the Treasury Solicitor intended to move forward with the prosecution. To allow time to prepare, he said, Treasury had requested an adjournment for another week.

Dudley, Stephens, and Brooks again sought to be released on bail. Tilly asked the magistrates to let "these unfortunate men" go home until the proceedings resumed. His clients were still "in a wretched state of health," he said, and the "small room" where they were being held was "ill-adapted" to their medical problems. Tilly argued that the magistrates should take into account that his clients were "only technically charged with" murder. There was not, he insisted boldly, "the slightest possibility that the charge alleged against them can hold." To support his argument for bail, he waded into the substance of the case for the first time.

Tilly told the magistrates that what his clients did was neither wrong nor a crime. In a situation in which two people's lives are at risk and one must inevitably die, he said, the law did not prohibit one from taking the life of the other. He cited the legal commentaries of Sir James Fitzjames Stephen, a respected conservative judge and philosopher who had argued that such a killing would be justified, Tilly said, by "the great universal principle of self-preservation which prompts every man to have his own life preferable to that of another." Tilly also invoked Sir Francis Bacon's opinion that it was justifiable in the ancient Greek hypothetical of the two shipwreck survivors for the one man to shove the other away from the floating plank to save his own life.

The court clerk reported that the Treasury Solicitor did not oppose bail and believed the decision should be left to the magistrates. Treasury's view generally carried considerable weight, and it would now on the question of bail. The magistrates retired for a few minutes, and when they returned, Mayor Liddicoat announced that the case would be remanded until the following Thursday, September 18, to give Treasury the time it had requested, and that the magistrates had decided to set bail in the amount of £200 for Dudley and £100 each for Stephens and Brooks. The spectators broke out in loud cheers.

The bail decision was the first positive sign the men had received from the authorities since their arrest. It was not a small one, given that defendants facing capital charges were so rarely released on bail. The magistrates—and more important, the Treasury Solicitor—appeared to be signaling that even if the prosecution went forward, the government did not regard this as an ordinary capital murder case.

Low as the bail was, it was not immediately clear whether Dudley, Stephens, and Brooks would be able to meet it. But John Burton, the proprietor of the Old Curiosity Shop, spoke up in open court and said he would put up the money. He paid the bond for all three, even though he did not know Stephens or Brooks. The men appeared to be overcome with emotion. Stephens hid his face in his hands. Richard Parker's brother Daniel again shook hands with Dudley, Stephens, and Brooks. To the spectators in the courtroom, these public handshakes might have looked like a sign of support from the Parker family, but that does not seem to have been the intention. Daniel was trying to collect his brother's unpaid wages and may have thought the cordial gesture would help. Members of the family would make clear what they thought of the prosecution soon enough.

When the hearing ended, Dudley, Stephens, and Brooks walked out of the Town Hall with an almost giddy feeling. They were free for the first time since their arrest at the Custom House five days earlier, and they were finally headed home. The men "appeared highly delighted at being liberated," the Cardiff *Western Mail* observed. When the men left court, "there was great excitement," Brooks recalled, with "people clapping in the hall."

Stephens and Brooks returned to the sailors' home, which had invited the three survivors to stop by on their way out of Falmouth. Once again, they were welcomed warmly as sailors in need of assistance. "They treated us very kindly there," Brooks recalled, "giving us tea before we left and paying our passage up."

Stephens and Brooks left town that afternoon on a 5:20 train, arriving in Southampton the next day. Stephens's mother and brother-in-law met him at the station. They found him much changed since his departure in May. He stepped off the train only "with difficulty" and "appeared quite prostrate," the London *Standard* reported, and he walked up from the station to the nearby roadway on his mother's arm. When he reached his home, a reporter on the scene found that "the meeting of Mr. Stephens with his wife and family was very affecting."

When Brooks, the only *Mignonette* survivor who had no wife or children, arrived at the station, his friends were waiting and greeted him warmly. "I thank God," he said, "that I am spared once more to see my friends." Able to walk on his own, Brooks left the station accompanied by "a considerable following," according to *The Cornishman*. The entourage proceeded to the County Tavern, where he was staying, close to Fay's Yard, where he had worked as a rigger before setting sail on the *Mignonette*.

Dudley, who was headed home to Sutton, also left Falmouth in the late afternoon. When his train pulled into London's Paddington Station at 4 a.m. on Friday, his wife was there to greet him. Philippa Dudley had been ill for days from "nervous excitement," *The Cornishman* reported, but she had "made a struggle" to make it to London to meet him.

The Dudleys traveled by cab from Paddington to Victoria Station to catch a 5:50 a.m. train, and they arrived in Sutton forty-five minutes later. There were few people at the Sutton station at that hour, but the ones who were there welcomed Dudley "most respectfully," according to *The Daily News*, most of them taking off their hats as he walked through the station. When Dudley arrived home, he saw his children for the first time in four months. Friends and neighbors dropped by to wish him well and to hear what he had gone through. One of the first things he did was to send for a doctor to tend to his various injuries.

Dudley had brought his wife a poignant souvenir: the farewell letter he had written on the *Mignonette*'s chronometer certificate. He also shared the letter with newspapers, which were eager to print it. It was a shrewd public relations move. The press had been focused on Parker's killing and the cannibalism that followed, but the letter shined a spotlight on the men's desperate struggle to survive and Dudley's tender feelings for his wife. His words, which included his hope "to meet you and all our dear children in heaven," were far from the ravings of an uncivilized cannibal.

Sharing the letter was also a good legal strategy. Dudley would be barred by the "incompetence of interested witnesses" rule from testifying at his trial, if there was one. That would make it difficult to win jurors' sympathy and show them his humanity, which did not come across in his statement at the Custom House. When the letter was printed in newspapers, a readership that might include jurors or even judges in the case would see his emotional account of his time in the lifeboat.

Reporters continued to descend on Dudley, Stephens, and Brooks's hometowns over the next few days to provide an eager public with updates. A follow-up story reported that Dudley "looks fairly well, but is still fairly weak." The newspapers offered detailed information on the condition of his legs and feet. When Dudley was rescued, his legs were "much swollen, and it was only after a long course of blistering and bandaging that they were reduced to a normal size," the London *Standard* said. Now he wore "slippers on his feet, as they are still too tender to admit of putting boots on." In Southampton, reporters found Stephens at home, where he was still ailing and "able to get but little sleep." His feet and legs were still badly swollen, they said, and he was suffering from pain in his limbs and congestion in his lungs. "The excitement attending his arrival home," which "bore him up wonderfully, has gone off, and a sort of reaction has set in which is attended with the most uncomfortable symptoms," the *Southampton Herald* said.

Brooks was not doing much better. His health was "shattered," the *Southampton Herald* said. His friends were visiting him regularly at the County Tavern, listening to his stories of the loss of the *Mignonette* and everything that followed. Brooks seemed to be getting an especially warm reception, perhaps because he had not participated in killing Parker. The *Essex Standard* reported that Itchen Ferry yachtsmen, people Parker might have worked alongside, were "making him quite the hero of the hour."

When they were not worrying about their health, Dudley, Stephens, and Brooks had to focus on their legal troubles. The immediate challenge was raising funds for a defense. Dudley was the best off financially, having kept most of the *Mignonette* pay for himself and also benefiting from the income of a working wife. Still, he did not have much. Stephens and Brooks were "quite destitute," according to *The Royal Cornwall Gazette*. Brooks was blunt about his situation. "As to defending myself, if there's a trial, I've got no money," he said in an interview. Brooks publicly put some of the blame on Dudley, noting, "Our wages were stopped from the moment" the *Mignonette* "went down."

Donations were still coming in from the lifeboat exhibit in Falmouth, where, the *Standard* reported, "visitors" had "contributed substantially." There were more advertisements soliciting donations, including one in the *Southampton Times* focused on the Stephens family, whose need was greatest. Stephens's Masonic lodge was also raising money for him. John Want, who had commissioned the ill-fated voyage, sent £100 from Sydney for the defense, the amount he was going to pay Dudley when the *Mignonette* was delivered.

The maritime community continued to rally around the men. Many sailors empathized with their plight as shipwreck survivors, enduring circumstances that presented them with few options. Sailors were familiar with cannibalism at sea, and they were beginning to speak out in defense of it through an array of communication channels. One of these channels was the sea shanty, the traditional work songs of sailors. Around this time, someone composed a shanty that circulated in printed form under the title "Fearful Sufferings at Sea. Lad Killed and Eaten." It began, "Just a few moments your attention I crave, / While I relate a sad death on the wave." The ballad presented a sympathetic portrait of Dudley, Stephens, and Brooks. It noted that while they killed the cabin boy "to preserve their own lives," the men "thought of their children, their homes and their wives."

Some of the men's supporters were sending letters and petitions to the Home Office lobbying for the charges to be dropped. Just a few days after the men had arrived in Falmouth, the home secretary received a personal letter from a yacht owner who had once hired Dudley as captain. He assured Harcourt that Dudley was a fundamentally decent man. "Whatever view the law may take of the act, Dudley could not have thought it unjustifiable," the yacht owner wrote. "Neither selfishness nor cruelty had any part in his character."

The men were grateful for the outpouring of support. "Our sufferings have commanded a considerable amount of sympathy on the part of those who are able in some measure to understand what we really have gone through," Brooks said in an interview. The survivors hoped that the popular support would cause the government to rethink the prosecution.

But not everyone was on the men's side, and they knew it. There were members of the public who considered them to be murderers and wanted to see them punished severely. Unlike the people who had gathered to cheer in the courtroom, they were not easy to spot at first, but clearly, there were influential people who did not want the three men freed. Mayor Liddicoat had ordered them arrested, and the Treasury Solicitor was bringing charges against them. The home secretary made clear that he considered the matter serious, and the attorney general favored prosecuting. There were still other sectors of society that had not been heard from much yet, but they were about to start weighing in, and they would see the case differently than the crowds filling the Falmouth courthouse.

On September 18, Dudley, Stephens, and Brooks returned to Falmouth to appear in court. The magistrates would hear more evidence and decide whether the case against the men was strong enough to warrant a full trial before a jury. Now that the Treasury Solicitor was involved, the prosecution was no longer a local matter. Lawyers had arrived in town from London to represent the Crown.

A large crowd of people gathered at the entrance of the Town Hall almost an hour before the start of the hearing, far more than could fit in the courtroom. The magistrates arrived at 11 a.m., and Dudley, Stephens, and Brooks took their places in the dock. This time, since they were out on bail, the men had come to court on their own, without law enforcement escorts. They were still "very weak, and only able to walk with difficulty," according to *The Royal Cornwall Gazette*.

William Danckwerts, junior Treasury counsel and expert on shipwreck cases, headed the prosecution. He was assisted by G. Appleby Jenkins, the town clerk of nearby Penryn. Jenkins had a better understanding of the local people and legal practices than the Londoners did, and he could advise them on how to pitch the Crown's case to the magistrates. Danckwerts was well aware he was an outsider in Falmouth, and he believed, his son would later say, that he might be in danger for prosecuting the men in a place where they had such strong support. After the death threat to the mayor, it was no idle fear.

The formal charge was read out. The prisoners, "on the 25th day of July, being subjects of our Lady the Queen, on the high seas feloniously, wilfully & of their malice aforethought did kill and murder one Richard Parker, against the peace of our Lady the Queen, Her crown and dignity." In keeping with English homicide law, it was a murder charge, with no room for a judge or jury to take the extreme conditions in the lifeboat into account and find the defendants guilty of a lesser crime. If they were convicted, the defendants would almost certainly be sentenced to death.

In deference to the sympathies of the spectators who had packed the courtroom, Danckwerts began on an empathetic note. He acknowledged that "no human" could "help feeling the most profound pity" for Dudley, Stephens, and Brooks after what they had experienced. But he said that the magistrates must not let themselves be "turned to the right or to the left by any feeling of pain of pity or any other sentiment than that of a sincere desire to further justice and nothing more."

The killing of Parker clearly met the legal definition of murder, Danckwerts said. That was true even though it occurred far from England, since the Maritime Act of 1850 established that the queen's law prevailed on British ships on the open sea. Danckwerts underscored that the magistrates did not need to decide whether the men's actions were justified by the necessity defense or on any other ground. These were jury questions, he said, "and it is to a jury of their countrymen that I ask you to send it."

Then Danckwerts did something unexpected: He dropped the case against Brooks. The prosecutor said he had carefully reviewed the seaman's actions and decided he should be not a defendant but rather a witness for the prosecution. The announcement came as a surprise to Brooks. The authorities had treated the three men identically up until this point, and it was their first recognition that Brooks was not culpable for Parker's death. Brooks was released from custody, and one news account reported that there was "loud applause" in the courtroom.

There were good reasons not to prosecute Brooks. The main one was obvious: that he had not been involved in the alleged crime. He had opposed killing anyone, he had not been included in the planning, and he had covered his face with his coat while the act was done. There was little more he could have done to separate himself from the crime that was about to occur. But Danckwerts also had a more practical reason: It would help with the prosecution of the other two men. The main evidence he had against Dudley and Stephens was their statements at the Custom House. It was likely the statements would be admissible in the prosecution, but the defense would no doubt object, and the court had not yet ruled on the question. If the statements were not allowed into evidence, the Crown might actually have trouble proving its case.

Even if Dudley's and Stephens's statements were admitted, they would not be the same as having a live witness. They were brief accounts of what happened, given as part of a shipwreck investigation. They did not answer the questions a judge or jury might have about what had occurred in the lifeboat, and the only living people who could do so were Dudley, Stephens, and Brooks. With the charges against Brooks dropped, he would be able to testify for the prosecution, and the Crown would have an eyewitness who could recount the events precisely.

The prosecution's first witness that day was Laverty, the harbor police sergeant, repeating his testimony from ten days earlier. On cross-examination, Tilly tried to get Laverty to support Dudley's claim that Parker was nearly dead when he was killed. He asked Laverty if he had overheard Dudley say at the Custom House "that the boy was very weak and nearly down to death's door." Laverty did not agree. "I heard him say that he was very weak," Laverty said, refusing to confirm the part about being near death's door.

Next was Cheesman, who recalled Dudley, Stephens, and Brooks coming to the Custom House shortly after they arrived in Falmouth. Danckwerts used him to lay the factual groundwork for admitting the men's written statements into evidence. Cheesman also testified about what Dudley had told him about the murder in their conversation after his official statement.

There was a moment of drama during Cheesman's testimony. As he was recounting how Dudley had acted out the killing for him in the Custom House, he was about to point to the side of his neck to show where Dudley had put the knife in. But he hesitated, saying, "I am not sure whether it was the right or left side." At that moment, Dudley interrupted, pointing to the left side of his neck, and called out, "It was on this side!"

The interjection was shocking. Defendants were not supposed to speak in court. But it was more than that. When Dudley declared which side of the cabin boy's neck he had slit open with his knife, his words and gestures brought the killing into the courtroom with a realness and immediacy that was impossible to ignore. One newspaper reported that when Dudley spoke out, Stephens "gave an involuntary shudder, and for a few moments covered his face."

Danckwerts said that if Tilly intended to object to the Custom House statements being used, he should do it now. Tilly did object. He argued that the statements had been taken as part of a shipwreck investigation under the Merchant Shipping Act and should not be admitted in a criminal case against the men who had willingly provided them. Danckwerts insisted there was no legal bar to using them as evidence. The magistrates discussed the objection in private and then ordered the statements read in open court. With that one ruling, much of the prosecution's work was done. The record would have the defendants, under oath, describing how they had killed Parker. That would likely be enough on its own to make the factual case, but the Crown now also had Brooks as a live witness to support the defendants' own admissions.

On cross-examination, Tilly tried to use Cheesman to discredit his clients' sworn statements. He got Cheesman to concede that he had not warned the men of the possible legal consequences of answering his questions. Cheesman insisted that he had had no idea at the time that the statements would be used against them in a criminal prosecution. He thought he was simply investigating a shipwreck. If he had known that it would lead to criminal charges, Cheesman said with tears in his eyes, he would never have questioned them.

Next, the prosecution called Julius Wiese, one of the sailors who had helped with the rescue. With an interpreter translating from German, Wiese told of seeing a piece of rib and some other flesh and bone. He recalled how they had thrown it overboard on his captain's orders. If Dudley's outburst had made the killing feel real, Wiese's grisly description of the remnants of Parker's body gave the magistrates and spectators a ghastly sense of what the cannibalism looked like.

The prosecution's final witness was the one the whole courtroom was waiting to hear from, able seaman Brooks. His testimony would be murder tourism of the highest order, as the spectators got to hear one of the notorious *Mignonette* castaways describe the killing of Parker in his own words. It would be far better than inspecting the *Mignonette* lifeboat—and many people had been willing to pay money to do that.

There was the added drama of what Brooks's testimony would mean for the case. As a prosecution witness, Brooks would be testifying against the men he had sailed with for months, the fellow castaways with whom he had survived a shipwreck. The words he was about to speak could cause his former shipmates to be hanged.

As if that were not enough excitement, Brooks would also be pulling the veil off the dark taboo at the heart of the *Mignonette* case: the cannibalism. The public might have been fascinated by murders, but murder trials were not altogether uncommon. The spectators in the courtroom in Falmouth were about to hear a proper Englishman describe in his own words how he ate another Englishman.

Brooks's testimony began slowly, with his decision to sign on with the *Mignonette*. He talked about the other crewmembers, including seventeen-year-old Parker. He said the crew worked together well, and he told how the voyage had gotten off to a promising start. That soon changed, Brooks said, and he recounted the sinking of the *Mignonette*. He described how all four men evacuated in the lifeboat, surviving on two tins of turnips and the turtle they caught. He recalled that Dudley proposed drawing lots and that the first time he did, Parker was not sick. "He was pretty well at that time," Brooks said. Brooks testified that Dudley continued to propose drawing lots and that he had opposed it, saying, "Let us all die together." Brooks said that the captain insisted something had to be done.

It was clear from his account why he was not being prosecuted. He recalled that after he said he would rather die than kill anyone, he was excluded from the discussions about killing

Parker. "I did not hear Dudley or Stephens discuss the question of killing the boy," he told the court.

Finally, Brooks gave up the gritty details of what he had witnessed. He told the magistrates that he was lying down in the front of the boat with his oilskin jacket over his head when he "heard a little noise." When he looked, he saw that Parker was dead, and he fainted briefly, he said. When he came to, just a minute or two later, he saw Dudley and Stephens drinking the cabin boy's blood. He could see that Parker's eyes were "quite white." Brooks said that he asked Dudley for some of the blood, and he received some, but it was congealed, and he had trouble swallowing much of it.

He told the magistrates that he did not see the killing itself, but he had no doubt about what had happened. "I did not at any time ask how the boy had been killed," Brooks said, but "I knew the captain had killed him because he said so himself soon after."

Brooks did not seem eager to testify against his former captain and mate. He spoke in such a low voice that he could barely be heard. The magistrates had to ask him more than once to speak more clearly. "The impression created by Brooks's manner was that he assumed the role of a witness rather reluctantly," a reporter observed, "and that the recital of the sad scenes in which he had been to some extent a participator was a painful and repugnant task." On cross-examination, Tilly elicited some praise for Dudley. "I have known Captain Dudley for 12 years by reputation as a good skipper and I have found him a kind and good captain," Brooks said. "On the 5th of July when the yacht foundered, he was the last to leave her."

Tilly tried to show that there was little difference in the actions of Brooks, who was not being charged with murder, and his clients, who were. Brooks conceded that while he did not help with the killing, he made no effort to stop it. "I did not by any act of mine attempt to prevent the boy from being killed," he told Tilly. "And after he was killed I shared his blood and flesh with the others."

But neither admission put Brooks on anything approaching an equal footing with Dudley and Stephens. The law did not require people to intervene to stop others from committing a crime. And in any case, Tilly gave no indication of how he thought Brooks could have stopped Dudley and Stephens from killing the cabin boy if he had wanted to. As for sharing the blood and flesh after Parker was already dead, that did not make Brooks part of the murder.

Tilly questioned Brooks about Parker's condition, trying to show that the cabin boy was near death when he was stabbed, and Brooks provided some help on that score. "The lad was in a great deal worse condition than any of us," Brooks said, adding that Parker had been lying with his head on his arm, not speaking or taking notice of what was occurring around him for hours. "To the best of my judgment," he ventured, Parker "appeared to be dying." He further aided Dudley and Stephens by saying, "But for the death of the boy I believe we should all have died from hunger and thirst."

Tilly also wanted Brooks to testify that Dudley had done the right thing by proposing to draw lots. "Supposing one has to die, is not casting lots the fairer way?" he asked. But on that score, Brooks offered no help. He was no more willing to support drawing lots in the courtroom than he had been in the lifeboat. Brooks repeated the words he had used before. "I should not like to kill anyone, and I should not like anyone to kill me," he said, adding, "I should prefer to die in the ordinary way."

On redirect questioning from Danckwerts, Brooks helped the prosecution on a critical point: While he said Parker was the "weakest of the four," he would not say he was sure the cabin boy was about to die. "I cannot say how long Parker might have lived," he said. Brooks would not help the defense make an argument that Parker was so close to death that killing him should hardly count as murder. Brooks's refusal also undermined the defense's argument that it was better for one person to die so four could live. If Parker was not on the brink of death, it was possible that all four men would have survived one more day, until it rained, and a little longer past that, until the German boat appeared.

When Brooks's testimony ended, Danckwerts told the magistrates he was done presenting the Crown's case. "I submit it will be your duty," he said, "to commit the prisoners for trial." It was now the defense's turn to put on its case, but Tilly was not sure there was any point. He thought the magistrates might have already decided that the prosecution should go forward. Tilly said that if their minds were still open, he was prepared to mount a defense, but if they had already made their decision, he would not waste their time. The magistrates retired for a few minutes. When they returned, Mayor Liddicoat said the charges were too serious to dismiss. He announced that the case would go to trial before a jury at the upcoming winter assize, or court session, at Exeter, about eighty miles northeast of Falmouth.

The mayor declared that Dudley and Stephens would remain out on bail. When he made that announcement, the spectators cheered loudly, and the police in the courtroom made little effort to quiet them. Burton continued to provide the bail money for the two prisoners who still needed it. With that, the hearing ended, more than six hours after it began.

The defendants had displayed different demeanors during the proceeding. Stephens was the more emotional of the two, burying his head in his hands at various points. Dudley was more stolid, watching "with keen interest," *The Cornishman* reported, and "never blanching even when counsel and witness recalled the crisis of the tragedy and pictured the revolting details." Dudley's composure broke, however, when the hearing was over. The captain, who had been "cool and collected" during the testimony, "lost command of himself and burst into tears," *The Cornishman* said.

Dudley and Brooks left town early the next morning by train, and Stephens left a little later by boat. All three men were headed home, but now there was a profound difference in their situations. Dudley and Stephens were out on bail, but they were facing a trial that could end in their being hanged for murder. Brooks, who had firmly resisted killing anyone in the lifeboat, was now a free man—and the star witness for the prosecution.

8

The Grand Jury Weighs In

Dudley and Stephens's case was moving through the legal system with impressive speed. The *Mignonette* survivors had arrived in Falmouth on September 6, a Saturday, and were brought before the magistrates on Monday morning. There was a hearing on September 11, at which they were released on bail, and another on September 18 at which the decision was made to prosecute them. Their case was now headed to a grand jury on November 3, when the next Exeter Assize began.

As that day of reckoning drew near, popular interest in the *Mignonette* saga remained intense. People from all walks of life continued to discuss it in their homes, on the streets, and in pubs. The press, which jumped on the story from the moment Dudley, Stephens, and Brooks set foot in Falmouth, still loved it and eagerly fanned the flames, focusing on the most lurid aspects. After the final hearing before the magistrates, the headlines were full of the one word the press could not get enough of. Only the words around it changed: "The *Mignonette* Cannibalism Case," "The Alleged Murder and Cannibalism," and "The Charge of Cannibalism Against a Shipwrecked Crew."

By now, everyone knew all the grim details. They were just the sort of things Victorians loved to read about. The newspapers reveled in the specifics of how Parker was killed, reporting that the defendants had agreed in the lifeboat that Dudley would "strike the blow" and "Stephens should hold the lad in case he moved." They wrote breathlessly about the moment when Dudley "ran a small penknife into Parker's jugular vein" and the men "caught the gushing blood" in tins and drank it. They did not shy away from the most grisly aspects of the story, including how the castaways cut out Parker's liver and heart and devoured them "while they were yet hot from the body." The *Derby Daily Telegraph* reported that the German captain ordered that the "putrid and mangled remains of the poor boy Parker" be "consigned to a watery grave."

As the proceedings in Exeter approached, the focus of the public and the press shifted perceptibly. The initial uproar over the shipwreck and "the terrible tale of cannibalism" had "considerably subsided," the *Southampton Herald* observed. Now "the chief topic of conversation," it said, was "what will be the fate of the survivors." The question of the moment was whether Dudley and Stephens would be convicted of murder.

News stories were generally sympathetic to the men, and public opinion remained strongly on Dudley and Stephens's side. According to the *Nottingham Evening Post*, "The public feeling at Falmouth, and, indeed, throughout the west of England, is one of deep sympathy for the unhappy men." There was, the paper said, "scarcely a word of condemnation of their desperate action . . . from any quarter."

That was an overstatement. Critics of Dudley and Stephens were starting to speak out, challenging the initial idea that the survivors were heroes. People were openly questioning Dudley's judgment in embarking on such a difficult ocean voyage in a tiny yacht. The *Essex Standard* reported that Dudley had ignored "his friends and associates at Tollesbury" who tried to dissuade him "from attempting the foolish and hazardous journey to Sydney, which it was predicted would be likely to bring ruin or disaster." More pointedly, Dudley and Stephens were being faulted for not following the custom of the sea. "The question which was the most extensively discussed by the public was 'Why did they not cast lots?'" *The Cornishman* wrote. "In the mind of a very large section a feeling of strong antipathy towards the survivors has been created on this point."

Parker's hometown of Itchen Ferry was a particular center of criticism of Dudley and Stephens. The residents' judgments were rooted, one newspaper said, in "a warm expression of pity for the lad, who was so well known" to them. Among these hometown critics were Parker's family. Parker's adoptive mother was "in a very excited and distressed condition of mind by what" had "happened," according to the *Liverpool Mercury*. "When I heard of his dreadful death I could not believe it," Mrs. Mathews told the paper. His death, she said, had "almost broken my heart, for he was as dear to me and to my husband as if he were our own son." John Mathews was "very downhearted," the *Mercury* reported, "and would speak to hardly anyone."

Mrs. Mathews did not share the view that Dudley and Stephens were heroes or that taking Parker's life was justified under the circumstances. "All I have to say about it is that I really do not think they should have killed him," she told the paper. "I can seem to see him looking up to Captain Dudley and saying, 'What me, sir?'"

John Mathews's nephew, himself a young yachtsman, agreed. "I know it may be argued that three lives are better than one," he said. "But the lad was an orphan, and we seem to think here that advantage was taken of him." He believed that Dudley and Stephens should be convicted of murder. "As to whether any punishment should be awarded," he said, "we say there should be a little," otherwise "anybody might go to sea and get into trouble and be killed." The *Mercury* reported that this view "may be said to be representative of public opinion at the Ferry."

Another group was starting to speak out against Dudley and Stephens, and it was a large and influential one: Victorian-era reformers. Their guiding principle was that the government had a responsibility to rein in humanity's worst instincts, to hold people to higher standards of conduct than they were likely to hold themselves to. Motivated by a commitment to greater fairness and equality in society, they were on the lookout for instances of the powerful using their advantages to oppress the weak. What had happened on the *Mignonette*'s lifeboat violated their most cherished principles. Powerful people had exploited a weaker person to advance their own selfish interests. They had resorted to brutal violence. An innocent person was intentionally killed. And adults had harmed a child.

To some reformers, the prosecution now underway was not simply a criminal case against two seafarers; it was a chance to put survival cannibalism itself on trial. All their reform instincts told them that just as society needed rules against exploitative factories, it needed a prohibition on killing and eating people under trying conditions at sea.

This perspective began to appear in newspapers—not so much in the news articles, where Dudley and Stephens were still largely being presented sympathetically, but in opinion pieces. One paper leading the charge was *The Spectator*, which had been founded in 1828 by a crusading journalist who, as one observer put it, had played "a prominent part in the discussion of every important reform achieved during" his time at the helm. *The Spectator*'s current editors believed that the magistrates had done a "public service" by sending Dudley and Stephens's case to trial. It was "high time" to bring an end to "the hideous tradition of the sea which authorises starving sailors to kill and eat their comrades," the paper said. Sailors should be taught once and for all "that the special dangers of their profession furnish no excuse for a practice as directly opposed to human as it is to divine law." *The Spectator* was hardly alone. The more radical *Reynolds's Newspaper*, a zealous advocate for worker's rights, saw the killing as an act of "selfishness," another version of the systemic oppression it saw throughout Victorian society.

An anonymous barrister framed the reformers' position sharply in a letter to *The Daily Telegraph*. Letting people kill others to save themselves was "exceedingly dangerous" and "highly immoral," he wrote. If the courts allowed such acts, it would leave anyone in a "tight place"—in a lifeboat or anywhere else—"at the mercy of any companion who happened to be stronger, heavier, better armed, or in any way more dexterous and unscrupulous."

The most unexpected letters to the editor came from Dudley himself. He wrote to several papers, nominally to thank the public for its support but more to advocate for himself. In the *Standard*, he declared that he and Stephens had been charged for "an act which certainly was *not* accompanied by either premeditation or malice . . . to that our consciences can affirm." In his letter to *The Times*, he was even more emphatic in asserting his innocence, referring to "our present torture under the ban of law." In the *Western Daily Mercury*, Dudley suggested that he and Stephens should be acquitted on the basis of mental infirmity. "I question," he said, "whether we could be considered of sound mind . . . under the extreme circumstances of the case."

Newspapers generally did not open their pages to criminal defendants to plead their innocence, but Dudley's case had attracted so much interest that papers were happy to publish him. It was one more precedent-shattering aspect of an already singular case. One lawyer said he believed it was "unique for a man awaiting trial for murder to comment on the impending proceedings in the columns of the daily press." Dudley would be legally barred from testifying in Exeter, but the letters allowed him to respond in his own words to the charges against him.

The prosecution, which was now formally known as *Regina v. Dudley and Stephens*—*regina* being Latin for "the queen," who was officially the prosecuting party—moved to the Exeter Assize on Monday, November 3. Exeter, a town with a rich history that was still visible in its Roman wall and Gothic cathedral, hosted the courts of assize by virtue of its status as the county town of Devon. The assize system, whose origins lay in the twelfth century, brought a high-quality justice system to rural areas in the form of county courts that were presided over by visiting judges from prominent courts in London. The jurors were drawn from the local population.

The Exeter Assize would consider Dudley and Stephens's case in two stages. First, a grand jury would decide whether there was a basis for prosecuting them. It was the same question the Falmouth magistrates had considered, but this time, the decision would be made by grand jurors, a crucial first step in bringing a serious criminal charge. If the grand jury found there was a basis, it would return a "true bill" of indictment. The case would then move on to a trial before a regular jury, formally known as a "petit jury."

The assize system was an elitist form of justice. The grand jury was drawn from male members of the landed gentry; the one that was being assembled to hear the case against Dudley and Stephens would include two members of Parliament, one of whom was a baronet. The petit jury that would hear the case at trial, if there was a trial, would be less socially elevated, but its members would still all be male property owners from the area.

The presiding judge at the November assize was Sir John Walter Huddleston, one of fifteen members of the Court of Queen's Bench of the High Court of Justice in London. Baron Huddleston had been born into relatively modest circumstances and had risen up through British society by his law career, becoming a wealthy criminal lawyer and serving in Parliament before becoming a judge. He climbed in social standing when he married Lady Diana De Vere Beauclerk, daughter of the 9th Duke of St. Albans, when he was fifty-seven and she was thirty-one. He ascended to the bench at a time when judges on some courts were awarded the honorary title of baron. The practice was discontinued soon after that, and Baron Huddleston's auspicious timing led to him being known as "the Last of the Barons."

Baron Huddleston was known for having strong opinions about the cases before him, and for usually getting his way. British judges were, on the whole, more inclined than American ones to help juries decide cases. One American lawyer who traveled to England to observe British trials wrote, "What impressed me, in the jury cases that I heard while I was over there, was that the judge on the bench . . . sat there to give the jury the benefit of his learning, and to help them weigh the evidence." But even among British judges, Baron Huddleston stood out. He was, one commentator said, "what is called a strong Judge, taking a view of his own, and almost invariably leading the jury to the same opinion."

The Dudley and Stephens prosecution would in some ways be familiar territory for Baron Huddleston. His father, Thomas, had been a merchant captain and had served in the navy. Baron Huddleston had himself been a judge advocate of the naval fleet, which gave him a working knowledge of many aspects of sailing life. As opinionated as he was, he could be expected to have some strong beliefs about how captains and crews should act.

At the grand jury proceeding, both sides had able counsel. Arthur Charles, Queen's Counsel (QC), appeared for the Crown, while Arthur John Hammond Collins, QC, appeared for the defendants. The change on the defense side was notable. Collins was a significant step up from solicitor Harry Tilly. The stakes were higher now that the men were directly facing capital charges, and they had more money to hire counsel from the fundraising on their behalf. Collins was one of the most prominent barristers in the region. He was highly respected for his legal skills, and his stature in the profession would help him advocate for Dudley and Stephens in the rarefied world of the Exeter Assize. Collins was well acquainted with the assize officials and likely would know many of the twenty-three grand jurors.

Baron Huddleston began by telling the grand jury the facts of the case: the shipwreck, the time the men spent in the lifeboat, the killing of Parker, and the cannibalism. His account was neutral and nonjudgmental, and he was generous in describing Dudley. The captain was, he said, "a man of exemplary character, great experience, and courage." Baron Huddleston then explained the relevant law. This was standard, and he was right to do it, but Baron Huddleston was unusually direct in stating what he believed the facts and law added up to. "It seems clear," he said, "that the taking away of the boy's life was carefully considered and amounted to a case of deliberate homicide."

Baron Huddleston knew that the necessity doctrine would be critical to Dudley and Stephens's defense, and he addressed it head-on. He dismissed the two main precedents the defendants were likely to rely on, the St. Kitts case of cannibalism at sea and *United States v. Holmes*, the case of the sailor who led the crew in pushing sixteen passengers out of the lifeboat of the *William Brown*.

The St. Kitts case, Baron Huddleston said, was not a precedent at all, because there was no reliable report of a legal decision. Everything that was known about it, he said, came from a Dutch physician's book of medical curiosities. There was no reason to believe, he added, that it was actually a holding of an English court. As for *United States v. Holmes*, Baron Huddleston said that it relied on the necessity doctrine, and unlike American law, British law did not provide any legal support for such a doctrine. Baron Huddleston also noted that Justice Henry Baldwin had only approved of sacrificing lives if lots were drawn. Dudley and Stephens had not drawn lots, so the *Holmes* case did not support their defense.

Baron Huddleston went further and directly repudiated the custom of the sea. He noted that Justice Baldwin had endorsed the drawing of lots as a basis for deciding who should be killed in an emergency at sea, seeing it as "in some sort, an appeal to God for selection of the victim." Baron Huddleston regarded Justice Baldwin's analysis as not only wrong but offensive. "Such a reason would seem almost to verge upon the blasphemous," he said.

Having rejected the necessity defense, Baron Huddleston went on to explain why the doctrine of self-defense did not apply. It was true, he said, that the law sometimes permitted people to kill to prevent someone from killing them. But that had not been the case in the lifeboat, he said. Dudley and Stephens may have been in danger of dying of hunger and thirst, but Parker, "at the bottom of the boat, was not endangering their lives by any act of his," the judge pointed out. As a result, it was "impossible to say that the act of Dudley and Stephens was an act of self-defense."

In his remarks to the grand jury, Baron Huddleston struck some of the main themes of the Victorian reformers, and this was the first time a judge was speaking about Dudley and Stephens from that perspective. Baron Huddleston argued that it was especially wrong to take the life of a young person as Dudley and Stephens had done. They had decided that Parker's life was less valuable than their own because he had no wife or children. On the contrary, young people's lives were *more* valuable, Baron Huddleston argued, citing ancient Rome's most famous lawyer. If somebody had to be sacrificed in an emergency, Cicero wrote, it should be the person least likely to contribute to the Republic. Baron Huddleston insisted that Parker, as the youngest person in the lifeboat, could be expected to live the longest and provide more service to England than the others.

Another broad Victorian reform principle that Baron Huddleston invoked was the importance of protecting the weak from being exploited by the strong. Baron Huddleston noted that Dudley considered Parker's illness to be a reason for sacrificing him, but he maintained that the opposite was true. "One would have imagined that the state of his health, and the misery in which he was at the time, would have obtained for him more consideration," he said.

Having covered both the facts and the law—with a strong dose of subjective moralizing—Baron Huddleston proceeded to firmly suggest to the grand jury what it should do. "I am bound to tell you that if you are satisfied that the boy's death was caused or accelerated by the act of Dudley, or by Dudley and Stephens, this is a case of deliberate homicide, neither justifiable or excusable," he said. "The crime is murder, and you, therefore, ought to find a true bill for that offense against both the prisoners."

Finally, the judge emphasized that the grand jury's role in the process was limited. He assured the grand jurors that if they returned true bills, Dudley and Stephens would have an opportunity later in the process to argue more fully that English law recognized a necessity defense. If the necessity doctrine was found to exist, he said, "the prisoners would have the benefit of it." Furthermore, if the defendants were convicted, there would be a path for them to overturn their convictions or reduce their sentences. "Under the peculiar circumstances of this melancholy case," they would be able "to appeal to the mercy of the Crown," Baron Huddleston said, referring to the "royal prerogative of mercy." The law, he reminded them, empowered Queen Victoria to pardon "particular objects of compassion . . . in cases of peculiar hardship."

With that, Baron Huddleston called attention to the fact that English criminal law at the time had two sequential stages. In the first stage, which they were in now, judges and juries would decide whether Dudley and Stephens were guilty of murder, which almost invariably meant a sentence of death. Judges were not supposed to impose any other penalty for murder. (That applied even to children convicted of murder; the death penalty for children was not ended until 1908.) If the men were indeed sentenced to death, there would be a second stage, in which the queen, on the advice of the home secretary, would decide whether they were deserving of mercy or should be sent to the gallows.

In Victorian England, that life-or-death decision was effectively made by the home secretary, though that had not always been the case. The roots of the royal prerogative of mercy lay in the reign of Edward the Confessor, the king of England from 1042 to 1066. The royal prerogative was, according to William Blackstone, the great legal commentator, part of the "power of the Sovereign of his pure grace to show mercy to an offender by mitigating or removing the consequences of conviction." The power was limited to less serious crimes at first, but over time, it evolved so the monarch could, and often did, use it to overturn death sentences. In some cases, the mercy power was considered to be, according to a legal scholar, "an acknowledgement of the fallibility of the judicial process."

Sovereigns could use any criteria they wanted to decide whether to grant mercy. But in practice, the prerogative had changed considerably at the start of Queen Victoria's reign. She was just eighteen when she was crowned, and it was not considered appropriate for such a young and inexperienced woman to delve into the details of capital cases and decide who should be hanged. To avoid this, Parliament established a new procedure by which the home secretary reviewed all mercy applications and made a recommendation, which effectively decided the matter. This change professionalized the process, since legal experts at the Home Office could analyze each case in a systematic way, and it brought the elected government in on capital punishment decisions.

As the de facto decision-maker, the home secretary generally looked at all aspects of a case, from the nature of the crime, to the state of mind of the defendant, to the severity of the sentence. Weighing the public's views was not formally part of the process, but it was inevitable that a political figure like the home secretary, who worked for the prime minister, would take note of popular opinion.

This unusual way in which English law treated capital cases put juries and judges in a difficult position. They were supposed to limit themselves to the question of whether a crime had been committed and leave it to the home secretary and the queen to decide whether mercy was appropriate. But that meant they ran the risk of causing the execution of a defendant they did not believe should receive capital punishment if it turned out that the queen and home secretary did not have the same degree of sympathy they did.

If the Victorian reformers had their way, this dilemma would not exist. They had been trying for years to end capital punishment entirely. In the early 1800s, the death penalty abolition movement succeeded in limiting capital punishment to just four of the most serious offenses: treason, murder, piracy with violence, and aggravated forms of arson. They also succeeded in ending public executions, which were a popular form of entertainment. They did so by waging a crusade against the barbarity of the practice. William Thackeray, the author of *Vanity Fair*, wrote about attending a public execution in his essay "Going to See a Man Hanged." He declared that it was "murder I saw done." A Royal Commission on Capital Punishment proposed ending executions in public settings, and in 1868 they were prohibited. From that year on, executions were held on prison grounds, out of the view of a gawking public.

The abolitionists pushed to end capital punishment altogether, but there was considerable support for the death penalty from conservatives as well as some liberals. Reformers brought their cause to Parliament repeatedly: Between 1840 and 1869, there were at least eight votes in the House of Commons on abolishing the death penalty. None of them succeeded.

The Victorian reformers also failed in their efforts to create a second category of noncapital murder, a change that could have helped Dudley and Stephens and other defendants charged with killings that had extenuating circumstances. The reformers pointed to the United States, which had different degrees of murder, and a royal commission supported their position. They tried to make their change in Parliament six times in twenty-five years, starting in 1866, but the opponents prevailed every time.

All this put the grand jurors in Dudley and Stephens's case in a bind if they were at all sympathetic to Dudley and Stephens. If they voted to convict, they would be starting a process that could end in the defendants' deaths. In mentioning the possibility of a royal grant of mercy, Baron Huddleston was giving the grand jury a preview of where the case might ultimately be headed. As he saw it, there was no question that the defendants were guilty of murder, but they could be spared from death if the queen and the home secretary exercised the royal prerogative of mercy. The problem was, Baron Huddleston could not say for certain whether mercy would be granted. As one scholar has observed, the legal system at the time was "almost whimsical in the way it awarded death to some, imprisonment to others." There was simply no way to know whether, if they returned a true bill, the grand jurors were setting Dudley and Stephens up for an acquittal, a conviction with a prison sentence—or hanging.

Baron Huddleston started to bring the proceedings to a close without ever allowing the prosecutors or the defense lawyers to address the grand jury about the facts or the law of the case. It was no great loss for the prosecution, since the judge had done their work for them, setting out all of the reasons the grand jurors should return a true bill. But it deprived the defense of the chance to present opposing arguments on the pivotal matters of necessity, self-defense, the court's jurisdiction, or anything else.

The judge's way of proceeding was in keeping with his reputation as a "strong judge" who did what he could to get the result he wanted. It put the defense at a serious disadvantage, since he was the only one advising the grand jurors what to do and he was telling them to return a true bill. It was not particularly fair to Dudley and Stephens, but there was no rule requiring the judge to let the lawyers speak or to present the grand jurors with the arguments for both sides.

In the end, the grand jurors did what Baron Huddleston wanted. They deliberated, and the same day that the proceeding began, they returned a true bill against both Dudley and Stephens on a charge of murder. The next step would be a trial before a petit jury, and Baron Huddleston scheduled one for three days later.

The day after the proceeding, a member of the grand jury paid an unofficial visit to Dudley. The visitor said he felt he and his fellow grand jurors had no choice but to return a true bill. It was not entirely clear what he meant by that cryptic comment. The whole point of the proceeding was that the grand jury was free to return a true bill or not. The grand juror may have been confirming what was so often said about Baron Huddleston, that he was adept at pushing jurors to his desired outcome. Or Dudley's visitor may have been saying that it seemed clear to the grand jurors that the defendants had in fact committed a crime—clear enough, at least, to meet the low bar of sending the case on to a jury trial.

The visitor was aware that he and his fellow grand jurors had put Dudley and Stephens on a path toward the death penalty. But the purpose of his visit was not to dwell on the impending death sentence but rather to put the defendants' minds at ease. The grand juror went on to tell Dudley to "rest assured," because "you will be granted a free pardon we all are sure." But these words of reassurance were not actually reassuring. The grand juror was predicting that Dudley and Stephens would be sentenced to death. As for the royal pardon, Dudley knew there was no way his visitor, or anyone else, could know for certain what William Harcourt, head of the Home Office, and Queen Victoria would do. He was worried his visitor might be right about the verdict and punishment but wrong about the royal pardon. "From that hour," Dudley later said in a legal filing, "I prayed for strength to bear that awful sentence."

9

A Special Verdict

On Thursday, November 6, three days after the grand jury met, Dudley and Stephens's trial began in a courtroom in Exeter Castle. The public's interest was as intense in Exeter as it had been in Falmouth. The courtroom was packed when Baron Huddleston took his seat, and many more would-be spectators had been turned away. The ones who made it in represented less than "a tenth of the eager clamourers for admission," according to one news account.

The crowd was overwhelmingly male, but the press noted that there were "not a few of the fair sex in the galleries of the court." Lady Diana Huddleston and several other prominent women were given preferential seating. "Some of the details of the case were hardly fit for ladies' ears," the London *Daily News* said, "but there being no real controversy as to the facts counsel on both sides were able to pass these lightly over."

The audience was "spellbound" when the proceeding began, according to one reporter on the scene. The spectators looked on intently when the prisoners arrived, excited to be in the presence of English cannibals. It had now been two months since the men had landed at Falmouth, and their health seemed to have improved. The *Gloucester Citizen* declared that they "looked tolerably well." Their mental state was harder to gauge. An old friend who met Dudley in town before the trial found him in surprisingly good spirits, and he still appeared upbeat when the trial began. In the courtroom, *The Daily News* found his "cheerful" demeanor "in rather striking contrast to the general surrounding" and attributed it to the captain's "apparent inability to realize as keenly as other people the gravity of his position." As for Stephens, the paper found that "there was more anxiety visible in" his "deportment." It reported that "his glances were throughout the case those of a man who was distressed by his position and eager to know what would be the outcome."

The differences between Dudley's and Stephens's comportment and their responses to what happened would be much commented upon throughout the proceedings, but appearances could be deceiving. The journalists in the courtroom did not appreciate how much anxiety Dudley was hiding behind a brave face. They could not see that he was deeply fearful of how the prosecution would end and that he was quietly praying for the strength, as he said, "to bear that awful sentence."

The trial began with a reading of the formal charges—that Dudley and Stephens "did feloniously kill and murder Richard Parker on the high seas." When their names were called, each man stepped forward and resolutely declared, "Not guilty." With that, the hearing was underway.

The case would be argued to a jury made up of twelve petit jurors, who could be expected to be more sympathetic to Dudley and Stephens than the grand jury. These jurors were respected male landowners from the Exeter area, which made them part of the local elite, but they were not all "gentlemen of the best figure in the county," as William Blackstone had called the grand jurors. The petit jurors' position one notch lower in economic and social class put them closer to the members of the general public who had mobbed the Falmouth courthouse and cheered in support of the three ragged sailors and further from the upper-class elites who were now prosecuting them.

The counsel for both sides, who had had almost nothing to do before the grand jury, would now take a far more active role in presenting the facts and law of the case. Arthur Charles, the lead prosecutor, delivered the opening argument for the Crown. He began by conceding that the jurors would almost certainly feel "the deepest compassion and sympathy for" the defendants "in their appalling sufferings," but he insisted that the jurors must not allow these sentiments to deter them from doing their duty. The men's sufferings could, he said, instead be used later on in "a most powerful plea" for reducing the sentence. It was the same point that Baron Huddleston had made to the grand jury. Charles was highlighting that in the end, the defendants would have an opportunity to ask the queen for mercy. He hoped, as Baron Huddleston had, that it would make the jurors feel more comfortable returning a guilty verdict against defendants whom they might not want to condemn to death.

Speaking softly, Charles recited the facts with what one observer called "a happy and effective conciseness," from the launch of the *Mignonette* to the defendants' return on the *Moctezuma*. In describing the killing and the short dialogue that passed between Dudley and Parker before it occurred, Charles emphasized one sobering fact for the jury. "Gentlemen," he said, "the poor lad, it appears, was conscious."

Charles said that much of the Crown's evidence would come directly from the defendants. He told the jurors that Dudley's and Stephens's own statements would be read in court. The men had "made no secret whatever of what they had done, and what they conceived they had a right to do." The heart of the case,

Charles said, was a question "of great importance and deep interest" that could "only be answered in one way." The question was whether the killing of Parker constituted murder. Parker was killed by someone "of sound mind" with "malice aforethought," Charles said. He explained that malice aforethought meant not spite or evil but deliberate and intentional action. There was clearly malice aforethought, Charles insisted, since Dudley had said in advance that a killing had become necessary and then "killed him with his own hand" after Stephens had agreed to hold Parker's feet.

As for the other element of murder, being of sound mind, the British legal test for sanity, known as the "M'Naghten rule," required that a criminal defendant know what he is doing and know it is wrong. In this case, Charles said, Dudley made clear he did by his behavior. "I say so gentlemen," Charles told the jurors, "for before he did the act he offered a prayer that he might be forgiven for what he was about to do."

Charles then argued that the killing could not be excused as self-defense. Echoing Baron Huddleston's instructions to the grand jury, he noted that Parker had never posed any threat to Dudley and Stephens. "Gentlemen, if a man assails you, you may kill him in order to prevent his killing you," Charles said. "That is self-defense." But in this case, "Parker was not assailing either of them," he said. "The boy was lying at the bottom of the boat, and had been lying there for many hours." Charles quoted legal authorities, starting with Blackstone's assertion that if a man is under violent assault and the only way to save himself is to kill an innocent third party, he has no right to do so. "He ought rather to die himself than escape by the murder of an innocent," Blackstone writes. The prosecutor pointed out that Dudley had done precisely what Blackstone decried: He had killed an innocent person.

In the defendants' opening statement, Arthur John Hammond Collins, Queen's Counsel, began by asserting a necessity defense. He cited the case of the British sailors in St. Kitts and the American case of the passengers killed on the *William Brown*, but Huddleston rejected both on the grounds that they were not rulings from a British court. When Collins would not give up, Baron Huddleston made clear that he did not intend to allow the jury to find that a necessity defense applied in this case. "I may say at once that is a doctrine which I cannot assent to because I have already expressed my opinion as to what is the law, and I shall tell the jury to act upon it," he announced.

But Collins still refused to yield. "I must address the jury on that point," Collins insisted. His defiance of Baron Huddleston was jarring, creating a sharply worded battle between two strong-willed men of the law. But it made strategic sense. The necessity defense was his clients' best chance of winning an acquittal. Since the jury's vote had to be unanimous, Collins only had to persuade one juror. And the fact was, he did not have any better arguments to offer on his clients' behalf. So Collins forged ahead. When Baron Huddleston again said he would rule "distinctly and absolutely" that Dudley and Stephens could not assert a necessity defense, Collins stood his ground. "I will address the jury upon my view of the case," he said. "Your Lordship will, of course, adopt what course your Lordship pleases after that."

In this exchange on one of the most crucial issues in the case, Baron Huddleston was again living up to his reputation as a "strong judge." But he did offer Collins the hope of trying his defense before a different court. "I shall take every opportunity that occurs to me to lay this case before a superior tribunal, that they may decide upon it," he said. Baron Huddleston said he believed "some definite rule of law by the highest authority ought to be laid down." In other words, although he would firmly direct this jury not to accept a necessity defense, he would try to give a higher court the final word.

Baron Huddleston then did something unexpected, even shocking. This was a jury trial, and the jury was supposed to reach a verdict of guilt or innocence. But Baron Huddleston had other plans. He announced that he wanted the jury to return a "special verdict," an arcane procedure that had not been used in an English court in nearly a century. In a special verdict, the jury only made findings about the facts in a case. It was left to a judge or a panel of judges to decide whether the facts the jury found constituted a crime. Baron Huddleston had the legal authority to suggest using a special verdict, since the law still allowed it. But it was a highly unusual move. He told the jury he had found the special verdict in "old books," and at least one commentator at the time referred to special verdicts as "obsolete."

Strictly speaking, Baron Huddleston was only making a suggestion. As a legal matter, the jury had the right to insist on deciding guilt or innocence. But Baron Huddleston does not appear to have told the jurors about their right to reject his suggestion, and it was unlikely they would know on their own that they could insist on delivering a verdict.

There were likely two reasons Baron Huddleston took the extraordinary step of proceeding by special verdict. The first is that he did not trust the jury to reach the guilty verdict he was hoping for. There was clearly a possibility of a "perverse verdict" or "jury nullification," the British and American legal terms for when jurors have strong feelings about the issues in a case or sympathies for the defendant and return a not-guilty verdict even when the law has clearly been broken, undoing an otherwise strong prosecution. Juries have the power to engage in jury nullification. That was established as early as 1670, when it was held that jurors could not be punished—as they once had been, with prison sentences and fines—for reaching a verdict that was at odds with the facts or the law. The Exeter jurors unquestionably could acquit Dudley and Stephens if they wanted to, no matter what the law said.

Baron Huddleston had good reason to suspect that this jury might hesitate to convict. Dudley and Stephens had far more popular support than murder defendants usually do. Members of the public did not generally make visits to the scene of a murder—in this case, the *Mignonette* lifeboat—and leave behind contributions for the killers. They did not usually launch fundraising drives to pay for defense lawyers or show up in large numbers in court, cheering when the defendants are let out on bail. It was not hard to imagine at least some of the Exeter jurors sharing these grassroots prodefense views, and indeed, before long, the jurors would make clear their sympathy for the prisoners. This was a particular concern because of the unanimity requirement: A single prodefendant holdout would derail the entire prosecution.

The jurors' potential hesitation to find Dudley and Stephens guilty would be made worse by the fact that a conviction would carry the death penalty. Victorian juries were reluctant to return guilty verdicts in capital cases, and Baron Huddleston would no doubt have been aware of that. Using a special verdict would avoid this problem by putting the decision in the hands of judges rather than jurors.

The second reason that Baron Huddleston wanted to proceed by a special verdict was likely the kind of ruling it would produce. A special verdict had the best chance of elevating the case from being a mere criminal prosecution to one that produced a landmark decision. If he was hoping to create a nationwide rule that survival cannibalism was a crime, this was the best way to achieve it.

A jury verdict of guilty or not guilty would not reform the law—and it certainly would not end the practice of cannibalism at sea. If the jury found Dudley and Stephens not guilty, it would send a message to the world that English law permitted killing and eating people in survival conditions. And it would send that procannibalism message in a particularly damaging way. Dudley and Stephens had not even respected the custom of the sea and drawn lots. Dudley had decided that the choice of who should be sacrificed was entirely his. If he and Stephens were acquitted, it would tell sailors that they could kill and eat people in extreme conditions without even having to choose their victims at random.

As a matter of legal precedent, though, the meaning of a not-guilty verdict would be unclear, because juries do not write legal opinions explaining their reasoning the way judges do. An acquittal might mean the jury had accepted the necessity defense. But it also might mean that they believed that Parker was so close to death that killing him was not really murder at all or that they believed survival cannibalism to be illegal but engaged in jury nullification purely out of sympathy for Dudley and Stephens. In short, there would be no way to know what the jury was thinking when it acquitted, and the verdict would not actually clarify the law on cannibalism at sea. In the end, the law would remain the muddle it was.

Similarly, if the jury found Dudley and Stephens guilty, there would also be no legal clarity. With no written legal opinion, the jury's reasoning would be no more transparent than it would be if they acquitted the men. The jurors might have decided that killing someone so others could survive was always murder. Or they might merely have believed, as Justice Henry Baldwin had in the *Holmes* case, that it was necessary to draw lots before sacrificing someone. There would be no way, based on the simple word *guilty*, to know what the jury's reasoning was. And again, the law would remain a muddle.

Baron Huddleston's strategy of proceeding by special verdict had the potential to produce something a regular jury verdict could not: a bold and authoritative legal opinion. The case would be decided by a judge or panel of judges, who would write an opinion that would analyze the legal issues and explain in detail whether survival cannibalism was a crime and why. A judge's opinion holding Dudley and Stephens guilty of murder would have the potential to change the law on a broad scale. Just as Victorian reformers had persuaded Parliament to enact laws that established new national standards for child labor and factory safety, Baron Huddleston and William Harcourt could use the prosecution of Dudley and Stephens to establish a new national policy on survival cannibalism.

The killing of Parker was in many ways an ideal vehicle for driving reform. It presented the issue of survival cannibalism in stark form: Dudley and Stephens freely admitted that they had killed and eaten the cabin boy to survive, so the facts were clear-cut. Parker's killing perfectly illustrated the power dynamics that usually prevailed in survival cannibalism—a captain and the highest-ranking crewmember had decided to kill the lowest-ranking, sickest, and youngest person in the boat. Adding to the case's appeal was the enormous publicity it was receiving. Any rule the court established would immediately be known across the country and indeed the world.

These advantages notwithstanding, there was a real problem with the use of the special verdict: It deprived Dudley and Stephens of a jury trial. There was a long and established English tradition of trial by jury. Blackstone had extolled juries, declaring that "the liberties of England cannot but subsist, so long as this palladium remains sacred and inviolate." The jury system was the greatest check on prosecutorial power, since it required the Crown to persuade an objective group of citizens that a defendant was guilty before he could be convicted and punished. When Baron Huddleston decided to use the special verdict, he deprived Dudley and Stephens of this important protection against unwarranted prosecution—and deprived the jury of its traditional role as the conscience of the community.

The fairer way for Baron Huddleston to proceed would have been to allow the jury not only to find facts but to decide the question of guilt or innocence. It would have been a gamble on his part, since it would have allowed the possibility that the jury might find Dudley and Stephens not guilty. But it would not necessarily have been such a great gamble. Even if the jurors began with sympathy for the defendants, Baron Huddleston was remarkably adept at steering juries to the result he wanted. By playing his usual active role at trial—and with the law of murder strongly on his side—it seems likely he could have led the jury to the guilty verdict he favored.

Troubling though the use of the special verdict was, there is also, it must be said, an argument on Baron Huddleston's side beyond how useful it could be for producing a clear and far-reaching precedent. In addition to the established English tradition of respect for jury verdicts, there was also another long tradition of concern about juries ignoring the law and reaching an incorrect verdict. As one scholar of English juries observed, "there has been an unbroken effort to avoid the rendition of unreasonable verdicts ever since the jury was first developed." In the sixteenth and seventeenth centuries, the Star Chamber, an elite court that sat at the royal Palace of Westminster, fined jurors for wrongly acquitting criminals. In some cases, jurors who reached an incorrect verdict were even sentenced to prison. The special verdict was a different sort of tool for protecting against jury verdicts that judges deemed to be erroneous. There are modern versions of this sort of tool in use today: Trials can be moved to another venue if the defense or prosecution can show that the local jury pool has been biased by prejudicial media coverage. Rather than move the trial to find a better jury, the special verdict placed the decision of guilt or innocence in the hands of judges.

By using this undeniably heavy-handed tactic, Baron Huddleston could help ensure that the prosecutors had a fair chance to prove their case. That was how the special verdict was designed to be used, and Baron Huddleston may have believed his decision was not only permissible but morally right.

Collins told Baron Huddleston that the defense would not consent to the use of a special verdict, but he would not argue against it. At first glance, that seems like a surprising position to take. It might have made sense for the defendants to object strenuously to the use of a special verdict, since it would take the decision of guilt or innocence away from jurors who were likely to be sympathetic to the defendants and put it in the hands of a judge or judges who were likely to be less so. But there were strategic reasons for not objecting. If Collins insisted on having the jury decide Dudley and Stephens's guilt or innocence, he might ultimately regret it. He may have decided that if the jurors were allowed to reach a verdict, Baron Huddleston would ensure it was a guilty verdict. If the trial proceeded by special verdict, it was not clear who would be appointed to decide Dudley and Stephens's guilt or innocence, but there was some chance that it might be a judge or judges who were not as antagonistic to the defense as Baron Huddleston was. It might even be ones who believed that defendants to a homicide charge were entitled to make a necessity defense.

Baron Huddleston was satisfied with Collins's response. What mattered to him was that the defense did not object to the use of a special verdict. He did not need Collins to actively give his approval. "I do not ask you to," Huddleston said in response to Collins's insistence that he could not consent to a special verdict. "I shall take it upon myself to do it."

The prosecution could also have objected, but Charles did not. "If your Lordship pleases," he said agreeably. There was no surprise there. Baron Huddleston's special verdict was likely the best possible path toward producing a verdict of guilty and one that would have a broad impact across the country. The other people in the courtroom who could have objected to the use of a special verdict were the jurors, but it does not appear that they knew they could. In the absence of any objections, Baron Huddleston proceeded with his plan.

The Crown could now start presenting evidence. Charles Mathews, another prosecutor, introduced the *Mignonette*'s register and articles to establish that it was a British ship; that Dudley was captain; and that Stephens, Brooks, and Parker were the crew. The jury was also given the defendants' statements from the Custom House, which set out most of the facts, and several versions of the account of the loss of the *Mignonette* and subsequent events that Dudley wrote and rewrote while he was still on the *Moctezuma*.

Brooks was the first witness, and he repeated the star turn he had delivered in Falmouth. His testimony, so dramatic the first time he gave it, was still riveting, as an Englishman's personal account of engaging in cannibalism was bound to be. But the actual facts he relayed were by now familiar to anyone who had followed the case in the press. He testified about the *Mignonette*'s journey, the shipwreck, and everything that followed. He once more provided eyewitness testimony about the key events, and he did not hold back. He told the jurors how Dudley killed Parker, and he freely admitted that he had immediately asked to share the cabin boy's blood.

Charles, the prosecutor, took advantage of the opportunity to underscore for the jurors the awfulness of what had transpired. "Then did you eat the boy's heart and liver between you?" he prompted. Brooks replied that yes, he had, adding, "We lived on the body nearly four days."

With this, Brooks once again had provided evidence that could condemn his captain and first mate to death. At the same time, he again made clear his sympathy for them. He said only positive things about Dudley and Stephens as men. Dudley was a "good skipper," he said, and "a kind and good captain."

In his cross-examination, Collins turned attention away from the killing, focusing instead on the grueling conditions the defendants had endured. Brooks gave Collins most of what he wanted. Driving home the point that all of the men were suffering from extreme thirst, Collins asked Brooks, "You could not resist the sight of the blood? I believe you asked for some, you were in such a state?"

"I could not," Brooks responded. "I was obliged to ask for some."

"Horrible as it was, you were obliged to have some?"

"Yes," Brooks said.

"And you were reduced to feeding upon the heart and the liver of the boy?"

"Yes," Brooks answered.

"I need scarcely say that you must have been in a fearful state at that time all of you?" Collins asked.

"Yes, we were," Brooks responded.

"For those four days was life kept in you by this unfortunate boy's body?" Collins asked.

"Yes, no doubt," Brooks said.

Brooks testified that the lifeboat was so cramped that the men could barely move around, a level of confinement that led to them developing sores and swollen limbs. He recalled that after they were rescued, it was days before Dudley or Stephens could lie down or walk, although Brooks was in somewhat better shape.

Collins was using Brooks to do something his clients could not do for themselves. Since the law barred Dudley and Stephens from testifying to the jury about the extreme conditions that drove them to kill Parker, Collins was getting Brooks to do it for them, and Brooks was obliging. Brooks's testimony could help win the jurors' sympathy for the defendants, and it might also establish the factual basis for a higher court to accept his clients' necessity defense. But on one important point, Brooks did not help the defendants. He had previously said that Parker appeared to be dying, but Huddleston pressed him further: "Did it appear to you that the boy was likely to die sooner than any of you other three?" Brooks responded that Parker "seemed weakest," something he had said in Falmouth, but he would not say that Parker would have been the first to die. With this response, Brooks cast significant doubt on Dudley's account of what had occurred in the lifeboat. Dudley had presented his selection of Parker as the natural choice, since the cabin boy was so close to death and would certainly be the first to die. Brooks's response reframed that as only one man's opinion—and not one he could confirm.

There was another reason Brooks's description of Parker's condition was important. Although the custom of the sea was not on trial, many members of the public wondered why Dudley and Stephens had not taken the more established and honorable route of drawing lots, and the jurors may have been wondering as well. Dudley had decided there was no need to draw lots, in large part because one of the four people in the boat was close to death. If Parker might not have been the first to die, Dudley's decision not to draw lots was harder to defend.

The remaining witnesses stuck closely to what they had already said in Falmouth. Julius Wiese, the sailor from the *Moctezuma*, again recalled rescuing the men and spotting "a small piece of rib, and there was some flesh attached," which he threw overboard. Baron Huddleston rushed the harbor pilot, Gustavus Collins, through his testimony, since it added little to Dudley's own statement about what occurred. Robert Gandy Cheesman, the collector of customs and receiver of wrecks, covered well-trodden ground. Even though the jury had written copies of the defendants' Custom House statements, the prosecutor asked to have them read aloud. The clerk also read the account that Dudley prepared while on the *Moctezuma*.

The prosecutors entered physical materials into evidence. They especially wanted to present the penknife that Dudley had used to kill Parker, and they called harbor police sergeant James Laverty as a witness and had him produce it. Becoming impatient again, Baron Huddleston bristled and asked, "What is this for?" Nevertheless, he admitted the knife, and it soon became clear what it was for. Although it did not have great legal significance—there was already plenty of evidence that there had *been* a knife—the appearance of Dudley's white penknife had a palpable impact on everyone in the courtroom. It "added to the horror . . . in the still court," *The Daily News* reported, as the "spectators were called upon to imagine" how it had recently been used.

Dudley's knife was the last piece of evidence that was introduced. "That is the case for the Crown," Charles declared. The prosecution rested.

The defense did not present any evidence. Dudley and Stephens had already spoken through their sworn statements, and they could not testify in person. The only other witness to the violent act at the center of the case, Brooks, had already been heard from. Collins did not call any witnesses who could speak to the defendants' state of mind or to the likelihood of the men dying if they had not killed and eaten someone—no doubt because he did not think they could make any legal difference against the charge of murder.

But the defense did have one more argument, and it was one with the potential to derail the entire prosecution. Collins asserted that the court did not have jurisdiction to hear the case because Parker was not killed on a British ship. The *Mignonette* was a British ship, he acknowledged, but Parker was killed on the lifeboat, which he said was not a "ship" at all. Invoking the rule that crimes committed outside of Britain had to be prosecuted in the countries in which they occurred, Collins insisted the case did not belong in an English court. This claim that the whole prosecution was illegitimate caused "some little bustle" in the courtroom, one reporter noted.

Baron Huddleston asked why the lifeboat should not be considered part of the *Mignonette*. Collins said that according to the Merchant Shipping Act of 1854, a ship was any vessel "propelled not by oars." The lifeboat, he said, *was* propelled by oars—and therefore it was not a "British ship," and the act did not give the courts jurisdiction over it.

Collins may have had a point based on the law's text, though it is hard to believe Parliament intended to extend Britain's law to all of its sailing ships but not to their lifeboats. The defense attorney's problem was that he was not able to cite any cases supporting his position that the lifeboat of a British ship was not also a British ship. "I cannot find the point has ever been raised before," he admitted.

Baron Huddleston was in no mood to see the whole case disappear. Did it not matter, he asked Collins, that the men on the lifeboat were English subjects? In the end, the claim that the court could not hear a case about a crime on a lifeboat was so unexpected that Baron Huddleston chose not to resolve it. He said he would proceed with the case and reserve the jurisdictional issue for the court that heard the case next.

After a short dispute among the lawyers over who should give the first closing argument, Collins addressed the jurors. He spoke to them as though they were going to deliver a verdict of guilty or not guilty, even though Baron Huddleston had already said they would be limited to finding the facts. As a result, much of his argument was spent asking the jurors to do something that, unless things changed dramatically, they would not have the chance to do—namely, to find his clients not guilty.

Collins was asking the jurors to ignore Baron Huddleston's decision to proceed by special verdict, despite the fact that he had not formally objected to the use of a special verdict earlier. He proceeded to mount a necessity defense—even while acknowledging that "my Lord," by which he meant Baron Huddleston, "is against me on this point." Collins argued that necessity could indeed justify actions taken in extreme circumstances of the sort that existed in the lifeboat, and he was therefore asking the jury to find his clients not guilty on grounds of necessity. "I submit that I am entitled to have your opinion upon it," he said.

Collins, however, was not merely making the usual necessity defense, that the defendants had chosen the lesser of two evils by killing one person rather than allowing four people to die. Collins took his argument in a harsher direction. He insisted that Dudley and Stephens had a right to save themselves because they were more likely to survive the ordeal. "In a case such as this is, if necessity is paramount, the weakest at the time must go to the wall and the weakest must fall for the protection of the others," Collins said. The weakest person in the lifeboat, he reasoned, was Parker, "a boy of 17 or 18 years of age . . . who, unfortunately for him," had ignored the advice of men who "knew better" and drank seawater, making himself sick.

With this argument, Collins was plugging up an important hole in the defense. The jurors might well be wondering why his clients decided Parker should be the one to die—and why they had not followed the custom of the sea. Dudley's answer had always been that Parker was on the brink of death and would have been the first to die. But Brooks had just cast doubt on this, saying that Parker "seemed weakest" but that he could not say if he would have been the first to die. Collins decided to explain the decision to kill Parker by saying that in situations of this kind, the right thing to do is to kill the weakest person.

He was, in effect, making a social Darwinist case for killing Parker. Social Darwinism, a popular philosophy of the day, held that society should actively favor the strong over the weak. It was best for all, its proponents argued, if the strong were able to survive—and it was acceptable to crush the weak along the way. The roots of this thinking lay in the work of Charles Darwin, the English naturalist and biologist who published *On the Origin of Species* in 1859. Social Darwinists took Darwin's ideas about evolution being driven by survival of the fittest and applied them to human relations in society.

Collins's social Darwinist reasoning sounded a lot like one of Dudley's arguments in the lifeboat for killing Parker. Rather than declaring that the healthiest people in the boat should do everything they could to nurse Parker back to health, Dudley had decided that because of Parker's physical weakness, his life was the least valuable and should be sacrificed to save the stronger ones. In the defense's view, there was a battle for survival in the lifeboat, as there was in all of life. In that lethal battle, the strong had an inherent right, even a duty, to use the weak to survive.

Collins then switched from social Darwinism to utilitarianism, another popular philosophy of the time—and the more traditional rationale for the necessity defense. Utilitarianism is rooted in the idea that moral actions are ones that produce the greatest good for the greatest number. Jeremy Bentham, the English philosopher who founded the movement, envisioned a sort of mathematical calculation, or "hedonic calculus," that assesses morality by the amount of pain and pleasure a particular act would produce.

The custom of the sea and other forms of killing to survive at sea are populist versions of utilitarian thinking applied to a specific situation. Sailors decided for themselves over the centuries, long before Bentham had written a word about utilitarianism, that the best outcome when there was a shortage of food and water was the one that would result in the most lives being saved.

Utilitarianism had its supporters, but many people saw it as eroding the moral values that had emerged throughout history, passed on by religious and national traditions. To these critics, there were some acts that were inherently wrong—such as taking an innocent life. Religions generally condemn these acts, and societies around the world make them illegal. The critics of utilitarianism did not believe these well-established moral lines should be erased by hedonic calculus.

Collins contended that utilitarian principles justified the killing of Parker. "Horrible as the repast was, disgusting as the food was, it saved these three men's lives," he said, "and if they had not done what they did not a single man of them would have been heard of." Sounding a lot like Bentham, Collins applied a hedonic calculus and argued that three survivors were better than none.

Before he ended his closing argument, Collins also made an appeal to legal precedent—or rather, to the lack of it. He emphasized that no captains or sailors had ever been charged with a crime for doing what Dudley and Stephens did on the *Mignonette* lifeboat. Further, he suggested that the customary unwillingness to prosecute people who, as he put it, "have been driven through stress of hunger and thirst to eat their fellow creatures," was essentially universal. "I believe I am right in saying," he told the jurors, "that in no civilized country has the government of the day ever prosecuted a single person for the offense, as is admitted by the Counsel of the Crown in this case."

Charles began his own far shorter closing argument for the prosecution by telling the jurors, "I will trouble you with but few observations." Responding to what the jurors had just heard, he rejected Collins's social Darwinism–infused contention that in extreme circumstances, "the weakest must go to the wall." Charles did not question its morality. He simply said he did not believe it to be "the law of England."

For Charles, the case was straightforward because the law that applied to it was. The killing of Parker, he said, had all of the elements of murder without any lawful excuse. He did not have to elaborate on why the necessity defense was invalid in this case, he said, because Baron Huddleston had already done so. That allowed Charles to end his brief remarks by saying, simply, "I leave the case to my Lord."

Baron Huddleston gave the jurors instructions on how to proceed. He began by saying that although they no doubt had "sympathy for these two men . . . standing in the dock," he had faith they would "discharge their duty" properly. Baron Huddleston conceded that Dudley and Stephens were inherently decent men, but he said that was not a question the jurors needed to worry about. "Outside the facts of this unhappy case," he said, "there is no reflection on either their character or their humanity." In their task of delivering a special verdict, he said, the jurors' role would be to decide what the important facts of the case were and set them out in an official finding. The next court to hear the case would use that finding of facts to make its decision about guilt or innocence. It would be that court, which would be appointed in London, Baron Huddleston said, that would "lay down the law."

Under the rules of special verdicts, the jury would have no say about the legal issues, but Baron Huddleston nevertheless gave his views on them. He told the jurors why he did not believe in the necessity defense in homicide cases. It was based, he said, on a faulty premise: "that a man may, in a certain state of things, arrive at a position when he will be justified in taking the innocent life of another who is doing nothing to him." Baron Huddleston was emphatic in his conclusion: "I know of no such law as the law of England."

Baron Huddleston rebuked the defense for its embrace of social Darwinist ideas to justify the killing of Parker. Collins, he said, advocated a legal rule that would "justify the stronger man taking the life of the weaker, and that if several men are in a position of peril, the weaker man should be put to the wall." That was, Baron Huddleston said, "a proposition from which I entirely dissent." There was no basis in the law, he insisted, for the idea that "the weakest is the first to be sacrificed."

The jurors accepted Baron Huddleston's plan to proceed by a special verdict. They might not have understood, despite Collins's argument for the necessity defense, that they had the right to insist on delivering a verdict of guilty or not guilty. But it is also possible that they simply wanted to avoid choosing between two troubling options. An acquittal would mean letting Dudley and Stephens go free, despite their confession to having killed and eaten an innocent and harmless boy. A guilty verdict could mean a death sentence for two men for whom they felt considerable sympathy. Whatever the explanation, when Baron Huddleston told the jurors what he wanted them to do, the jury foreman simply responded, "Yes, my Lord."

Baron Huddleston produced a draft special verdict he had prepared in advance. He told the jury, "Be kind enough to follow me in the facts that I have prepared and give your consent to each paragraph as I read them to you." When they were done, the findings of fact would be sent on to the court that ultimately decided the case. The judge invited both sides to make suggestions as they went along.

From this point on, Baron Huddleston led an editing session in which he went through his document paragraph by paragraph and asked if the jury agreed with it. The first paragraph began, "That on the 5th July 1884 the prisoners with one Brooks, all able-bodied English seamen, and the deceased, a boy between seventeen and eighteen years of age, the crew of an English yacht, were cast away in a storm on the high seas." The jurors consulted with each other each time Baron Huddleston paused at the end of a paragraph. In most cases, they simply exchanged signs of approval among themselves. When they reached agreement on a paragraph, the foreman nodded to Baron Huddleston to indicate their assent.

The document remained largely as Baron Huddleston had written it. But the jurors did raise concerns about a few paragraphs, and one produced a notable exchange. Reading from his draft, Baron Huddleston said that if the men had not eaten Parker's body, they "would . . . have died of hunger." He then explained the passage he had just read to the jurors, saying that the evidence "would seem to show that, in all probability," if the men had not eaten Parker's body, they would have died before they were rescued. When the time came for the jury's response, the foreman said that it was their view that the men "would have died if they had not had this body to have fed on." At this point, Baron Huddleston did something odd. He said, "That is as I put it. Now I will read the paragraph again." He then read from the draft findings of fact again, saying, "If the men had not fed upon the body of the boy, they would, probably, not have survived to be picked up and rescued." Although Baron Huddleston said he was just rereading his original paragraph, he had actually added the word *probably* to it. When Baron Huddleston was done, the foreman accepted this version—the one with *probably* in it.

This addition of the word *probably* mattered. It would weaken Dudley and Stephens's necessity defense. There was a great deal of difference between "We killed the cabin boy because otherwise we *would* all have died" and "We killed the cabin boy because otherwise we *probably would* all have died." The second wording leaves the listener—even one of a utilitarian frame of mind—wondering whether anyone actually had to be killed at all.

It is possible that in the laborious process of a judge and jury jointly drafting a complex statement of fact, Baron Huddleston simply became confused and made an honest error. But it is also not hard to believe that he was intentionally prodding the jurors toward what he believed to be the right outcome, whether they wanted to be led there or not. That would have been fully in keeping with his reputation as a "strong judge" inclined to bring juries to his own desired result. If Baron Huddleston was in fact misleading the jury, it was clearly a case of judicial overreach. One thing that could be said in Baron Huddleston's defense, though, was that however it came about, the judge's inclusion of the word *probably* made the sentence more accurate. There was no way that twelve jurors in an Exeter courtroom could say for certain who would have lived or died on a lifeboat in the South Atlantic months earlier. The version Baron Huddleston pushed for had the advantage of being true.

Another sentence in the draft appears to have been included expressly to undermine the defendants' attempt to use a necessity defense. "Assuming any necessity to kill anyone," Baron Huddleston read to the jury, "there was no greater necessity for killing the boy than any of the other three men." This statement was aimed at Dudley's decision to choose Parker to die. As Huddleston saw it, the necessity defense required showing not merely that someone had to be eaten but that specifically Parker had to be killed. "The necessity of something to eat does not create the necessity of taking and excuse the taking of the boy."

In addition to undermining the necessity defense, the judge's wording was another rebuke to the defense's recourse to social Darwinism. Indeed, Baron Huddleston told the jurors, there was a strong ethical argument that people "ought not to allow the stronger to have power over the weaker, but they ought all, morally speaking, to have the same chance." Baron Huddleston was now sounding like a Victorian progressive reformer speaking out about the equal rights and dignity of everyone in society, including those at the bottom. "Was there any necessity of taking that boy rather than drawing lots?" the judge asked. Once again, he let the jurors know the answer he expected: "I should think you would consider no."

The jury agreed to language saying there was no greater necessity "for killing the boy than any of the other three men." It was a valuable sentence for the Crown. When the next court met to decide the survivors' guilt or innocence, this would give it another reason to see Dudley and Stephens as having acted not only illegally but immorally. The defendants had not only killed an innocent boy; they had chosen him because they believed that stronger people had the right to exploit—and even kill—the weak if it meant saving themselves.

After Baron Huddleston finished going through the text he had drafted, he asked the jurors to end with a sentence reflecting what the next step of the special verdict process would be. He provided the wording: "But whether, upon the whole matter, the prisoners were and are guilty of murder the jury are ignorant, and refer to the Court." The jurors accepted Baron Huddleston's wording. In the end, the foreman nodded to indicate their endorsement of the whole draft. These agreed-upon statements became the jury's formal findings of fact.

Baron Huddleston then spoke to a feeling he sensed in the jury. "I see what you are going to suggest to me," he said, "that you wish to accompany your finding with some expression . . ."

"That is just my idea," one juror said.

"And mine," said another.

"And I take it," Baron Huddleston said, "you are very desirous that I should convey to the proper quarters your strong feeling of compassion for the position these men are placed in."

"Yes, my Lord," the foreman said.

Baron Huddleston assured the jurors he would convey their feelings of compassion to "the proper quarters." He was referring again to the "royal prerogative of mercy," the Crown's power to grant clemency. The jury's view on the matter might well have an impact on the home secretary and the queen, but it might not. Asking for mercy, even with the support of a jury and a judge, did not mean receiving it.

Baron Huddleston released Dudley and Stephens on bail pending a verdict of guilt or innocence to be handed down by a judge or judges yet to be named. Once again, the two men had a patron who offered to put up their bail. This time, it was a lawyer from Glasgow named Thomas Houston Kirk, who had employed Dudley as a captain on his yacht. The men were freed as soon as the proceeding ended.

The members of the public who were crowded into court in Exeter Castle seemed pleased with what they had seen. *The Daily News* said that "curious as it was," the special verdict "appeared to spectators a welcome way out of the wood." The general feeling was one of "compassion," the article continued, and much of the audience would have been upset if the proceeding had ended "with the awful ceremony associated with the black cap," a reference to the black hat English judges traditionally wore when pronouncing a sentence of death. The audience members also approved of Baron Huddleston's decision to release Dudley and Stephens on bail. The men "left the dock amid every manifestation of satisfaction by the spectators," the *Manchester Times* reported.

The jurors seemed just as satisfied with how the case, or at least their part of it, had ended. If they were unhappy with being denied the right to make a decision on guilt or innocence, they did not show it. "These twelve men . . . appeared grateful to Baron Huddleston for the neat way in which he interposed to save them from a decision involving consequences so abhorrent," *The Daily News* said.

Baron Huddleston also had reason to feel good. He had invoked a near-obsolete procedure without running into opposition from counsel for either side or from the jury, and in doing so, he had laid the groundwork for a written opinion that could establish a new national rule on survival cannibalism.

The press gave Baron Huddleston generally positive reviews. *The Times* had no problem with his use of the special verdict or anything else he had done to produce the findings of fact. This was "a very remarkable case, unique in the history of English criminal law," the paper said, and the judge "had to do what English judges have frequently to do—under the guise of interpreting the law he had to make it."

The Times also praised the hard line the judge took against survival cannibalism and the necessity defense. It was clear that he was leading the case in the direction of progressive reform, and *The Times* approved. "The English law as laid down by Baron Huddleston is averse from entertaining the notion that peril from starvation is an excuse for homicide; and it seems best to adhere to this rule," the paper said. "It would be dangerous to affirm the contrary, and to tell seafaring men that they may freely eat others in extreme circumstances, and that the cabin boy may always be consumed if provisions run short."

10

The Lord Chief Justice Rules

For the first time since their arrest in Falmouth, Dudley and Stephens did not know where their case was headed next. The special verdict had hit them with a new element of uncertainty. Baron Huddleston had said that after the jury signed off on its finding of fact, another judge or judges would take over the case and deliver a verdict. But he did not say who those judges would be, and it had been so long since a special verdict was last used that no one seemed to have any idea what should happen now. Baron Huddleston scheduled a hearing to decide the question.

On November 25, the lawyers who had represented the Crown and the defense at the Exeter Assize appeared before him in his regular court at the Royal Courts of Justice in London. In an imposing display of the importance of this next stage of the case, they were joined by the attorney general, Sir Henry James. Baron Huddleston and the lawyers started discussing right away who should decide Dudley and Stephens's guilt or innocence.

The attorney general acknowledged that there was "some little difficulty in determining positively what is the right course." In the time since the special verdict was last used—almost a full century—Parliament had passed a series of laws that reorganized the English court system. Any precedents for how special verdicts were handled in the past would no longer apply. Baron Huddleston, however, was not suffering from any doubt. He declared that his own court, the Court of Queen's Bench of the High Court of Justice, was the best place to decide the case. The judges of the Queen's Bench were able to sit in multijudge panels, and they could issue decisions that established a legal standard that applied to the whole country. As he saw it, all that remained was to decide which of its judges should decide the case.

The lawyers started discussing the possibilities, but again Baron Huddleston already had his answer. He said he had spoken to the lord chief justice of England and Wales, who had advised him that the two of them should serve on a panel of judges, and the lord chief justice would himself select three more judges to sit with them. He ended up choosing those judges based on seniority. The actions of two obscure seamen in a small dinghy drifting in the South Atlantic would be decided by some of England's most exalted jurists.

On December 4, the case resumed before the Court of Queen's Bench, in the lord chief justice's court. Once again, a throng of spectators showed up to witness proceedings in a case that *The Times* had declared to be unique in the history of English criminal law—and that also, of course, featured Englishmen engaging in cannibalism. Presiding over the case was the lord chief justice himself, joined by Baron Huddleston, along with justices Charles Edward Pollock, William Grove, and George Denman.

If Baron Huddleston had been trying to take the decision away from the jurors of Exeter and put it in the hands of England's legal elite, there was no one better suited for the role than the lord chief justice, John Duke Coleridge, 1st Baron Coleridge. Lord Coleridge had one of the most august pedigrees in all of English law. His father had been a barrister and judge, and his great-uncle was the poet Samuel Taylor Coleridge, who wrote *The Rime of the Ancient Mariner* and knew a few things about being thirsty at sea. His own life's voyage had been a smooth one through the elite ranks of English society, from Eton to Oxford—where he was president of the Oxford Union, the distinguished debating society—then on to the House of Commons and solicitor general, then attorney general, and finally, in 1880, lord chief justice.

Like Baron Huddleston, Coleridge was a member of the Liberal Party and had been an outspoken progressive his entire career. He was an outspoken advocate for women's suffrage, and in his first speech in Parliament, he had argued for Catholics and Jews to be admitted to Oxford University on the same basis as Anglicans. Coleridge was a man of strong political ideals, and if his past sympathies for the disadvantaged were any guide, he might be expected to sympathize less with Dudley and Stephens than with Parker. He might well want to send a message to the nation that "seafaring men," in the words of *The Times*, should not feel "that the cabin boy may always be consumed if provisions run short."

In background and temperament, the lord chief justice was a lot like the other man who was playing a leading role in deciding Dudley and Stephens's fate—the home secretary, William Harcourt. Both were from the upper echelons of British society. Harcourt had gone to Cambridge and was president of the Cambridge Union five years after Coleridge's term at the Oxford Union. Both men were former members of Parliament from the Liberal Party. More to the point, they shared a reformist spirit and a deep sympathy for society's dispossessed. They had both proven their willingness to take bold stands on behalf of the underdogs they championed. And both men believed that the law should be a vehicle for building a more just and equitable society. Given the immense influence these two men would have on what was to come, Dudley and Stephens were not only on trial for murder—they were on a collision course with late Victorian-era progressive reform.

The attorney general, James, headed up the prosecution in the Court of Queen's Bench. He brought a team of lawyers with him who knew the case well—Arthur Charles, Charles Mathews, and William Danckwerts. James and his team arrived early with a small library of legal tomes to help make his arguments in this case that would be developing new law for the entire nation. Dudley and Stephens were again being represented by Arthur John Hammond Collins. He was backed up this time by Henry Clark and Lionel Edward Pyke, lawyers who were experienced in admiralty law. They brought their own stockpile of books, which, "notwithstanding the resources of the Treasury, were hardly less imposing than those of the Counsel for the Crown," according to *The Daily News*.

Two people who were conspicuously absent from the crowded courtroom were Dudley and Stephens. The defendants were still out on bail, and no one had told them they were required to attend. The attorney general asked the justices if they wanted the men to be present. "I believe they are in the neighborhood of the court," he said.

Collins did not appear eager to make his clients sit through the proceedings. He told the justices that the men had never been formally summoned. Lord Coleridge settled the matter, declaring briskly, "I think they had better be here."

Ten minutes later, Dudley and Stephens appeared. Their expressions suggested that they had different reactions to being present for the occasion or that the captain was doing a better job of hiding his feelings. "Dudley still preserved the easy satisfied demeanour which was so much remarked at Exeter," one journalist reported. Stephens, whose manner had been more varied throughout the prosecution, "showed much less composure than his fellow-prisoner," the reporter said, "and obviously regarded the whole proceedings with serious concern."

The attorney general suggested that the justices have a court officer read the record that was created at Exeter Assize. Lord Coleridge ordered that it be done. The master of the Crown Office unscrolled a long parchment to read aloud the indictment, the trial proceedings, and the special verdict. It was a dense recitation, weighed down with archaic legal language. The master listed a lengthy series of purposes for which assizes were "holden," or held. They included not only the sort of serious charges Dudley and Stephens faced—"murthers," in the pronouncement's dated wording—but "unlawful meetings and conventicles, unlawful uttering of words, assemblies, misprisions, confederacies, deceits, and all other evil doings, offenses, and injuries whatsoever." The master gradually worked his way to the Exeter jury's findings of fact. The presentation "necessarily consumed much time," a reporter noted.

After the reading, Collins objected to several words that he said did not belong in the findings of fact. He noticed that at some point after the jury had approved the text, it was not clear when, Baron Huddleston had added two phrases. One was that the *Mignonette* was a "registered British vessel." The other was that the boat the men had escaped in when the *Mignonette* sank was one "belonging to the said yacht." These changes helped the prosecution by providing a stronger factual basis for holding that the lifeboat—the scene of Parker's killing—fell under the jurisdiction of the English courts. It appeared to be another way in which Baron Huddleston, the strong judge, was doing everything he could to convict Dudley and Stephens. But as with his addition of the word *probably* earlier, at least the words he added were accurate. The *Mignonette was* a registered English vessel, and the lifeboat *did* belong to it. The additions, suspect though their timing may have been, made the findings of fact a more accurate record on which to decide the case.

Collins argued that the words added after the jury approved the findings of fact should be removed. But the attorney general defended the additions. The jury had evidence, he said, that the boat was English and that it belonged to the yacht. Baron Huddleston was permitted to modify the statement of facts the jury produced, he insisted. "The notes of the learned judge who tried the case were, I believe, intended to be rough notes," the attorney general said. Still, he had no objection to removing the words. Baron Huddleston, who admitted that he had added the words, agreed with the attorney general that judges had the right to do so, and he cited legal authority in support. In any case, he added, he did not believe the words were "of the slightest importance."

The lord chief justice ordered the removal, "by consent," of the words Collins had contested but showed no signs of conceding that his court lacked jurisdiction. He entertained a few arguments about technical issues and directed that the hearing begin.

The attorney general told the justices that the case was a simple one: Dudley and Stephens murdered Richard Parker. He conceded that the men "believed that if they did not have an opportunity of consuming" Parker's "flesh and drinking his blood their own lives would be lost from want of sustenance." But he insisted that one more thing had to be accepted: When the defendants killed Parker, there was still a chance his life could have been saved. At any point before Parker died, he said, a ship could have appeared to rescue all of them.

Turning to the legal issues, the attorney general argued that the defendants' acts could only be viewed as murder. There were a limited number of instances in which the law countenanced taking a life, he said, and he proceeded to list them. One was an executioner carrying out a death sentence, and another was a soldier killing an enemy combatant—but Dudley and Stephens were not executioners or soldiers. A third circumstance, the attorney general said, was self-defense.

Lord Coleridge interjected, "Self-defense against that particular person whose life is taken." The attorney general agreed. The two men were making the same point about the self-defense doctrine that Baron Huddleston had made in Exeter. While English law recognized a right to self-defense, it applied only to killing a person who was posing a threat—which Parker was not doing. The threat menacing Dudley and Stephens came from hunger and thirst—not from the harmless young cabin boy.

Once it was established that self-defense would apply only if Parker had actually attacked the defendants—which he clearly had not—the attorney general could turn to necessity. The matter was simple, he argued: English law did not recognize dire necessity as a legitimate excuse for taking a life. Dudley and Stephens killed Parker for one reason only, the attorney general said: to use him as food. But English law did not allow people to steal food when they were hungry, he said. If Parker had possessed food and Dudley and Stephens took his food, they would have committed theft, and if they had killed him to take his food, they would have been guilty of murder. Why should it be less of a crime, he asked, if the defendants "kill the boy . . . in order to obtain the food of which the body was composed?"

"Great writers on criminal law," he said, "all concur in the view . . . that no necessity of hunger will justify the killing of a man." At that, the lord chief justice stepped in. "I have consulted my learned brethren," Lord Coleridge said, "and the proposition is so entirely novel and startling to every one of us . . . that, unless this can be shown not to be murder it clearly is murder by the law of England." The lord chief justice was saying that he and his fellow justices were already in such agreement with the attorney general that there was no need for him to say any more.

Nevertheless, before concluding, the attorney general wanted to address a case that had been mentioned in public discussions and at trial. The incident from St. Kitts in 1641 was the only one, he said, in which there was a question of an English judicial body accepting a necessity defense in a case of this kind. But there were serious misconceptions about it, he said. His research at the British Museum had established that the sailors were pardoned by an administrative officer based in St. Kitts and that no judge was involved. The attorney general clearly wanted the court to know the historical record was pristine: No British court had ever countenanced the sort of cannibalism Dudley and Stephens had engaged in.

The lord chief justice then asked Collins to speak for the defense and to limit his argument to the charge of murder. The defense had so far not attempted to argue that the killing of Parker was manslaughter or any other lesser crime, which could have led to a sentence less than death. Lord Coleridge did not want it to start making such an argument now. "It is murder or nothing we all think," he said.

Collins began by invoking the necessity defense, despite Baron Huddleston's insistence at the Exeter Assize that English law did not allow it. "If to save their lives, it is necessary to kill one, they are not guilty of the crime of homicide," Collins told the court. He proceeded to cite cases and legal scholars in support of a necessity defense, going back to Henry de Bracton in the 1200s. But there was not much to work with, and the justices quickly disagreed with his interpretation of some of his sources. Their real resistance, though, was centered on fundamental principles of justice. The lord chief justice rejected the idea that saving one's own life was the highest obligation and could justify taking someone else's life. In his view, such reasoning could be used to excuse far too many immoral actions. Its logical extension, Lord Coleridge said, was that "no act, however base, however wicked, is punishable, if a man can save his life by doing it."

"That is for the jury," Collins responded.

The lord chief justice asked Collins what authority he could cite to support a contention "that it is a necessity that you should prefer your own life to that of another person."

"I should have thought," Collins replied, "the great instinct of self-preservation."

With that, Collins was again invoking a worldview steeped in social Darwinism—a view that envisioned the human condition as a battle in which everyone had the right, even the duty, to fight for their lives and in which the strongest would be the ones that survived. As the social Darwinists saw it, an unending series of battles of this kind would produce a better, fitter human race.

This "great instinct" was not a principle the justices endorsed. There was something missing from it according to the lord chief justice—or many things. Lord Coleridge said that Collins was assuming that there was such a great duty to save one's own life that people were free to "disregard every other moral or religious obligation." But there were principles, he insisted, such as the injunction not to kill and the duties owed to one's fellow humans, as well as kindness and charity, that argued against this sort of killing.

With the central legal argument clearly not going his way, Collins once again raised the jurisdictional issue he had brought up in Exeter, asserting that the court did not have the authority to hear the case. Having won the removal of Baron Huddleston's language describing the maritime crime scene as a "registered British vessel" and the lifeboat as "belonging to the said yacht," Collins insisted there was nothing in the record of the case to indicate that the *Mignonette*'s lifeboat was a British ship. "For aught we know these may have been Englishmen in a Chinese boat or any boat we choose," Collins said.

"Does it make any difference?" Baron Huddleston jumped in.

Baron Pollock insisted that since the men were "upon on the high seas as British sailors, they [were] amenable to the British law." This time, it was the justices who did not cite any authority for their position, but being the judges in the case, they did not need to. The lord chief justice was not persuaded by Collins's jurisdictional argument, and he did not want to spend any more time on it. Turning to the prosecution, Lord Coleridge told the attorney general that if the justices wanted to hear the Crown's response to Collins's jurisdiction argument, they would let him know. He then adjourned for lunch.

After the break, Lord Coleridge came back with a bold announcement. He had conferred with the other justices, and they had agreed that "the convictions should be affirmed." He said the court would explain its reasoning in writing later.

The announcement was a bombshell—and inaccurate. The court could not "affirm" Dudley's and Stephens's convictions, since they had not yet been convicted of a crime. The Exeter jury had ruled only on the facts. With Lord Coleridge's announcement, the court had actually just decided for the first time that Dudley and Stephens were murderers.

It was a powerful moment and a great blow to Dudley and Stephens. Just three months earlier, when the men arrived in Falmouth, they had been so convinced of their right to kill Parker that they freely talked about it to everyone they encountered. The centuries of tradition that they had relied on as a justification for killing and eating Parker had been stripped away in a few words from a powerful judge. Now the act of killing Parker had led to murder convictions—and in a few days' time, the convictions would presumably be followed by death sentences, the mandated punishment for murder.

But right now, there was not even agreement on which court would hand down the sentences. The lawyers discussed whether it should be this panel of the Queen's Bench or if the case should go back to the Exeter Assize. The justices conferred, and Lord Coleridge said that on Tuesday he would both deliver a written opinion on the guilty verdicts and sentence Dudley and Stephens.

The importance of the moment was underscored when the attorney general asked what should be done with the defendants in the interim. The lord chief justice replied, "We have considered that and I think that they must remain in the custody of the Court now."

Collins still hoped Dudley and Stephens might be allowed to remain at liberty. "We have bail for them," he said.

The lord chief justice denied the request. "It was a very different thing before today," he said. When the men had been released in Exeter, "my brother"—meaning Baron Huddleston—"had not decided" guilt or innocence. Now the men had been found guilty of murder. "We are all of the opinion," Lord Coleridge said, "that it would not be right to free them from custody."

The lenient treatment the men had been receiving since mid-September, when they were released on bail, had come to an end. Now they were being treated like ordinary criminal defendants, and they had to wonder, as they were taken away, whether they would ever be free men again.

Even so, the men might have found one glimmer of hope when Lord Coleridge announced that they were to be remanded to London's Holloway Prison. The lord chief justice said that he had selected "the most comfortable prison that can be provided for them." This was an unusual statement from a judge who had just pronounced defendants guilty of capital murder. It was another small act of leniency, suggesting that the legal system might still regard them as better than the worst kind of murderers—and perhaps, in the end, might not hang them.

When they settled in at Holloway Prison, Dudley and Stephens were allowed visitors. A friend of Stephens went to see him on Saturday, two days after he was convicted of murder. He found Stephens to be in an anxious state. Stephens asked what was being said about him and Dudley on the outside. The friend told Stephens that the press was not making any firm predictions, but people he spoke to believed Dudley and Stephens would be pardoned. Stephens did not seem to share his friend's optimism. "Deep lines of anxiety had worn themselves into his otherwise pleasant face," the friend said.

Asked about his wife and children, Stephens said his wife was bordering on a state of frenzy. She had wanted to accompany him to London but had decided it was better not to. The friend promised to write to her; Stephens had permission to write to her but said he was often too distressed to do so. Another visitor, who came with the friend, reminded Stephens of the many brave things he had done over the course of his career at sea, which seemed to cheer him up.

"If I could have saved the poor boy's life by the loss of my own, I would have done so," Stephens told his friend, "but he was too far gone." It was a noble sentiment, possibly said to assuage his guilt or in hope that his words would somehow make it to Lord Coleridge, who was about to sentence him, or to the home secretary and the queen, who would decide his appeal for mercy. But it does not appear that it had any basis in fact. On the lifeboat, when Dudley had insisted on killing Parker, Stephens never suggested sacrificing his own life.

The lord chief justice and the home secretary were, just then, considering what should be done with Dudley and Stephens. Coleridge was writing his legal opinion explaining the court's guilty verdicts, which would set a new national policy on survival cannibalism, and he was preparing to deliver Dudley's and Stephens's sentences. At the Home Office, Harcourt was working under the assumption that the lord chief justice would sentence Dudley and Stephens to death. He was weighing what he should do when he was presented with the defendants' inevitable request for mercy.

Lewis Harcourt, serving as his father's private secretary, was convinced his father would not allow Dudley and Stephens to be hanged. The death sentences "of course will be at once reprieved," Lewis wrote in his journal. "The only question is what their punishment is to be." His confidence was perhaps partly a matter of statistics. The royal prerogative of mercy had the appearance of being an exceptional act, the sovereign personally stepping in to stay the executioner's hand, but in fact it was used quite often. The younger Harcourt also knew a great deal about how his father felt about capital punishment in general. Given what he did know, it is notable that beyond expecting that the men would not be executed, he had no real sense of how harshly they would be punished.

There was no formula for how Harcourt would go about deciding what to do. A Home Office internal memorandum written a decade earlier acknowledged that the office's recommendations with respect to the royal prerogative of mercy were "governed by no fixed rules." But the Home Office had developed guidelines over the years. It was more likely to grant mercy when a jury recommended it, and much more so when the trial judge did. Both of these factors would work in Dudley and Stephens's favor, but requests for mercy were no guarantee, and there were other factors that would work against the men.

In the end, the decision would be more about policy than law, which meant it would owe a great deal to the home secretary's personal priorities. These life-or-death decisions ultimately came down, one scholar observed, to "the values" that particular home secretaries "sought to protect." Harcourt's personal values pulled him in different directions. As a general matter, he opposed capital punishment, and he had worked to reduce its use. Three years earlier, he had introduced a bill to restrict the death penalty to murders in which there was a demonstrated intent to kill. Yet as home secretary, he did not try to stop all executions. He believed that since capital punishment was part of the laws of England, he had a duty to accept it.

When Harcourt considered a request for mercy in a capital case, he examined the facts closely. He believed some crimes, such as young mothers who killed their babies, were categorically deserving of mercy. There were also circumstances, such as mental impairment, that he considered clear reasons for clemency. Dudley and Stephens did not exhibit the serious mental defects that were required for an insanity plea under England's M'Naghten rule, but they were certainly under extraordinary duress when they killed Parker.

At the same time, there were aspects of this crime that would incline Harcourt toward supporting either the death penalty or lengthy prison sentences. One was the matter of intentionality. The killing of Parker, for all of its unusual circumstances, was undeniably intentional. And in other respects, too, its perpetrators had acted in ways opposed by Harcourt and many Victorian reformers. In the lifeboat, the people at the top of the hierarchies—by rank, age, wealth, and health—had decided, without drawing straws, that the boy at the bottom of these hierarchies should be sacrificed.

And there was the matter of the influential precedent that would be set. This was no run-of-the-mill murder in which an act of clemency would be deemed to be only a judgment of the specific facts of the case. Dudley and Stephens's punishment would be seen as an overarching statement by the government about survival cannibalism at sea—and the necessity doctrine more broadly. Harcourt would have to consider that if the men were punished too lightly, it would encourage more people in extreme circumstances to kill others to survive at sea or elsewhere.

The decision was not Harcourt's alone. Even though the home secretary was the de facto appeals tribunal for death penalty cases, he also had to consider the views of the queen, who often took a harder line toward criminality than he did. Queen Victoria did not share his opposition to capital punishment or his broad sympathies for criminal defendants. The queen was "disturbed at what she felt was his undue tenderness to offenders," Harcourt's biographer Alfred George Gardiner notes.

Dudley and Stephens's mercy request arrived while Harcourt was still deciding what to do and before the lord chief justice and his fellow justices had decided on their sentences. On

December 5, the Home Office received "The Humble Petition of Thomas Dudley Late Master and Edward Stephens Late Mate of the Yacht 'Mignonette.'" It must have been the pressure of rushing to make a plea for clemency that led the advocates who filed it to use the wrong name for their client, Edwin Stephens.

In the appeal, the lawyers set out the facts of the case and made a plea. "Your petitioners most humbly hope," it said, "they may under all the circumstances of this unfortunate case be considered as proper objects of the Royal mercy which your Petitioners most humbly pray you Sir will advise Her Majesty to extend to them by granting them the Royal Pardon." Dudley and Stephens each signed the petition.

Meanwhile, Dudley and Stephens's supporters had begun lobbying the Home Office, sending petitions urging mercy. Newspapers continued to report that the public was on the men's side. At least one paper predicted that it would be hard for the home secretary to ignore vox populi. "We think we are justified in saying that public opinion would not permit any severe punishment being passed upon these men," the *Derby Daily Telegraph* wrote.

Harcourt was also receiving advice from closer to home. The attorney general wrote to him on December 5 arguing against not only the death penalty but also life sentences, which the home secretary was considering recommending. The letter continued the lenient line that James had taken in his first letter, back in September, when he had joked that he would be nervous sitting near any man with a large appetite if Dudley and Stephens were not prosecuted. In that letter, he had also said that "when convicted we can let them off."

Now the attorney general was advocating just that. He reminded Harcourt that when the men killed Parker, they were "in a state of comparative phrensy quite upsetting the ordinary balance of the mind." In James's view, what Dudley and Stephens did was properly viewed as less than murder. He argued that if they had been convicted of manslaughter rather than murder, a judge would have sentenced them to just three months. Indeed, having successfully prosecuted the case, the attorney general was suggesting a complete pardon. Going beyond the newspapers' sense that the public would not accept a severe punishment, he said that popular opinion was so strongly on Dudley and Stephens's side that it would be impossible to sentence them to prison at all. "If you announce a commutation to penal servitude for life or even to any other term you will never be able to maintain such a decision and you will have to give way," James wrote.

In his response to the attorney general the next day, Harcourt gave an indication of his thinking. He began by saying that while he valued James's counsel, "in so grave a case as this, the responsibility of decision must rest with me and it is I who shall be called to account." Harcourt did not dispute that Dudley and Stephens had considerable popular support. It simply meant less to him than it did to James. "Everybody knows that the vulgar view of this subject at first was that these men had committed no crime," Harcourt wrote. It was "exactly to withstand an erroneous and perverted sentiment on such matters that we are placed in situations of very painful responsibility." Directing the attorney general's attention to the actual law of the case, he reminded James, "You and I accepted our several shares in the prosecution because we were convinced the men were guilty of Murder." They were right to have viewed Parker's killing that way, Harcourt insisted, and he was troubled that James now appeared to believe that Dudley and Stephens had only committed an offense "in law." Their crime, the home secretary insisted, was a real one. The court's verdict made clear that "to slay an innocent and unoffending person to save one's own life is not a justification or excuse," he wrote. It was "therefore upon moral and ethical grounds, not upon technical grounds, that the law repels the loose and dangerous ideas floating about in the vulgar mind that such acts are . . . anything short of the highest crime known to the law."

Harcourt's response to the attorney general did not sound like the words of someone who was inclined to recommend a full pardon or a highly reduced sentence. Lewis Harcourt, writing in his journal (and using initials for his father's title) confirmed that "the H.S. feels very strongly that they ought to have a severe punishment."

Lewis was, like the attorney general, an advocate for mercy, and likely the most influential one. The younger Harcourt was just twenty-one years old, but his advice carried considerable weight with his father. "I feel that there will be a great though unreasonable outcry if they have any sentence," he wrote in his journal, but he thought it would be "altogether wrong" for the men to be set free with no prison time. "I do however think that they should not be severely punished and have tried to impress this as strongly as possible on the H.S. but he is averse to leniency," he wrote. On December 8, Lewis had a long talk with his father in which he made his case.

On Tuesday, December 9, the Court of Queen's Bench reconvened to deliver its legal opinion and sentence Dudley and Stephens. Despite a steady rain, a crowd had assembled at the entrance to the Royal Courts of Justice's public gallery. The governor of Holloway Prison delivered Dudley and Stephens to the courtroom at a little after 10 a.m. The defendants were seated between two uniformed prison guards, whom they talked to while they awaited their fate. The Holloway Prison governor sat in the jury box, ready to take the defendants back if they were sentenced to prison or to death. At 10:20 a.m., the public

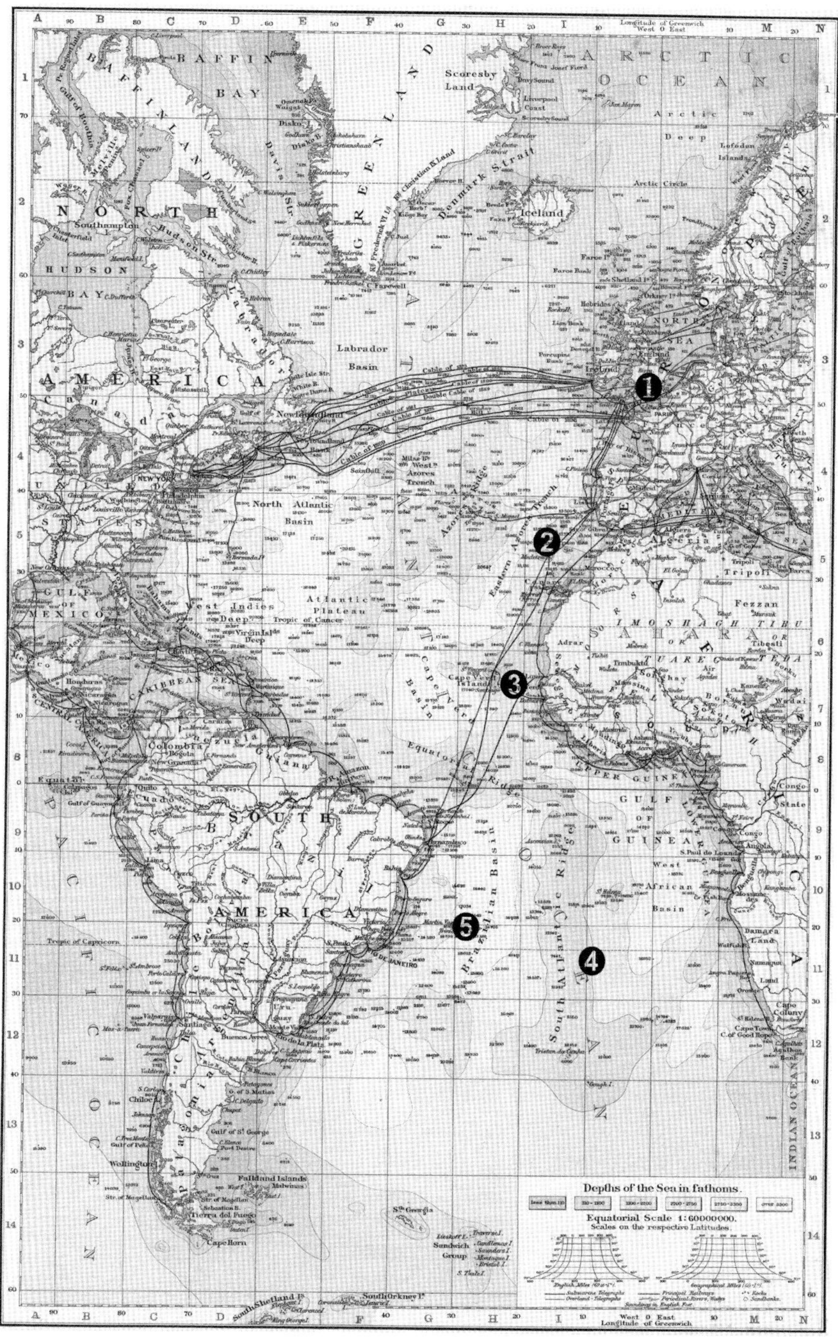

Map depicting the route of the *Mignonette*, whose voyage began in Southampton, England (1) on May 19, 1884. The crew then visited Madeira (2) and the Cape Verde islands (3) before sinking off the Cape of Good Hope (4) and being rescued farther north and west twenty-four days later (5). Map by Richard Andree. Courtesy of the David Rumsey Historical Map Collection.

Image of Captain Thomas Dudley, commander of the *Mignonette* (*Le Voleur*, 1885).

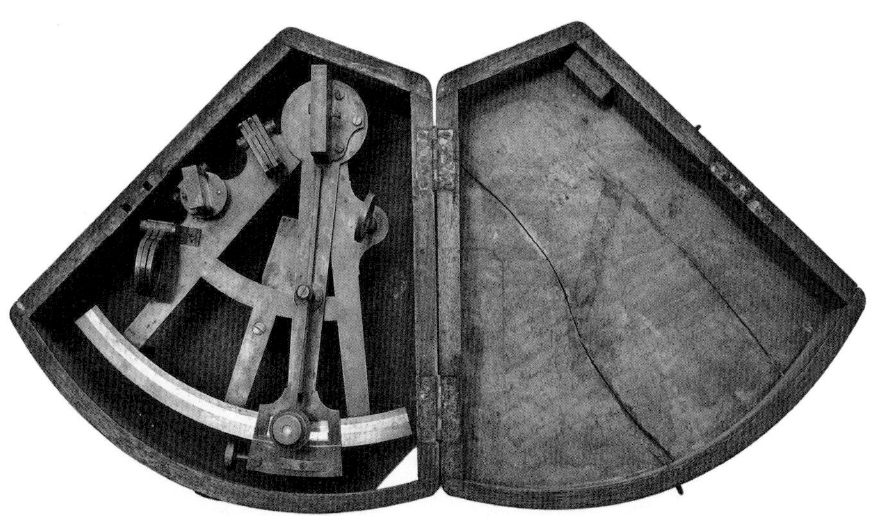

Photograph of Captain Dudley's sextant from the ill-fated yacht *Mignonette*. Courtesy of Charles Miller Ltd., Specialist Marine & Scientific Auctioneers.

Sketch of the *Mignonette* done by Thomas Dudley in 1884 from The National Archives, UK.

Opening page of the *Mignonette* crew agreement from The National Archives, UK.

List of crewmembers and their signatures from the *Mignonette* crew agreement from The National Archives, UK.

The sinking of the yacht *Mignonette*, based on drawings by Edwin Stephens. Originally published in *The Illustrated London News*.

THE ILLUSTRATED LONDON NEWS.

REGISTERED AT THE GENERAL POST-OFFICE FOR TRANSMISSION ABROAD.

No. 2370.—VOL. LXXXV. SATURDAY, SEPTEMBER 20, 1884. WITH EXTRA SUPPLEMENT | SIXPENCE. By Post, 6½d.

THE LOSS OF THE YACHT MIGNONETTE.—FROM SKETCHES BY MR. EDWIN STEPHENS, THE MATE.

The way in which they stowed themselves in the dinghy.

Sailing before the wind: How the dinghy was managed during the last nine days.

How the dinghy was managed in the heavy weather: with the stern sheets up aft, and the "sea anchor," made of the water-breaker bed and the head-sheets grating.

Newspaper story from 1884 showing sketches of the dinghy by Mr. Edwin Stephens, the mate. Originally published in *The Illustrated London News*.

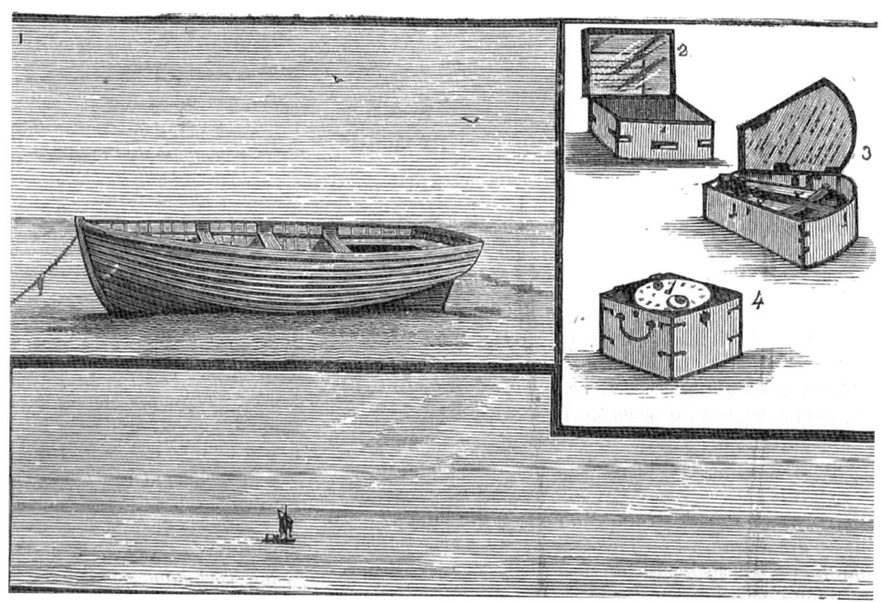

Images of the lifeboat; the chronometer lid, with Thomas Dudley's letter to his wife; the sextant, with writing on the lid; and the chronometer. Originally published in *The Illustrated London News*. © Chronicle/Alamy.

Inq. 1.

ISSUED BY THE BOARD OF TRADE, MAY, 1879.

EXAMINATION ON OATH

Relating to the "Mignonette"

IN PURSUANCE OF THE 432ND SECTION OF THE MERCHANT SHIPPING ACT, 1854, 17TH AND 18TH VICTORIA, CAP. 104, AND OF THE 32ND SECTION OF THE MERCHANT SHIPPING ACT, 1876, 39TH AND 40TH VICTORIA, CAP. 80.

1. Names of Deponent at full length.

1. Thomas Dudley *being duly sworn, deposes as follows; namely,*

2. State whether Deponent is "Master," "Mate," &c., of the Ship; the name of the Ship; and particulars as to her Tonnage and Official Number.
If the Ship is a Steam Ship, the fact should be stated, as well as the nominal horse power of the Engines, and whether Paddle or Screw.

2. That he was the Master *of the Ship* "Mignonette" *of the Port of* London *of the Register Tonnage of* 19 *Tons, her Official Number being* 56845

3. Names and Residence of Owners.

3. That the said Ship is *owned by* Jno Henry Want *residing at* Sydney Australia *in the* ✓ *of* ✓

4. Particulars of rig, build, age, and class of Ship.

4. That the said Ship was *rigged as a* Cutter *that she was built of* wood *at* Brightlingsea *in the year* 1867*, and that she ______ classed in ______ as ______ years.*

5. Particulars as to the Number of hands composing Crew, and as to the Certificate of Deponent.

*5. That the Crew consist*ed *of* four *hands, including deponent, that the deponent's Certificate is a Certificate of* competency as Mate *and is numbered* unknown

6. Particulars of Cargo, and Shippers and Consignees.

6. That said Ship had on board ~~a~~ no *Cargo of* ✓ *of the weight of* ✓ *tons, shipped by* ✓ *of* ✓ *and consigned to* ✓ *of* ✓

7. Depth of Water.

7. That the draught of water of the said Ship was ✓ *feet forward and* ✓ *feet aft.*

8. Number of Passengers on board.
NOTE.—*If the Wife and Children of the Master or of any Officer of the Ship are on board, the fact should be stated.*

8. That said Ship had on board in addition to the Cargo aforesaid no *Passengers.*

9. Date, and state of Weather at time of sailing.

9. That said Ship proceeded from Southampton *on her intended voyage as named below, on the* 19th *day of* May *last past, at* 4.30 P. *M.; the tide at the time being* high Water *the weather* fine*, and the wind blowing a* light breeze *from the* S. E.

Examination on oath of Thomas Dudley, captain of the *Mignonette*, from The National Archives, UK.

Image of the home secretary, William Harcourt, who insisted that the killing of Parker be prosecuted as murder. © Chronicle/Alamy.

Sir John Walter Huddleston, the judge who presided over the grand jury proceedings and jury trial of Thomas Dudley and Edwin Stephens in Exeter. Originally published in *The Illustrated London News*.

Sketch of the Exeter Castle gate during the trial.

Sketch of the trial of Thomas Dudley and Edwin Stephens.

Thomas Dudley, Edwin Stephens, and Julius Wiese (from left to right). Wiese was one of the German sailors who had helped with the rescue and testified at trial.

Edmund Brooks in the witness box, testifying against his former crewmates, Thomas Dudley and Edwin Stephens.

Sir John Walter Huddleston during the trial.

FEARFUL SUFFERINGS AT SEA.

LAD KILLED AND EATEN.

A fearful tale of suffering and shipwreck has just come to light, by the landing of three of the men at Falmouth, by a German barque. They were part of the crew of the yacht 'Mignonette,' bound for Australia, which foundered in a storm, and they were twenty-four days in an open boat. Their sufferings were so great that they killed a lad named Parker, and lived on him for several days.

Air—Driven from home.

Just for a few moments your attention I crave,
While I relate a sad death on the wave;
God help poor sailors--for we cannot see
What they go through when alone on the sea.
A terrible story, alas, has been told,
A worse one I'm sure we never could unfold,
Of the sufferings of sailors on the ocean alone,
What they went thro' may never be known.

The waves rose like mountains round the poor ship-
wrecked crew,
Starving and thirsty, oh, what could they do,
They thought of their children, their homes and their
wives,
They killed the poor boy to preserve their own lives,

It was but a vessel fragile and small,
Not fit to sail the atlantic at all,
The 'Mignonette' yacht was a speck on the wave,
A coffin to carry poor men to their grave.
A storm she encountered she could not withstand
She sank on the ocean for, far from the land;
The captain and crew in on open boat lay
Exposed to the weather by night and by day.

For twenty-four days they were tossed on the sea,
Expecting each moment their last it would be,
Five days without water seven days without food,
By ravenous sharks the boat was pursued,
Mad with the thirst and the hunger as well,
What they did then is fearful to tell,
Between life and death on the desolate wave,
They killed the poor boy their own lives to save.

The captain went to him as he laid on his side,
" Dick your time's come," to him he cried,
I pray God forgive me for what I must do,
The story is terrible but alas! it is true.
The poor lad was stabbed, they drank his life's blood,
He died as his manhood was yet in the bud,
Only nineteen he drew his last breath,
To give life to others he met with his death.

They lived on the body of the ill-fated boy,
To satisfy hunger his limbs did destroy,
It may seem strange to me and to you,
But we cannot tell what hunger will do.
What must it be when day after day,
Starvation slowly takes life away,
The burning sun on them, 'tis fearful to think
Tho' surrounded by water not and drop to drink

The captain and mate are now on their trial,
To killing the boy they give no denial,
'Tis a terrible story which they have to tell,
How they have sufferd and how the boy fell.
They will never forget those days on the sea,
As long as they live, wherever they be
Good bless poor sailors alone on the wave,
The ocean alas, is too often their grave,

Image of a ballad recounting the events on the *Mignonette*, circulated while Thomas Dudley and Edwin Stephens were facing murder charges, which takes a sympathetic view of the defendants' actions. Reproduced with permission from materials on loan to the National Library of Scotland from the Balcarres Heritage Trust.

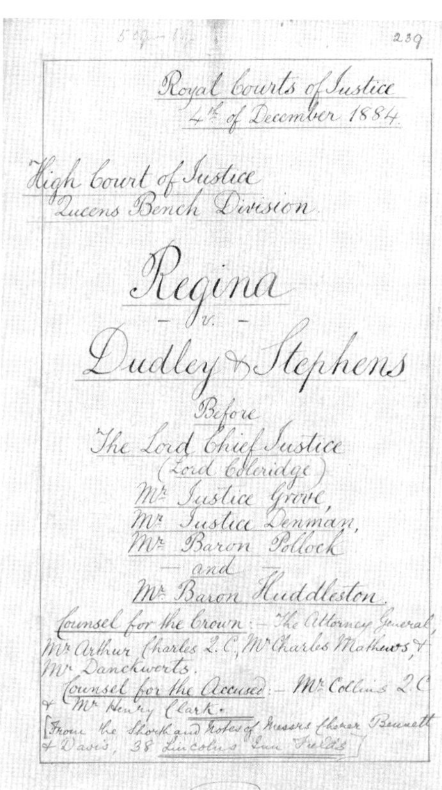

239

Royal Courts of Justice
4th of December 1884.

High Court of Justice
Queens Bench Division.

Regina
– v. –
Dudley & Stephens

Before
The Lord Chief Justice
(Lord Coleridge)
Mr. Justice Grove,
Mr. Justice Denman,
Mr. Baron Pollock
– and –
Mr. Baron Huddleston.

Counsel for the Crown: – The Attorney General, Mr. Arthur Charles Q.C., Mr. Charles Mathews, & Mr. Danckwerts.

Counsel for the Accused: – Mr. Collins Q.C. & Mr. Henry Clark.

[From the Shorthand Notes of Messrs Cherer Bennett & Davis, 38 Lincolns Inn Fields]

1

Opening page of the record of the argument in *Regina v. Dudley and Stephens* before the lord chief justice from The National Archives, UK.

A life drawing done in 1887 of John Duke Coleridge, the lord chief justice of England and Wales. Illustration for *The Graphic*, October 29, 1887. © Look and Learn / Illustrated Papers Collection / Bridgeman Images.

L. P.
C. 6.

PRISON COMMISSION
RECD 8 JAN 1885

A 36934 / 1M

H. M. C. P., M. 6—80

PETITION.

Name, Age, Register No., and where confined. } Thomas Dudley — ~~33~~ 31 — 5331

H.M. PRISON, Holloway.

Convicted.		Crime.	Sentence.	Remarks.
When	Where			
Dec 9, 1884 ~~H.C.J. Queens Bench Division (Winter Assize County No 14) Cornwall~~	H.C.J. Queen's Bench Division (Winter Assize County No 14. Cornwall)	Felony and murder.	Death. commuted to 6 months simple Impt from Dec 4, 1884	[signature] Governor 7.1.85

The Petitioner not to write on this margin.

To the Right Honourable Sir William Vernon Harcourt Her Majesty's Principal Secretary of State for the Home Department.

The Petition of Thomas Dudley, a prisoner ~~in the~~

Humbly Sheweth—

Sir

With the Governors permission I beg to present this Petition on my behalf the charge against me is sad indeed to think about much more to endure & I beg your further consideration in my unhappy case

On Nov 4th at Exeter Mr Collings J.P. one of the Grand Jury came & saw me after the True Bill had been found & he explained to me how necessary for them to do so. but said Dudley you have our sympathy but prepare for the awful sentence which must be passed to uphold the laws of England But rest assured as soon as things can go through their form you will be granted a free Pardon we all are sure. Now from that hour I prayed for strength to bare that awful sentence which was given me but You know the Judge would not take upon himself to pass it at Exeter on Nov 6th

I beg to call your attention what our terrible sufferings while in our 13 feet boat for 24 days the only food we had for the first 11 or 12 days was one half pound of Turnips & say at the most three pounds of raw Turtle each & you may say next to no water only our owen Urin to drink day after day & for the next 8 days not any food whatever & five days of which not one drop of water Can any one on shore judge the state of our bodys & what must our poor brain & mind have been when that awful impulse came to put the poor lad out of his mesry & for he was dying at the time the salt water killed him & the terrible

Petition for a pardon from Thomas Dudley to William Harcourt, the home secretary, from The National Archives, UK.

Your Petitioners most humbly hope they may under all the circumstances of this unfortunate case be considered as proper objects of the Royal mercy which your Petitioners most humbly pray you Sir will advise Her Majesty to extend to them by granting them the Royal Pardon for the said offence.

And your Petitioners as in the strictest gratitude and duty bound shall ever pray &c

Thomas Dudley

Edwin Stephens

Joint petition for a pardon from Thomas Dudley and Edwin Stephens from The National Archives, UK.

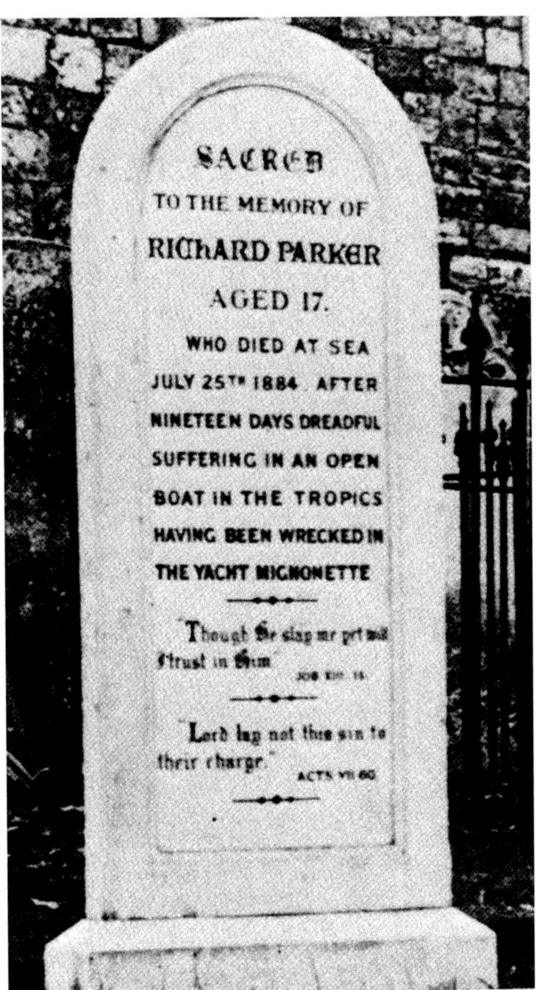

Memorial to Richard Parker, the cabin boy, in Southampton.

Lifeboat of the *Mignonette*, exhibited in Falmouth in 1884.

gallery doors opened, and the seats filled quickly with a group of spectators who were, this time, entirely men.

Dudley once again appeared to be in better spirits than the occasion warranted. The *Essex Standard* noted that he "wore his apparently habitual smile, somewhat incongruous in view of the fact that he was within half-an-hour," most likely, of receiving a death sentence. But Dudley's smile was masking considerable anxiety and fear. A recent visitor to the prison reported that he was "dreadfully harassed by the suspense." Stephens, as usual, was more obviously perturbed. The tension showed on his face. His "bold forehead" was "knit," the *Essex Standard* noted, "showing a seriousness and anxiety, that earned for him considerable compassion."

At 10:40 a.m., cries of "silence, silence" rang out and a hush fell over the courtroom. The justices filed in, wearing wigs and black robes, and sat at five individual desks. The skies were darkening outside, giving the proceeding an ominous feeling. "In the gathering gloom the rows of white faces peering anxiously down from the gallery wore an almost ghastly aspect," *The Cambridge Independent Press* reported.

A court officer announced the case of "The Queen against Dudley and another." The room was silent, and Dudley and Stephens rose to stand before the justices. The lord chief justice began to speak. The men had been laughing at something when they arrived in the courtroom, but as one observer noted, they became "very anxious and serious during the delivery of the judgment of Lord Coleridge."

The lord chief justice started by reading aloud the Exeter jury's special verdict, which he said presented the facts of the case with "cold precision." He began his own comments with sympathetic words. It was clear that "the prisoners were subjected to terrible temptation," he said, "to sufferings which might break down the bodily power of the strongest man, and try the conscience of the best." He added, "Other details yet more harrowing, facts yet more loathsome and appalling, were presented to the jury, and are to be found recorded in my learned Brother's notes," a reference to the Exeter findings of fact that Baron Huddleston had presided over.

Lord Coleridge then pivoted to giving his own interpretation of the crime at the heart of the case. "This," he said, "is clear, that the prisoners put to death a weak and unoffending boy upon the chance of preserving their own lives by feeding upon his flesh and blood after he was killed, and with the certainty of depriving him of any possible chance of survival."

The justices did not see this as a hard case. They were convinced from the beginning, Lord Coleridge said, that Parker's killing was murder. "The contention that it could be anything else was, to the minds of us all, both new and strange," he said. He had stopped the attorney general from responding any further to the defense's arguments because they appeared to the justices to be "at once dangerous, immoral, and opposed to all legal principle and analogy." The defense had offered two main arguments why the killing of Parker was not murder, and the lord chief justice now resoundingly rejected each of them. One was self-defense, and Lord Coleridge did not spend much time on it. That defense could not be used to excuse killing someone who did not pose a threat, he said—and Parker clearly had been no threat to his shipmates. The lord chief justice noted that the defense claimed to have "books of authority" stating that it was permissible to kill an innocent person to save one's own life, but those books, he declared, "will not be found to sustain this contention."

Lord Coleridge had more to say about the defendants' main legal argument: the necessity defense. He insisted, as Baron

Huddleston had at Exeter, that he knew of no English court ruling that supported the necessity defense against a charge of homicide. The St. Kitts case carried no weight, he said, since it dated to 1641, when France and England shared the island, and the only report of it was in a medical treatise published in Amsterdam. It was, all in all, "as unsatisfactory as possible" as a precedent. He put no more stock in the case about the *William Brown* passengers thrown overboard, an American ruling that had no authority in English courts.

The law of England provided no support for a necessity defense to a charge of homicide, Lord Coleridge said, and for his own part, he thoroughly rejected the reasoning behind it. Dudley and Stephens's necessity defense was based on their conviction that one had an absolute duty to save one's own life, the lord chief justice said—and he himself did not believe there was any such necessity. "To preserve one's life is, generally speaking, a duty," he said, "but it may be the plainest and the highest duty to sacrifice it," as when a soldier dies to protect women and children or a captain gives his life in his duty to save his crew and passengers.

Lord Coleridge supported his argument for the virtue of sacrifice with two examples dear to the hearts of Victorian reformers. One of these was what he called "the noble case of the *Birkenhead*." The HMS *Birkenhead* was a troopship that was carrying about 640 men, women, and children when it crashed into rocks and sank off the coast of South Africa in 1852. The soldiers famously stood at attention on the deck while the women and children were evacuated to safety. The ship slipped under the waves, and more than four hundred men lost their lives. It was one of the earliest examples of the maritime tradition of saving women and children first, a practice sometimes known as the "*Birkenhead* drill." Rudyard Kipling immortalized the sacrifice in his poem "Soldier an' Sailor Too" with the line "to stand an' be still to the *Birken'ead* drill is a damn tough bullet to chew."

Directly contrary to the self-centered imperative invoked by Dudley and Stephens's defense team, the soldiers and sailors of the *Birkenhead* had been guided, Lord Coleridge said, by "the moral necessity, not of the preservation, but of the sacrifice of their lives for others." The judge's second famous example was none other than Jesus Christ. Lord Coleridge pointed out that Jesus did not argue that others should be sacrificed to save him—quite the reverse, he gave his own life to save mankind. "It is enough in a Christian country to remind ourselves of the Great Example whom we profess to follow," he said.

The wording Lord Coleridge used to disparage the necessity defense sounds archaically moralistic to the modern ear. We no longer expect captains and crews to rush to throw away their own lives in times of danger. Nor, when we develop our legal standards, do we ask people to act as Jesus did. Lord Coleridge's language and analogies have led some modern critics to call his opinion "sanctimonious" and sermon-like, but despite its antiquated reference points, his conclusions about the defendants' necessity defense remain as valid today as they were when he wrote the opinion.

Dudley and Stephens were trying to invert the powerful moral principle of self-sacrifice and say instead that others had the duty to be sacrificed to save *them*. That was an ethical proposition, or perversion, that the lord chief justice was categorically rejecting. If the only way to stay alive was by killing an innocent person, there was no duty to keep living, he insisted—and in fact, staying alive that way was a crime.

Lord Coleridge did not directly address the utilitarian argument that the killing of Parker was justified because a larger number of lives were saved, but his reasoning implicitly rejected such calculations. He did not believe individuals, even ones in dire circumstances, should be able to take the law into their own hands and decide that killing someone produced a greater net good than not killing someone. There would be an "awful danger," he said, to allowing calculations of this sort. "Who is to be the judge of this sort of necessity?" he asked. "By what measure is the comparative value of lives to be measured? Is it to be strength, or intellect, or what?"

The lord chief justice was, by position and temperament, a man of the law, and to him the necessity defense represented a dangerous form of lawlessness. Instead of the moral clarity of a prohibition against murder, it allowed people to make their own decisions about whether and when it might be right to kill someone. To Lord Coleridge, a society operating by such rules was not merely misguided—it was immoral, because it allowed evil deeds to be committed and excused. To drive this point home, he ended his opinion with a quotation from no lesser authority on perfidy than John Milton's *Paradise Lost*, the classic literary exposition of the biblical fall of man, describing the ways of the Devil:

> *So spake the Fiend, and with necessity*
> *The tyrant's plea, excused his devilish*
> *deeds.*

The lord chief justice insisted he did not mean "in this particular case the deeds were 'devilish.'" What would be devilish, he said, was the society that would be established if the law embraced the necessity defense against murder charges. Lord Coleridge was not thinking just of starving men in a lifeboat; he was imagining all the future wrongdoers who would invoke the necessity defense if the court recognized it and made it the law of England. Once society's rules were made contingent, there would be no end of far worse wrongdoers—cold-blooded murderers and other miscreants—who would try to use the new rule to exonerate themselves from their crimes.

The defense's arguments had now been decisively rejected by Britain's highest-ranking judge. All that remained was for the lord chief justice to decide what should be done with Dudley and Stephens. He was not suggesting, he said, that there were no extenuating circumstances to their crime. But he explained that it was not up to this court to make the decision about how much such extenuation should matter. English law had a designated process for determining when special allowances should be made, he said. If the law appeared too severe in a particular case, judges must "leave it to the Sovereign to exercise that prerogative of mercy which the Constitution has intrusted to the hands fittest to dispense it," he said. In other words, the defendants would have to make their plea for mercy to the queen.

Lord Coleridge was now ready to pronounce the legal judgment of the court. When he began, *The North Devon Journal* reported, all of the commotion fell away and there was "the deepest silence" in the crowded courtroom. "The prisoners' act in this case was wilful murder," he said, and "the facts as stated in the verdict are no legal justification of the homicide." The five judges were unanimous in their decision.

A half hour after he had begun reading out his opinion, Lord Coleridge was done. He asked the attorney general if he had anything to say.

"My lord, it is my duty now to pray the judgment of the court," he said.

Dudley and Stephens were ordered to rise, and a court master said, "You stand convicted of the crime of murder." He asked if either of them had "anything to say why the Court should not give judgment of death according to law?"

Dudley and Stephens had survived many turns of the wheel in the last seven months—embarking on a sailing adventure under fine conditions, their ship being smashed out from under them on the stormy ocean, drifting helplessly, nearly dying of thirst, resorting to murder and cannibalism, being rescued by a passing ship, returning triumphally to England, being unexpectedly arrested, receiving outpourings of public support, enduring a trial, and now facing convictions for murder. As a result of the last of these, they found themselves standing before the lord chief justice of England and Wales, pleading for their lives.

Dudley, speaking so softly he almost could not be heard, said, "What I have to say my Lord is this. I hope you will take into consideration the extreme difficulties I was in when the deed was committed," adding that he hoped to "have the mercy of the court." Stephens added simply, "I also say the same, my Lords."

Lord Coleridge allowed the seriousness of the moment to register, and then he addressed Dudley and Stephens directly. "You have been each of you convicted of the crime of wilful murder, but you have been recommended most earnestly to the mercy of the Crown," he said, "a recommendation in which I understand my learned brother who tried you and we who have heard this argument unanimously concur." This was no small bit of largess for two convicted murderers. A unanimous recommendation for mercy from the lord chief justice and his four fellow justices could be expected to carry enormous weight with the home secretary and the queen.

But having endorsed mercy from the Crown, the lord chief justice offered none of his own. "The sentence of the Court upon you," he said, "is that you be taken to the prison whence you came and from thence on a day appropriate that you be taken to a place of execution; that you be there hanged by the neck until your bodies be dead; and that your bodies, when dead, be buried within the precincts of the prison."

It was a foreboding recitation, but reading between the grim lines the lord chief justice had just delivered, there were subtle signs that all might not be lost. One was that Lord Coleridge did not wear the black cap that judges generally wore when they imposed a death sentence. Another was that he omitted a traditional phrase about recommending the condemned men's souls to mercy. All this led some observers to speculate that Lord Coleridge's imposition of the death penalty was simply pro forma—something the law required him to do once the defendants were found guilty of murder, but not a sentence Lord Coleridge expected would be carried out. It was not unusual for judges to sentence a prisoner to death even if they did not believe it was warranted under the facts of the case, relying on the sovereign to exercise her prerogative of mercy afterward and prevent the men from being hanged. The problem was, there was no way to be certain what the home secretary or the queen would decide. For now, the sentence for Dudley and Stephens was death.

Dudley had been tormented by the prospect of being hanged at least since the day the Exeter grand jury returned the "true bill"—when, as he said, he began praying "for strength to bear that awful sentence." If he was afraid then, his distress at hearing the lord chief justice personally order his hanging and burial on the grounds of a prison must have been nearly unbearable.

With their duties now fully discharged, the justices left the courtroom. Moments later, two Holloway Prison guards ushered Dudley and Stephens out of the courtroom. With that, the *Gloucester Citizen* said, "a most solemn scene came to a close." From there, the men were transported back to Holloway.

Dudley and Stephens did a good job of hiding their distress. One reporter on the scene observed that they "bore themselves up wonderfully well, and presented a perfectly composed exterior."

If there was any consolation for Dudley and Stephens on that grim day, it was that there was no danger they would be executed before the queen could consider their appeal. Home Secretary Harcourt had directed in a handwritten note that "the prisoners are to be kept in prison, where they are for the present + not to be moved, or placed in condemned cell, or anything of the kind." Their sentences would be "respited," or paused, until word arrived of, as Harcourt put it, the "Queen's pleasure."

The opinion of the Court of Queen's Bench, which ran ten pages in the *Law Reports*, fundamentally changed the law in important ways. Most obviously, the convictions of Dudley and Stephens marked the first time that an English court, and perhaps any court in the Western world, had tried a case of survival cannibalism at sea and found the perpetrators guilty of homicide. More broadly, it strengthened English law in rejecting the necessity defense, particularly for homicide cases. In doing so, it struck a blow against the idea that murder could be justified when it could be presented as the lesser of two evils.

There were a few issues the opinion did not address. It did not rule on the legality of the actual custom of the sea. There was a simple reason for this: Dudley and Stephens had not followed it when they killed Parker. But the logic of Lord Coleridge's opinion suggested that the outcome would have been the same even if lots had been drawn. The premise behind the custom of the sea was that in some circumstances it was necessary to kill someone for a greater good. The lord chief justice said that apart from times of war, it was never necessary to kill an innocent person to save other lives. It might be necessary to sacrifice one's own life but not to take someone else's.

The opinion also did not take on the issue of consent. What if there had been a drawing of lots to which everyone in the boat consented, and they all agreed to sacrifice their lives if they lost? That was not what happened in the *Mignonette* lifeboat, but what if a captain did get everyone's consent? At a theoretical level, it could be argued that the law should be forgiving if everyone agreed—there would be no person in power excusing a "devilish deed." But in practice, it is hard to imagine that such a pristine process would ever occur. Captains were not in the habit of seeking universal consent, and even if they did, history showed that the drawing would very likely be rigged. There was little reason for the lord chief justice to engage in such abstractions, and he did not.

Although the ruling was occasioned by an instance of cannibalism at sea, the lord chief justice had made clear that he saw the decision as having broader impact. He was concerned, he said, about what the larger implications would have been if Dudley and Stephens had succeeded in invoking the necessity defense. As he said, if such a defense were recognized, it might well "be made the legal cloak for unbridled passion and atrocious crime."

The opinion was largely received in this spirit. *The Times*, in an editorial, focused on what the ruling meant for society. "One may be pretty sure that there will not often be a literal repetition of the revolting incidents which took place in that open boat last July," the paper said, but there were other situations in which the new rule would apply, "at sea, and on land, too." There were overcrowded vessels, like the lifeboats of the *William Brown*, in which the strongest people on board might decide to throw the weakest overboard. And there were mining disasters in which miners trapped underground without food and water might be tempted to overpower their comrades and eat them. In the past, people in such circumstances might have been tempted to kill to save themselves and then try to defend themselves with "vague, uncertain ideas as to necessity," the paper said. But now "that there is a clear ruling upon the subject, that plea, such as it is, will be wholly taken away."

The court's landmark ruling was another brick in the progressive legal edifice being built by Victorian-era reformers. *Queen v. Dudley and Stephens* was a victory for a movement that had brought about the Chimney Sweepers and Chimneys Regulation Act of 1840 and the Factories Act of 1867. It bolstered a whole set of values the reformers were working to spread throughout English society. For one, it took a strong stand against the injustices of hierarchy. The lord chief justice viewed the killing of Parker as rooted in the hierarchies on the *Mignonette* and in the lifeboat, taken to a deadly extreme. Dudley and Stephens had, he said, killed "the weakest, the youngest, the most unresisting." The murder was a product of the most powerful people in a social structure believing they had the right to oppress, and even take the lives of, the least powerful.

In a similar vein, Lord Coleridge expressed the Victorian reformers' compassionate concern for young people. In his opinion, he emphasized Parker's youth, calling him a "weak and unoffending boy" and asking if it was necessary to kill him rather than one of the "grown men" in the lifeboat. Lord Coleridge was clearly disturbed that Dudley and Stephens had taken the life not just of an innocent person but of an innocent *child*.

In championing the weak, the lord chief justice was seconding Baron Huddleston's repudiation of the social Darwinist worldview. He was saying that societies—including the small society that had formed in the lifeboat—should not be ordered around helping the strong to survive and thrive. This was a firm rebuke to the assertion, made by Dudley and Stephens's lawyer in Exeter, that in difficult times "the weakest must go to the wall."

Lord Coleridge's opinion was also a refutation of the utilitarian thinking that was then in vogue. He did not directly take on Jeremy Bentham's contention that morality required promoting the greatest good for the greatest number. He instead rejected the idea that calculations of this kind could have any validity, asking, "By what measure is the comparative value of lives to be measured?" He did not believe that hedonic calculus could lead to the conclusion that a killing was "necessary," or legally forgivable.

There was something even more fundamentally reform minded in the lord chief justice's opinion: its championing of human dignity and human rights. The battles the Victorian reformers were waging were ultimately against the forces of dehumanization: factories that oppressed workers and treated them like automatons, procurers who turned women into prostitutes, and a society that ground the life out of the poor. Dudley and Stephens had engaged in a particularly literal version of that process: They had turned Parker from a person into meat to feed upon.

Lord Coleridge's message was, in the end, about the value of people. Dudley and Stephens's greatest offense was that in their single-minded focus on preserving their own humanity, they denied Parker his. The lord chief justice's opinion was, on the whole, a tour de force of the Victorian reform ethic. Its fundamental underlying principle was that the law of England would always punish the killing of the innocent because it was wrong. That was true no matter how young, or poor, or lowly, or sick the person being killed was. In the language of modern times, the court stood up for equality and championed the human rights of the cabin boy—and everyone else like him. The lord chief justice's opinion was not simply a legal ruling in a murder case. It was the latest step forward for England down a path of progressive reform. The court was working, alongside the crusaders for workers' rights and women's rights and children's rights, to build a society with more justice and fewer "devilish deeds."

11

Fading Away

The news of Dudley's and Stephens's death sentences quickly spread around the globe. In Australia, *The Sydney Morning Herald*, a paper the men of the *Mignonette* might have been reading if their voyage had been a success, reported that the prisoners had been sentenced to death in a story about what it called "The Mignonette Affair." *The New York Times* put the sentencing of "The Mignonette Cannibals" on its front page. And in Wheeling, West Virginia, *The Wheeling Daily Intelligencer* reported in a subheadline that the defendants had been "Sentenced to Be Hanged" amid "an Impressive Scene in the Court." At home in London, *The Times* reported that Dudley and Stephens's "crime is judicially declared to be in strictness nothing less than murder."

With the dire sentences now known, the discussion turned to whether the men would actually be hanged. Many commentators believed that the men would only have to serve a few months in prison or even be freed outright. That was the prediction of the *Northern Echo* in Darlington, England. "The most probable conclusion of the melancholy matter will be that the men will receive a free pardon," the paper declared. "Public feeling would be against any lengthened term of imprisonment, even if it extended to six months." The *Belfast News-Letter* reported that "it is expected that after a few months' imprisonment the convicts will be set at liberty."

It was certainly possible to comb through the details of the case and conclude that some form of mercy might come. The Exeter jury had recommended it, and Baron Huddleston had as well. The lord chief justice had publicly said that he and the other justices all supported bestowing the royal prerogative of mercy. Noting that Lord Coleridge had not worn the black cap, news stories took it as a sign that Dudley and Stephens would not be executed. But all this was just guesswork and supposition. In predicting a pardon, newspapers may simply have been telling their readers what they wanted to hear. "The men were virtually pardoned by public opinion before they were put on trial," *The Daily Telegraph* observed. Now there was "universal agreement," *The Daily News* reported, that the death sentence should not be carried out.

But there remained a sizable divergence between mass opinion and the views of the elite. This gap had existed since the men first stepped ashore in Falmouth. While the general public sympathized with Dudley and Stephens, the mayor and magistrates of Falmouth, along with Baron Huddleston and the High Court of Justice, had all sided against them, moving the prosecution forward. Newspaper opinion pages, which had already published extensive condemnation of the men, were now running more. Few of the critics actually wanted to see the men put to death, but many did want the point to be firmly made that in the future, actions like the killing of Parker would not be taken lightly. *The Times*, which generally spoke for the upper echelons of English society, regretted that Dudley and Stephens had become "the subjects of somewhat mawkish, ill-directed sympathy." The paper did not object to the men's sentences being reduced, but it insisted that "it would be a great scandal to justice if any one who hereafter yields to a similar temptation to that to which Dudley and Stephens yielded should be looked upon as entitled to the same mercy."

The radical *Reynolds's Newspaper* was worried that if Dudley and Stephens were not punished, claims of necessity could start to show up in coal mine collapses and other work accidents because the strongest people might believe they were entitled to kill the weakest to survive. The paper lambasted the "sickly, pernicious sentiment" of the "silly people who looked upon the murderers of Richard Parker as heroes" and said it was important for working people that the men receive a substantial punishment. "Nobody, of course, wishes Dudley and Stephens to be hanged," *Reynolds's Newspaper*'s editors said, but they believed letting them off would set a dangerous precedent. "It would not be proper to allow Dudley and Stephens to escape some punishment," the paper insisted, "less with a view of pain to them than as an example to others."

Some newspapers did sympathize with Dudley and Stephens, arguing that the court had imposed too high a standard of conduct on them. *The Daily Telegraph* suggested that the justices who found them guilty should have put themselves in the place of "the wretched beings as they were on that twentieth day of starvation, and then pass judgment upon them." It was "a trial to the judicial temper if lunch be late," the paper said caustically. What would the judges do "if breakfast, lunch, dinner, and supper, too, were to be denied for a whole day, for two days, or even for a week?" To keep Dudley and Stephens "imprisoned even for a short term would have been a shock to the conscience and common sense of the nation," *The Daily Telegraph* insisted.

Taken as a whole, though, the newspaper opinion pages were a reminder that much of the nation's elite still felt strongly that killing Parker was wrong. These were people who traveled in the same intellectual and social circles as the home secretary, whose recommendation would almost certainly decide their fate, and many of them were hoping for a punishment with some teeth in it.

Dudley and Stephens were now back in Holloway Prison, awaiting their fate. Their spirits were buoyed by the stream of letters and telegrams they were receiving from relatives, friends, and strangers and by the reports they were receiving on petitions being filed on their behalf. Dudley, whose mood had risen and fallen sharply over the last few months, was now optimistic—overly so, as it turned out. His wife visited him on December 12, and Dudley told her that he expected to receive a pardon from the queen imminently. He hoped, he said, that he would be able to return home to Sutton on Sunday.

The newspapers were reporting plans for a memorial to Richard Parker. A Mr. John F. Haskins presented a "mural tablet" to Captain Mathews, Parker's foster father, to be placed over Parker's parents' graves in Itchen Ferry's Pear Tree Churchyard. The engraving on it read, "Sacred to the memory of Richard Parker, aged 17, who died at sea July 25, 1884, after nineteen days dreadful suffering in an open boat in the tropics having been wrecked in the yacht Mignonette." It also contained two biblical quotations: "Though he slay me yet will I trust in him.—Job XIII 15" and "Lord lay not this sin to their charge.—Acts VII 60." The tablet received extensive publicity, and in a newspaper article on December 13, it was reported that the second quotation "was added at the special desire of a brother of the deceased," though it did not say which brother.

The second quotation could have been read as an indication that the Parker family, after its critical comments about Dudley and Stephens, had come around and now wanted them freed. If so, that would have been a fast reversal, and the family does not appear to have made any public statements indicating a change of heart. Or it might have reflected the opinion of one rogue Parker brother. But given the timing, it looked a lot like an attempt by Mr. Haskins, or other supporters of Dudley and Stephens, to influence the home secretary, who was about to make his recommendation to the queen.

On Friday, December 12, the home secretary, William Harcourt, reached his decision. He recommended that the queen commute Dudley's and Stephens's death sentences, but he stood up to members of the general public—and his own attorney general—who wanted the men to be set free immediately. He proposed that the men serve six months' imprisonment without hard labor, with the time running from the day of their conviction, December 4.

It was a compromise that embodied the Victorian reform spirit. Harcourt stuck to his conviction that Dudley and Stephens had committed a serious crime. In doing so, he was siding with the sick seventeen-year-old Parker, the lowliest person in the lifeboat, and insisting that taking his life was murder—"the highest crime known to the law." By calling for Dudley and Stephens to face serious punishment, Harcourt was sending the message that Victorian reformers hoped the case would deliver: that murder at sea in conjunction with survival cannibalism was still murder and would be punished as such—even if it was the captain doing it and the cabin boy being killed. If the queen adopted Harcourt's recommendation, a centuries-old tradition of allowing survival cannibalism would come to an end.

At the same time, Harcourt's bid to reduce Dudley's and Stephens's sentences to six months reflected another aspect of Victorian reform. The home secretary had spent his career urging understanding for criminals and delinquents, and he believed it was necessary to look at the underlying reasons a crime was committed. Once the castaways' crime was clearly identified as murder and the message was sent to society that people in power could not kill weaker people in survival conditions, Harcourt could demonstrate the sort of sympathy that he and other Victorian reformers generally showed to convicted criminals.

The next morning, at Holloway Prison, Dudley and Stephens learned of Harcourt's decision. The men were relieved that Harcourt was recommending mercy, but they had been hoping for more. Only a day after telling his wife he expected to be free on Sunday, Dudley had to send her a telegram saying that the home secretary was recommending six months' imprisonment. A disappointed Philippa Dudley told a reporter that she had thought her husband would receive a full pardon and be released immediately. She pointed out that he had originally assumed he would not be charged at all.

On December 15, Queen Victoria formally accepted Harcourt's recommendation and reduced Dudley's and Stephens's sentences to six months' imprisonment without hard labor. It is not clear how she made her decision or even how much time she spent on it. There is, one historian has noted, "no evidence that she took any interest" in Dudley and Stephens's case at any point.

The Home Office prepared a written conditional pardon. "We in consideration of some circumstances humbly represented unto us are graciously pleased to extend our grace and mercy unto them and to grant them our pardon for the crime of which they stand convicted," it read, "on condition that they be imprisoned without hard labor for the term of six months." When the governor of Holloway Prison received the queen's pardon, he formally reduced the sentences. With that, the case of

Queen v. Dudley and Stephens officially came to a close. All that remained was for Dudley and Stephens to serve out the remainder of their six months.

The order reducing Dudley's and Stephens's sentences had the odd effect of worsening their conditions in prison. When they were sent to Holloway as prisoners who were convicted but not yet sentenced, they were allowed to have visitors, to exercise together on the prison grounds, and to eat food brought in from outside. These conditions continued while the queen was deciding whether to pardon them. Now that the sentences were final, those privileges ended, which was an emotional blow. Philippa Dudley reported that the prospect of being treated like a common prisoner had been weighing heavily on her husband, who was now "evidently," *The Daily News* reported, in "a depressed condition."

The changes happened quickly. When Philippa Dudley received her husband's telegram on Saturday morning, she was preparing for a visit, but it was not allowed under the new rules. She wrote to the governor of the prison that same day to ask when she would be able to visit her husband. The governor replied that they could not communicate during the first three months of his sentence. He would then be allowed to receive one letter, write one in reply, and have one visit of no more than twenty minutes from up to two visitors. As it turned out, Philippa Dudley was allowed one twenty-minute visit before Christmas by special permission of the home secretary, whose own sad history made him sympathetic to separated husbands and wives. After seeing her husband on December 23, Mrs. Dudley described him as looking pale, thin, and careworn.

While he was confined in Holloway Prison, Dudley began to think more about starting a new life in Australia. He was hoping he would be able to take over the chandlery business his aunt had offered him and leave all the troubles of the past year behind. But he was worried his incarceration might lead to the offer being withdrawn. Meanwhile, Dudley's family was struggling. They had only Philippa Dudley's salary to live on, and a Plymouth newspaper reported that Dudley's legal expenses "proved a heavy drain on his slender means."

Far less was known about how the Stephens family was doing. Ann Stephens was still not speaking to reporters the way Philippa Dudley was, but the press had a sense that things were not going well. A news story said, "It is feared that Mrs. Stephens and her children are living in a distressed condition at Southampton."

While Dudley was locked up in Holloway Prison, he made an appearance in virtual form in one of the most-trafficked parts of London. On December 28, *The Sunday Times* reported in its "Gridiron Gossip" section that "an excellent portrait model of Captain Dudley" was "one of the latest attractions at Madame Tussaud's Exhibition." Madame Tussaud's grandson, Joseph Randall Tussaud, had spent hours in the courtroom studying Dudley to make his likeness out of wax. The sculpture was placed in the wax museum's Chamber of Horrors—a dubious honor Dudley shared with James Greenacre, who had murdered a young woman and cut her body to pieces, "concealing the fragments in various parts of the metropolis," and Mary Ann Cotton, also known as "the poisoner," who was said to have "killed off husbands and children with the unconcern of a farm-girl killing poultry."

While the public gawked at his wax statue, the real Dudley had not given up hope of being freed early. On January 7, he handwrote an appeal on a preprinted prison form, asking to be released immediately. After filling out the boxes for "crime" (where he wrote "felony and murder") and "sentence" ("death, commuted to six months"), Dudley wrote that "the charge against me is sad indeed to think about much more to endure + I beg your further consideration in my unhappy case." He said he wanted to call the home secretary's attention to "our terrible sufferings" while in the lifeboat "for 24 days," with only the turnips and turtle meat to eat and "no water only our owen [*sic*] urine to drink day after day." Dudley asked, "Can anyone on shore judge the state of our bodies + what must our poor brain + mind have been when that awful impulse came to put the poor lad out of his misery for he was dying at the time the salt water killed him." Dudley asked Harcourt for a full pardon, which would not only free him from prison but give him a measure of personal and professional redemption, including clearing the way for him to resume work as a captain. A pardon would allow him, he said, to "return to my happy home and get my living honestly as I have done at sea since I was ten years old."

In this personal appeal to the home secretary, Dudley did something he had refrained from previously: He expressed remorse about killing Parker and eating him, and even went a step further. "It makes my blood run cold to think about it now," he wrote, "and would to God I had died in the boat."

Stephens wrote a petition that was shorter but similar in content. Remarking that he had "suffered great hardships and privations (the facts of which are already well known)," he noted that the judge and jury in Exeter had both recommended leniency. He hoped that "some portion" of his sentence "may be remitted." Dudley and Stephens's supporters also continued to advocate for their freedom. On January 14, a newspaper reported that petitions from Falmouth and Southampton had been forwarded to the home secretary seeking the men's immediate release. There were five hundred signatures from Falmouth alone. Harcourt denied the requests.

There was only one place left to go. Dudley and Stephens's supporters petitioned the queen directly. The men had influential allies in making their appeal: Ellis Lever, a prominent businessman and philanthropist, and his sister, Alice Lever. Alice, who seems to have enlisted her brother in the cause, was moved when she read about Dudley and Stephens. She wrote to the Home Office on December 24, urging that Harcourt recommend the men to the queen for a full pardon and enclosing £50 to be sent to their families. "While we are met together as families to enjoy the festivities of the Christmas Season," she wrote, "it is very distressing to think of the poor fellows Dudley and Stephens who are undergoing a term of six months' imprisonment and to learn that the families of these men are in poverty."

The home secretary did not appreciate being asked to forward money. He wanted Dudley's and Stephens's prison sentences to punish them for killing Parker and to send a message about their actions, not to spur sympathy and financial support. "I do not wish to encourage presents of this kind," Harcourt told his staff. The money was returned, with the address of a defense fund working on the men's behalf. Through the fund, Alice came into direct contact with Philippa Dudley.

Ellis Lever, who supported cultural institutions and social welfare campaigns, such as relief for unemployed cotton workers, took up the cause more directly. He wrote an appeal to Queen Victoria on the Dudleys' behalf, which he enclosed in a letter to the home secretary. Lever said he "should be happy to think that, as the Queen's advisor on these matters," Harcourt might "feel it consistent with" his "duty to support the prayer." He added that he was sure his "individual signature" on the letter "represent[ed] a great" amount of "popular feeling" across the country.

Lever's appeal to the queen began in florid style. "To Her Most Gracious Majesty Victoria, of the United Kingdom of Great Britain, Ireland, Queen, Empress of India," he wrote. "May it please your majesty," he said, he was writing "in the hope and with the prayer that your majesty" might "extend your Royal clemency to this prisoner by curtailing his sentence." Dudley was being punished, Lever said, for his honesty. "It should not be forgotten," he wrote, that Dudley "unreservedly and voluntarily stated to his own terrible disadvantage the whole circumstances" of what he had done. Lever did not mention that when Dudley admitted his actions, he had no idea he would be arrested for them.

Lever also informed the queen that Dudley's friends and associates were prepared "with the full consent and even desire of the prisoner to facilitate his settlement in Australia." He said that even before the *Mignonette* voyage, Dudley's relatives in Sydney had offered him "a promising interest in a ship chandlery business in that city, which they had stated that, in his favor, they would be ready to relinquish." If Dudley were freed, he would "be in a position to start for the Colony . . . quickly," Lever said. This mention of Dudley relocating to Australia had a subtext. Britain had long engaged in "convict transportation," relocating convicted criminals to far-off lands rather than holding them in prison. Australia was one of the main destinations, and British prisoners were sometimes allowed to shorten their sentences by agreeing to be transported there. The practice had ended in 1868, in large part due to opposition from Victorian reformers, who regarded it as morally wrong. Lever was suggesting that if Dudley were released, he would transport himself—in effect, contritely accepting the ongoing punishment of that old-style exile.

The heart of Lever's appeal was a handwritten statement he included from Philippa Dudley that he hoped Queen Victoria would read, which extolled her husband's heroic role in the tragic events. "Without wishing to speak slightingly of his fellow sufferers, but in justice to my husband," she wrote, he was the one who "stayed in the yacht till almost too late, procuring provisions." It was Dudley, she said, who "constructed the sea anchor with which to break the force of the huge waves + prevent them engulfing them." He "cut off the bottoms of his trousers to stop the hole in the boat; he urged the men to give up a garment apiece to be used for sails."

In Philippa Dudley's telling, her husband was not merely *not* a criminal; he was a shining hero. "The men, hopeless + tortured, were bent on committing suicide," she wrote, in what was either a moment of exaggeration or a detail never before mentioned publicly. They were, however, "buoyed up by him," she said, "+ after the deed was committed, both Brooks + Stephens grasped his hands" many times "saying he had saved their lives and how they would show their gratitude on reaching home, if they ever did so."

Dudley's honesty about his actions was another important point in his favor, his wife insisted. When they landed, "Tom immediately made his deposition before the magistrates, not palliating a single circumstance, though entreated never to divulge it." This phrasing suggested that one of the other survivors, Stephens or Brooks, might have tried to keep the fact that Parker was killed and eaten a secret, though she provided no more details. More openly, her letter tried to lionize her husband at Brooks's expense, pointing out that though Brooks had not participated in the killing of Parker, he did share in the cabin boy's flesh and blood. "That the bravest + most honest should suffer most seems hard," she wrote, "when one who, too cowardly to do, was not too scrupulous to share, yet could be permitted to go unpunished."

This was another inaccurate framing of events—and unfair to Brooks. He had made clear from the beginning that he did not believe Parker, or anyone else, should be killed, and he was willing to take the risk that as a result, he might die of thirst or hunger. Philippa Dudley scorned as "cowardly" a stance that appears to have been deeply principled, even brave. She also complained in her letter that Brooks had been willing to make "a market out of the misery of his companions" by doing public performances in amusement shows that played on his grim experiences on the *Mignonette* voyage. Her husband, she said, had turned down similar opportunities to perform in "Public Places of Amusement," for which he had been offered "large sums of money."

Once again, Philippa Dudley's statement omits some uncomfortable facts. Dudley had decided to stop paying his crew as of the day the *Mignonette* sank. That was the main reason Brooks was in such dire financial shape that he had to appear in public to support himself. Dudley had been able to keep most of the £100 he had received in advance, since he had not paid Brooks, Stephens, and Parker for the part of the voyage that was not completed or for the time they spent returning on the *Moctezuma*.

Mrs. Dudley included a piteous description of the toll the events of the past year had taken on her husband. "The publicity and misery of the tragedy have been too painful almost for human endurance," she wrote. Her husband's health had been eroded by the travails at sea and his time in prison. "I feel doubtful if he will ever be so strong as before," she said.

The home secretary received Lever's appeal to the queen and, within it, the elaborate *apologia* from Philippa Dudley, and he forwarded the documents to Windsor Castle. But he did not urge the queen to take any further action. In a letter of March 2,

Harcourt advised Queen Victoria, "This is a melancholy case but the sentence is a light one and cannot be altered." The letters were returned to the home secretary from Windsor Castle with a note saying they "had been laid before the Queen." Queen Victoria did not appear to care any more about Dudley and Stephens's case now than she ever had, and she did not free them.

On May 20, 1885, Dudley and Stephens were released from Holloway Prison, a year and a day after the *Mignonette* set sail. "Both men looked well, but appeared anxious," according to the *Daily Gazette for Middlesbrough*. Two days later, they requested new Board of Trade certificates to replace the ones they lost when the *Mignonette* went down. The board had so far refused to issue new ones, likely out of concern that the men could use them to flee while out on bail. Now that they had served their sentences, the board restored Dudley's certificate as master and Stephens's as mate. They could finally resume sailing and put the horrors of the past year behind them.

It was not long before Dudley, Stephens, and Brooks returned to obscurity. Brooks, who had played no role in killing Parker, had the easiest time of it. He had been free since September 18, when the charges against him were dropped and he became a witness for the Crown. His life soon returned to something resembling what it had been before the ill-fated voyage. He lived the rest of his life out of the spotlight, with one notable exception. As Philippa Dudley mentioned in her letter for Lever, he appeared in public at some point in a performance or exhibition playing off the notoriety of the *Mignonette* shipwreck. Philippa Dudley viewed it as an unseemly attempt to profit from the "misery of his companions," but to Brooks it no doubt felt like appropriate recompense for all he had suffered—and a needed source of income at a difficult moment.

Although he had considered moving to Australia before the *Mignonette* voyage, Brooks spent the rest of his life in and around Southampton. There were reports that he returned to work at Fay's Yard. At the time he left on the *Mignonette*, Brooks did not have a wife or children. Six years later, in 1891, he married Sarah Anne Cox, a widow who was the daughter of a seaman. There is no record that he had children.

Brooks was said to have carried the events of the *Mignonette* lifeboat with him throughout his life. His friend Albert Bedford, who was related to the Parker family by marriage, recalled that when Brooks got drunk at night, he would yell loudly that he "didn't do it." Brooks died in 1919, almost exactly thirty-five years after the *Mignonette* sank.

After Stephens was released from prison, he went home to Southampton to rejoin his struggling family. In 1886, he returned to sea with his new Board of Trade certificate. His experiences on the *Mignonette* did not discourage him from undertaking long and arduous voyages. That year, he worked on the *Sareca*, a steam yacht bought by the Egyptian government, which he helped deliver to Alexandria. But he too was said to have remained deeply affected by the *Mignonette* traumas. Although he sailed for several more years, he reportedly fell into depression and alcoholism. He died on June 25, 1914, in Hull at the age of sixty-six, a poor and broken man.

Dudley had the shortest and most eventful life after the *Mignonette*. In her statement accompanying Lever's letter to the queen, Philippa Dudley had written that her husband was "eager to leave England as soon as possible: we trust soon to settle our affairs + make a fresh start in Australia." As soon as Dudley was released from prison, the family began making preparations. They traveled to Sydney in 1885 on the steamship *Austral*, completing the transoceanic journey the *Mignonette* had failed to. Dudley's aunt handed over her business, and Dudley began making and selling sails and other boating supplies near the waterfront, under the name T. R. Dudley and Co. The company prospered, and by 1890 it had a staff of forty. The Dudley family also thrived. Philippa gave birth to three more children in Australia. One, a son, died young, but two daughters survived. Two of Philippa's sisters, both teachers, also moved to Sydney to join the family.

But the good times did not last. In the mid-1890s, a bubonic plague pandemic broke out in Asia. When it reached Hong Kong, a major trading hub, it spread widely by ship, including to India, where it would kill six million people between 1898 and 1908. The plague was transmitted by fleas on rats, and when large numbers of dead rats began appearing near the Sydney waterfront in 1900, it was clear the disease had arrived in Australia. In January, Sydney already had its first case of an infected human. The victim was a man who worked near the waterfront. The city tried to contain the spread, advising people who lived and worked near the harbor on safe methods for disposing of rats and hiring a ratcatcher.

Dudley's shop was located in a building near the waterfront. It had a defective sewer system, it turned out, which allowed rats to climb up through the drainpipes into the rooms where Dudley and his family slept, bringing lethal fleas with them. On February 17, Dudley fell ill. He received medical care, but at the time, treatments for the bubonic plague were primitive and ineffective. Five days later, he was dead at the age of forty-six.

Dudley's was the first official death of Sydney's bubonic plague epidemic of 1900. It went on to take 103 lives in the first nine months of that year and 535 in a series of outbreaks that recurred through 1925. To combat transmission of the disease, there were strict rules about the burial of victims. Dudley's body sat unattended for days, then was wrapped in sailcloth soaked in 5 percent sulfuric acid, placed in a watertight coffin with more acid, and wrapped again in acid-soaked sailcloth and a layer of asbestos cloth. The body was then taken by skiff to a cemetery in the city's remote quarantine station and unceremoniously deposited in a grave of "unusual depth."

As the city's first official casualty, Dudley's name was widely reported in the news. If there was any larger meaning to be gleaned from Dudley's inglorious end, any sense that the score had been evened for what he had done years earlier to his cabin boy, the press did not notice it. With his move to Australia, Dudley had managed to put the killing of Richard Parker and his murder conviction behind him. Virtually none of the news accounts of Dudley's death mentioned his past life, and the official public health report referred to him simply as "Captain Dudley, a sailmaker."

AFTERWORD

In *Life of Pi*, the bestselling novel and Hollywood movie, the hero, Pi, survives a shipwreck and shares a lifeboat with a Bengal tiger named Richard Parker. The author, Yann Martel, said that he named the tiger after the cabin boy on the *Mignonette*—as well as the Richard Parker of Edgar Allan Poe's novel *The Narrative of Arthur Gordon Pym of Nantucket* and a third Richard Parker who died on the *Francis Spaight* in 1846. Martel said that he chose the name because "so many Richard Parkers had to mean something."

To some people, *Queen v. Dudley and Stephens* is above all a tragedy, with the doomed cabin boy at the center. Richard Parker is, in every way, the story's innocent victim. He was an orphan who put his faith in a captain who presented himself as a father figure, and that faith was cruelly exploited. While Parker was sick, the adults around him schemed to kill him and use his body to save themselves. When he was murdered, after uttering the haunting words "What, me, Sir?" Parker became the embodiment of the price that some people are forced to pay for the schemes of others.

Other people see *Dudley and Stephens* as a dark comedy—and not just law students. Over the last century and a half, the cannibalism jokes have found their way to even the most cultivated places. The highbrow *Times Literary Supplement* once published an essay on the case under the headline "Cabin Boy Cutlets."

For literary people, *Dudley and Stephens* is part of one of the greatest coincidences of all time. In 1974, *The Sunday Times* commissioned Arthur Koestler, the Hungarian-born novelist and journalist who wrote *Darkness at Noon*, to judge a competition for the greatest coincidence submitted by a reader. Nigel Parker, a schoolboy, won the £100 prize for his entry noting the parallels between the deaths of his great-grandfather's cousin, Richard Parker, and Poe's character in *The Narrative of Arthur Gordon Pym of Nantucket*, who lost a drawing of lots at sea and was eaten, decades before the *Mignonette* set sail. *The Sunday Times* called the coincidence "spinechilling." And there were yet more Richard Parkers. As Martel noted, there was also a Richard Parker who died on the *Francis Spaight*. Another who should be added to the list is a legal scholar who has been teaching the Dudley and Stephens case at Harvard Law School for decades—the same professor who taught it to my law school friend who first told me about the case—also named Richard Parker.

For lawyers, the trial of Dudley and Stephens has enduring significance because it has had a powerful impact on Anglo-American law. In England, the case overturned the long-standing tolerance for survival cannibalism at sea, a practice that had been accepted for centuries in the world of sailing and in literature—and by the legal system. It also helped turn English law against the necessity defense. Though it has not been completely eliminated, necessity is rarely invoked with any success. In a 1971 case, Lord Denning, one of England's most respected judges, cited *Dudley and Stephens* to reject a defense of necessity. Sounding a lot like the lord chief justice, John Duke Coleridge, he said that if one were recognized, it would "open a door which no man could shut" and "would be an excuse for all kinds of wrongdoing."

The impact in the United States has been even more pronounced. American law had expressly accepted the necessity defense before 1884. Justice Henry Baldwin made that clear in 1842 in *United States v. Holmes*, when he said that Alexander William Holmes would have been found not guilty if he had drawn lots and started out by tossing crewmembers overboard rather than passengers. No less an authority than Oliver Wendell Holmes, the scholar-turned-Supreme Court justice, wrote in his classic 1881 treatise *The Common Law* that "even the deliberate taking of life will not be punished when it is the only way of saving one's own." This principle was not uncontroversial, Holmes wrote, but he said that it "has the support of very great authority."

The rule changed as American courts began to follow *Dudley and Stephens*, especially in homicide cases. In 1931, Benjamin Cardozo, another great scholar and Supreme Court justice, wrote that "where two or more are overtaken by a common disaster, there is no right on the part of one to save the lives of some by the killing of another." In 2012, a criminal law professor wrote that the "traditional position" in American law—followed by most, though not all, courts—is that "the necessity defense is barred in all intent to kill homicide prosecutions, no matter how extreme the circumstances, and even if the killing of an innocent person would save a greater number of innocent lives." He attributed the adoption of this rule in significant part to "the influence of D & S"—that is, the *Dudley and Stephens* case.

The reason *Dudley and Stephens* has remained an object of fascination for close to a century and a half, though, is not its pathos, its humor, its coincidences, or even its impact on the law of homicide, significant though all those things are. It is, rather, that the case stands as an almost perfect real-world experiment about one of the great fault lines in philosophy: the debate between utilitarianism and rights-based moral theories. As moral philosophy professor Michael Sandel has been telling Harvard undergraduates for many years, each side in *Dudley and Stephens* represents one of these worldviews. On Dudley's side, he notes, are those who believe the killing of Parker is morally justified on the basis of providing "the greatest good for the greatest number." On the side of the Crown's prosecutors, he says, are those who believe it is "categorically wrong" because "murder is murder—it's always wrong."

"The Case for Cannibalism," as Sandel puts it in his course, is actually the case for a utilitarian approach to the predicament Dudley and Stephens found themselves in. *Dudley and Stephens* delivered a powerful argument for the other side—the case not so much against cannibalism but against cold-blooded cost-benefit analysis.

The decision in *Dudley and Stephens* came about because of the concerted efforts of three great Victorian-era reformers. When they learned about the events in the *Mignonette* lifeboat, they saw not only a human tragedy and a criminal act but a chance to bring an end to a practice they abhorred. Beyond that, they saw an opportunity to rewrite the laws of society in what they saw as a more ethical and humane way.

Sir John Walter Huddleston, the trial judge, believed that the killing of Parker was murder, and he was seemingly intent on handling the prosecution of Dudley and Stephens in a way that not only led to a conviction but established a national legal standard. He wanted a high court to rule that cannibalism at sea was murder and that a claim of "necessity" could never justify killing an innocent person.

William Harcourt, the home secretary, insisted that the killing of Parker be prosecuted as murder. When the defendants were convicted, he stood up to public pressure and the recommendation of the attorney general and refused to release them without punishment. Harcourt did not want the men to be executed, which was formally the only prescribed punishment for murder in England at the time, but he insisted that there should be real punishment, to make clear that cannibalism at sea was a real crime.

But it was the lord chief justice, the author of the decision in the case, who decided what the case would stand for. His opinion is one of the great refutations of the use of the necessity defense to a charge of murder—but it is also something more. It is, more broadly, a powerful rejection of utilitarian thinking. Lord Coleridge's written words have reverberated down through the ages. There will always be people who believe it is "necessary" to kill someone else—that taking away one life will result in saving the lives of others. *Dudley and Stephens* is firmly on the other side.

Lord Coleridge eloquently insisted that utilitarian calculations, like the decision to kill Parker, must be resisted, and he explained why. For one thing, he did not trust the way these calculations were done. "Who is to be the judge of this sort of necessity?" he asked. "By what measure is the comparative value of lives to be measured? Is it to be strength, or intellect, or what?"

There is always a bias when lives are weighed. Dudley said he believed that it was better to sacrifice one life rather than to let four die—a classic example of utilitarian hedonic calculus. When he put it that way, it sounded like he was treating all four lives as equal, but he never actually did. In the lifeboat, Dudley argued that Parker's life was less valuable than the other three because he had no wife and children—and later, because he was ill.

Lord Coleridge was skeptical of Dudley's decision that Parker should be the victim. He observed pointedly that the captain had chosen "a weak and unoffending boy" to sacrifice. That was certainly no accident. Dudley's lawyer was all too honest at the Exeter Assize when he told Baron Huddleston that "the weakest must fall for the protection of the others."

It is a powerful critique of utilitarianism in practice. The utilitarian says, "Trust me, I have worked out a procedure that will ensure that everyone is treated equally, and the outcome that is chosen will produce the greatest good for the greatest number." The response—for all the cabin boys, enslaved people, foreigners, and others at the bottom of one hierarchy or another—in Lord Coleridge's view should be *No, we do not trust you.*

The lord chief justice understood something else about utilitarian calculations: They rely on dubious and convenient claims about the future. Dudley asserted that it was right to kill Parker because it would save three lives. Killing him entailed one death, the captain insisted, while not killing him would have meant the deaths of four. But Lord Coleridge pointed out that Dudley could not know that if he did not kill Parker, then all four of them would have died. Events might have unfolded in other ways. "They might possibly have been picked up next day by a passing ship," he observed, and in that case killing Parker would have meant one death instead of none, and it would not have increased net happiness at all. In fact, shortly after Parker was killed, it rained, and the men were able to capture a considerable amount of freshwater, which perhaps might have allowed all the men to survive.

Most of all, though, the lord chief justice saw through the self-serving logic of Dudley's utilitarian calculation, or as he referred to it in his opinion, "necessity." It was an attempt to justify something awful, the cold-blooded murder of a harmless seventeen-year-old boy, by claiming a higher imperative. The simple, unalterable truth, Lord Coleridge said, was that there was no higher imperative and that any such killing was irreducibly wrong. He noted, with a quote from *Paradise Lost*, that bad actors often used appeals like these to excuse "devilish deeds."

Lord Coleridge's opinion in *Dudley and Stephens* changed the law of cannibalism at sea forever. That was a historic transformation and the end of an era, but it was not enormously important compared to other problems in Victorian England, and indeed it was fading in significance as the Age of Sail drew to a close and shipwrecks became increasingly rare. Although cannibalism was a subject of considerable popular fascination, it was not a societal problem on a large scale, like abusive factory working conditions or the oppression of women.

But Lord Coleridge was a reformer, in the best mold of the Victorian era, and he wanted the *Dudley and Stephens* opinion to be a force for societal progress beyond the narrow issue of cannibalism at sea. He was taking aim at the necessity defense and at all the utilitarian calculations that people make about why it is "necessary" to do evil things that serve their own interests.

The significance of *Dudley and Stephens* is very different now from what it was in 1884, when it was the much-anticipated resolution to a notorious cannibalism case. Today, the case stands as a soaring legal tower at one end of a great philosophical divide, because it represents the principle that human rights are critically important and lives should not be sacrificed based on utilitarian calculations. But the decision's lessons are far from merely academic. They speak powerfully to the real world, especially today.

Dudley and Stephens's main holding, about the need to defend individual rights in the face of utilitarian calculations, is an important moral and legal touchstone. Dictators have, throughout history, sought to justify atrocities through hedonic calculus. Adolf Hitler and Joseph Stalin insisted that their concentration camps, planned starvations, and other forms of mass murder were a step on the way toward building a better world. There will always be tyrants who argue that the dead bodies piling up will promote the greatest good for the greatest number. *Dudley and Stephens* represents a firm rebuke to all of them.

These days, though, utilitarian thinking is just as likely to be found in more mundane places. Today's Dudleys and Stephenses are liable to be corporate policymakers and faceless bureaucrats who crisply phase out individual lives with mathematical models and computer code. The killing can be done not with a penknife to the neck but with an iPad Pro.

Utilitarianism, it must be said, is not always a bad guide in setting public policy and making private choices. A strong case can be made for taking into account how many people will live or die, in the aggregate, when we set highway speed limits or ban an effective but dangerous pesticide. It makes sense to try to save as many lives as possible in the abstract—and, yes, to promote the greatest good for the greatest number. But utilitarianism becomes more problematic when there are identifiable victims who can be named in advance and when the utilitarian calculations collide with basic human rights.

One area where skepticism about utilitarianism is important is medicine. In health care, utilitarianism is often the default method of making decisions—we generally want to approve drugs that save lives and to prohibit hospital practices that cost them. But as Lord Coleridge explained in *Dudley and Stephens*, there are other considerations that must be taken into account, ones that can and often should override mere utilitarianism.

This ethical tension made a notable appearance at the start of the COVID-19 pandemic, when there was a shortage of ventilators in England. The British Medical Association, the doctors' trade union, declared that health professionals might have to remove ventilators from patients who were "stable or even improving" but had a "worse prognosis than other patients who required the same resources." It was a purely utilitarian calculus: Take the ventilator away from the patient whose life it might be saving and give it to a stronger patient with a better chance of surviving.

John Harris, a professor emeritus of applied philosophy at the University of Manchester, wrote a scathing response to the British Medical Association in the *Cambridge Quarterly of Healthcare Ethics*. The policy the union was asking its members to follow was "shockingly callous," he objected. It was also, he said, "almost certainly . . . unethical."

As Harris explained, a patient who was "stable or even improving" was presumably benefiting from the ventilator. If a doctor took it away and gave it to another patient, the first patient could die. Patients in the health care system "rightly expect to be treated and are entitled to the best of their doctors' and that system's abilities," Harris said. "They do not expect to be abandoned by those doctors in favor of other patients with a higher survival probability."

The policy the British Medical Association urged was not just immoral, Harris said; it was illegal. In explaining why, he reached back 136 years to the lord chief justice's ruling in *Dudley and Stephens*. And he entitled his essay "Why Kill the Cabin Boy?" Harris understood that the essential issue in the hospital and the lifeboat was the same: Someone had decided that if they could just end a particular person's life (or put it at heightened risk of ending), better things would result.

There are many more such examples in medicine. In a world of limited resources, there is always pressure to ration care. In discussions over how to allocate medical dollars, there are debates over how to value individual lives and parts of lives. There are debates over whether too much medical spending goes to the final years of life—and how much better it would be for some people if other people would shuffle off this mortal coil a little more quickly. At its extreme, this utilitarian thinking can be used to argue for involuntary euthanasia. This is hardly a hypothetical. There have been reports, notably from the Netherlands and Canada, of people put to death who have not given consent.

Medical care and medical ethics are subjects that are too complex to lend themselves to easy or absolute answers. It is said that doctors should consider "multiple ethical frameworks to find the right course of action." In this interplay, the rights-based position charted in *Dudley and Stephens* provides a crucial counterpoint to the always-present pressure from utilitarian budgeters. It stands on the side of those whose right to live might be silently given up through a hidden hedonic calculus.

The approach of the court in *Dudley and Stephens* bolsters the argument that a hospital should not move a patient who is benefiting from being in the ICU simply because a different patient might have better odds of benefiting from it, that an insurance company should not deny coverage for an expensive lifesaving drug simply because there are ways of spending the money someone might deem more efficient, and that no one should be rushed to die because a bureaucrat has decided the value of keeping them alive another year is not worth the cost. In all these scenarios, and many more, it argues that people have individual rights that should not be calculated away.

International human rights is another area where providing a counterpoint to utilitarianism has never been more important. Nations relentlessly pursue their own interests, which they reflexively equate with the greater good, and they often see human rights as an obstacle. The presumption that nations always have the right to pursue their interests is so strong that the question is often asked whether there are any absolute human rights at all: Do people have any rights that are so fundamental that nations cannot override them through hedonic calculus?

A classic debate on the issue is over whether people have a right not to be tortured, and it includes a famous hypothetical, the "ticking time bomb." After the terrorist attacks of September 11, 2001, there was considerable discussion of whether torture should be allowed as part of the war on terror. The question was posed whether, if there were a ticking time bomb in a major city, it was acceptable to override the usual prohibitions and torture a captured terrorist for the purpose of trying to find and defuse the bomb. Many academics and elected officials lined up to endorse the use of torture in these circumstances. The arguments in favor were utilitarian. Richard Posner, a professor at the University of Chicago Law School and a federal judge, sounded a lot like Dudley's lawyers arguing for killing Parker when he wrote, "There is such a thing as a lesser wrong committed to avoid a greater one." The right not to be tortured was not categorical, he said, and could be rescinded in the face of someone's calculation of the greater good.

Dudley and Stephens offers a basis for resisting these claims about torture and other incursions on human rights. The lord chief justice's dissection of Dudley's and Stephens's hedonic calculus regarding the killing of Parker sheds light on the ticking bomb. If he were around today and applied the same logic, Lord Coleridge would question the calculations that seek to defend the torture of another human being. How do you weigh the pain inflicted through torturing someone against the possibility, perhaps quite remote, that he might yield information to avert a catastrophe? He would also question the predictions about the future: How could anyone say whether the suspect knows the location of the bomb, whether the torture would elicit the information, and whether the information would have any effect on whether the bomb went off and did damage? Above all, he would question the whole enterprise of removing the categorical prohibition on something evil, like torture, to achieve some preferred outcome. He would be worried that it would become a cloak for "atrocious crime."

Arguments like the lord chief justice's can be effective. Utilitarian formulations like "the greatest good for the greatest number" sound attractive, but most people appreciate the value of individual rights. When the BBC conducted a poll asking more than twenty-seven thousand people in twenty-five countries whether torture should be allowed in order to obtain information that could save innocent lives in a terrorist attack, 59 percent said no. Even when presented with the potential benefits of such instances of torture, the BBC reported, most "agree[d] that clear rules against torture in prisons should be maintained because it is immoral and its use would weaken human rights standards."

The area in which *Dudley and Stephens* and its championing of individual rights may be most needed in the days ahead is in the brave new world that artificial intelligence is ushering in. This will be a highly contested realm because the rules for machine behavior must be thought through in advance, and there is as yet no agreement on what they should be. It is easy to fall by default into utilitarianism. There is a superficial appeal to the idea that the best thing to do is to produce machines coded to produce the greatest good for the greatest number. But the problem with any such hedonic calculations is that they overlook the importance of individual rights. A utilitarian designing a self-driving car would likely program it to minimize the loss of life when it gets into a dangerous situation. So if a car carrying four passengers is forced to quickly decide whether to crash into a wall and kill the four people in the car or swerve and run over a single pedestrian, it would kill the one pedestrian. The car designer would, like Dudley in the lifeboat, insist that losing one life was better than losing four.

Viewed through the frame of the *Dudley and Stephens* ruling, the flaw in this logic is readily apparent. The pedestrian is not in the car and has not assumed the risks that driving in an autonomous car entails. The pedestrian may not approve of autonomous cars at all. As the pedestrian walks down the sidewalk, happily living the life of a luddite, by what right does a self-driving car coder decide that the pedestrian's life will be sacrificed to save four people who have chosen to travel in a driverless car?

Some ethicists argue that the companies that set the algorithms for self-driving cars should move "beyond harm minimization." They call for rules that would prevent self-driving cars from swerving onto sidewalks or other places where they would violate the rights of "uninvolved" people who are not benefiting from self-driving cars. In this view, uninvolved people have the same right as Richard Parker should have had: to not lose their lives because someone else decided that killing them would save more lives and thereby serve the greater good.

Utilitarianism will always be with us, and as the world grows more complicated and more decisions are made for us by nameless policymakers and computer coders—and by artificial intelligence—we are likely to see more of it. *Dudley and Stephens* provides a model for pushing back. As Harris recognized at the start of the COVID-19 pandemic, it is always available to resist other people's calculations of what produces the most "good" and to insist on saving the cabin boy.

People who read the lord chief justice's opinion in *Dudley and Stephens* sometimes say that it is very much a product of its time, and it is. It was written in 1884, and that shows in many ways: the florid language about how people should stand ready to sacrifice their own lives, the insistence that England is a Christian nation whose entire population (regardless of individuals' personal religious beliefs) must model themselves on Jesus, and the romanticization of British soldiers who insisted that women and children evacuate first on their way to fight an imperialist, colonial war in Africa.

Those are some of the ways the decision reflects the worst of Victorian England, but in its most important elements, it represents the best of that era. The lord chief justice wrote his opinion at the height of an age that achieved a great deal of social and legal reform. In most places and times, governments work to advance the interests of the powerful. As Jean-Jacques Rousseau observed, "The universal spirit of laws, in all countries, is to favor the strong in opposition to the weak, and to assist those who have possessions against those who have none." In Victorian England, though, the government often did the opposite.

The Victorian reformers were driven by two overarching goals. They fought to lift up those at the bottom of society, and they worked to establish a set of legal rights that would protect people from being oppressed by those with more power. The ruling in *Dudley and Stephens* did both of these things. It made clear that the law would not countenance Dudley and Stephens's selection of the lowliest person in the lifeboat to be sacrificed. Rather than siding with the "strong," as Rousseau lamented society generally did, the ruling established a national standard protecting the interests of the young, sick, unsuspecting cabin boy, the weakest person in the lifeboat.

In standing up for Parker, the lord chief justice was coming to the defense of everyone at the bottom of a social hierarchy. He was striking a blow for every enslaved person, every Black man, every fourteen-year-old boy, and every Spaniard or dark-skinned Italian on a ship of Englishmen over the centuries who had been told that a decision had been made, and they would be the one to be sacrificed.

The fundamental principle underlying it all was the Victorian reformers' commitment to what would today be called human rights. Lord Coleridge believed Parker had the right to his own life—to live it and to keep living it as long as he was able to. And he believed it was a crime for Dudley and Stephens to take it away from him based on their self-serving calculations.

One thing that can be said about life is that, contrary to the assumptions Dudley was willing to make when he decided it was time to kill his cabin boy, there is no way of knowing how things will turn out. The lord chief justice pointed this out when he said that all four of the men might have been picked up the next day by a passing ship. Justice Cardozo expressed this idea more eloquently in a book about law and literature. "Who shall know," Cardozo asked, "when the masts and sails of rescue may emerge out of the fog?"

And so it was with Parker as Dudley moved toward him and brought a knife up to his throat. Dudley's actions reduced Parker to a thing to be bargained away in a cost-benefit analysis—no longer a shipmate or a young friend to be aided through their shared ordeal but merely food to keep him and two other men alive. Parker saw himself differently, as a human being who wanted to survive and might still. Sick though he was, the seventeen-year-old Parker never wavered in his will to live. He "expressed hope every day," Stephens recalled, "that we should see a ship." Had he lived just a few more days, he would have.

It was that hope of staying alive to live a full life that Dudley and Stephens stole from him. They did it by self-interested calculations and an appeal to necessity, which the lord chief justice likened to the strategy of John Milton's Devil. In the view of the progressive reformers of the Victorian era who produced this momentous decision—as in the view of human-rights champions in our own time—no matter how low people are on the economic or social hierarchy, no matter how young, or how hungry, or how sick, their lives belong to them and them alone. They have the right, until they breathe their last breath, to stare out into the fog undisturbed, searching for a mast and a sail.

NOTES

The key phrases (in boldface) correspond to the first words of the relevant paragraph in the text.

Introduction

xi **On September 6:** "Frightful Privations at Sea," *Daily News* (London), September 8, 1884.

xi **When Dudley, Stephens, and Brooks arrived:** "Frightful Privations."

xii **Sailors had long been killing:** A. W. Brian Simpson, *Cannibalism and the Common Law: The Story of the Tragic Last Voyage of the Mignonette and the Strange Legal Proceedings to Which It Gave Rise* (Chicago: University of Chicago Press, 1984).

xii **What followed:** G. H. Harrington, letter, *Singapore Daily Times*, November 13, 1874, quoted in A. W. B. Simpson, "*Queen v. Archer and Muller* (1875): The Leading Case That Never Was," *Oxford Journal of Legal Studies* 2, no. 2 (Summer 1982): 186.

xiii ***Queen v. Dudley and Stephens:*** Queen v. Dudley and Stephens, (1884) 14 QBD 27 (DC).

xiii ***Dudley and Stephens:*** Michael Sandel, "Justice," Harvard University, https://scholar.harvard.edu/sandel/justice.

xiv **Not least:** Luis A. Cordon, *Freud's World: An Encyclopedia of His Life and Times* (Santa Barbara, CA: Greenwood, 2012), 166.

xiv **People have always liked:** Scott Harshbarger, "Grimm and Grimmer: 'Hansel and Gretel' and Fairy Tale Nationalism," *Style* 47, no. 4 (Winter 2013): 490; Piers Paul Read, *Alive: The Story of the Andes Survivors* (New York: William Morrow, 2002).

xiv **Cannibalism is also:** "Lifeboat (Cannibalism) as Featured in *Monty Python's Flying Circus* Episode 26," https://web.archive.org/web/20090908023935/http://orangecow.org/pythonet/sketches/lifeboat.htm.

xv **But the main reason:** Exodus 20:13; James P. McDermott, "Animals and Humans in Early Buddhism," *Indo-Iranian Journal* 32, no. 4 (October 1989): 229, 271.

xv **Spiritual and moral traditions:** "Just War—Introduction," BBC, https://www.bbc.co.uk/ethics/war/just/introduction.shtml; David Kopel, "Self-Defense in Asian Religions," *Liberty University Law Review* 2, no. 1 (2007): 107, 140; Exodus 22:2; David Kopel, "The Torah and Self-Defense," *University of Pennsylvania Law Review* 109 (2004): 27; Niaz A. Shah, "The Use of Force Under Islamic Law," *European Journal of International Law* 24, no. 1 (2013): 343; *The Holy Bible, Containing the Old and New Testaments: The Revised Berkeley Version in Modern English: A Completely New Translation from the Original Languages*, trans. Gerrit Verkuyl (Nashville: Gideons International, 1974).

xvi ***Dudley and Stephens* presents:** Katell Berthelot, "A Classical Ethical Problem in Ancient Philosophy and Rabbinic Thought: The Case of the Shipwrecked," *Harvard Theological Review*, April 2013, 171, 173–75.

xvii **Dudley's rationale:** "Jeremy Bentham," in *Stanford Encyclopedia of Philosophy* (Stanford University, 1997–), https://plato.stanford.edu/entries/bentham/.

xvii On the other side: Michelle Cotton, "The Necessity Defense and the Moral Limits of Law," *New Criminal Law Review: An International and Interdisciplinary Journal* 18, no. 1 (2015): 47.

xvii In the end, England's High Court: Queen v. Dudley and Stephens, (1884) 14 QBD 27.

1. The Voyage Begins

1 By 1883: A. W. Brian Simpson, *Cannibalism and the Common Law: The Story of the Tragic Last Voyage of the Mignonette and the Strange Legal Proceedings to Which It Gave Rise* (Chicago: University of Chicago Press, 1984), 20.

1 In an era when ships: Lincoln Paine, *The Sea and Civilization: A Maritime History of the World* (New York: Vintage Books, 2013) 538; Simpson, *Cannibalism and the Common Law*, 20.

1 The younger Want: Simpson, *Cannibalism and the Common Law*, 17–21; Queen v. Dudley and Stephens (Murder on the High Seas) Official Record (Bound Volume), National Archives DPP 4/17, p. 13 (Dudley, "Account of Foundering 'Mignonette'") (hereafter cited as Queen v. Dudley and Stephens OR).

2 There were some fine things: Queen v. Dudley and Stephens OR, National Archives DPP 4/17, pp. 21–22 (Form Number 19 MRVS); Simpson, *Cannibalism and the Common Law*, 17–19.

2 The *Mignonette* came with a wooden dinghy: Simpson, *Cannibalism and the Common Law*, 19; Queen v. Dudley and Stephens (Murder on the High Seas) Official Record (Bound Volume), National Archives DPP 4/17, p. 8 (Examination of Dudley).

3 The *Mignonette* had one other: Queen v. Dudley and Stephens OR, National Archives DPP 4/17, p. 13 (Form Number 19 MRVS) and 4/17, p. 8 (Examination of Dudley); "Thrilling Narrative of Shipwreck," *Belfast News-Letter*, September 8, 1884.

3 **After Want bought the *Mignonette*:** Simpson, *Cannibalism and the Common Law*, 21.

3 **Want made clear:** Jamie L. Bronstein, *Caught in the Machinery: Workplace Accidents and Injured Workers in Nineteenth-Century Britain* (Palo Alto: Stanford University Press, 2007); Ike Matthews, *Full Revelations of a Professional Rat-Catcher After 25 Years' Experience* (Manchester: Friendly Societies' Printing, 1898), part 3, https://www.gutenberg.org/files/17243/17243-h/17243-h.htm.

4 **The London Yacht Agency:** Simpson, *Cannibalism and the Common Law*, 19, 21, 40; Queen v. Dudley and Stephens OR, National Archives DPP 4/17, p. 13 (Dudley, "Account of Foundering 'Mignonette'").

4 **The yacht agency's search:** Asha Hornsby, "Nautical Metaphors and the Late-Victorian Literary Culture," *Review of English Studies* 75, no. 320 (2024): 334–53; Robert Foulke, "Life in the Dying World of Sail, 1870–1910," *Journal of British Studies* 3, no. 3 (1963): 105.

4 **From England's earliest days:** David Loades, review of *The Safeguard of the Sea*, by N. A. M. Rodger, *War in History*, November 2000, 481.

4 **When Britain's sailing ships:** Peter E. Pope, *The Many Landfalls of John Cabot* (Toronto: University of Toronto Press, 1997); Foulke, "Life in the Dying World of Sail," 105–36.

5 **For centuries:** Beverly Lemire, "'Men of the World': British Mariners, Consumer Practice, and Material Culture in an Era of Global Trade, c. 1660–1800," *Journal of British Studies* 54, no. 2 (April 2015): 288, 291.

5 **Now the Age of Sail was ending:** Paul Bairoch and Gary Goertz, "Factors of Urbanisation in the Nineteenth Century

Developed Countries: A Descriptive and Econometric Analysis," *Urban Studies* 23 (1986): 288.

5 **Signs of transformation:** Foulke, "Life in the Dying World of Sail," 105–36; Simpson, *Cannibalism and the Common Law*, 21, 40; Max Fletcher, "The Suez Canal and World Shipping, 1869–1914," *Journal of Economic History* 18, no. 4 (December 1958): 558.

6 **The year 1883:** Fletcher, "Suez Canal and World Shipping," 562; Foulke, "Life in the Dying World of Sail," 105.

6 **New technologies:** Foulke, "Life in the Dying World of Sail," 128, 134; Graeme J. Milne, "The Steamship and the Making of a Globalized World," *Topmasts*, special issue (2020): 6; Thomas Brassey, *British Seamen: Recent Parliamentary and Official Documents* (London: Longmans, Green, 1877), 326.

6 **Working conditions:** Milne, "Steamship and the Making of a Globalized World," 5–6; Frank Knight, *The Sea Story*, quoted in Foulke, "Life in the Dying World of Sail," 106, 136; Joseph Conrad, *An Outcast of the Islands* (London: Dent, 1923), 13.

7 **Individual sailors:** Foulke, "Life in the Dying World of Sail," 136; Tim Carter, "From Sail to Steam: Changing Risks and Requirements for Seafarers," *Topmasts*, special issue (2020): 12–13; Milne, "Steamship and the Making of a Globalized World," 6.

7 **As it happened:** Queen v. Dudley and Stephens OR, National Archives DPP 4/17, p. 13 (Dudley, "Account of Foundering 'Mignonette'"); Simpson, *Cannibalism and the Common Law*, 21–23; "The Survivors of the Mignonette," *Western Mail* (Cardiff, Wales), September 11, 1884.

8 **In some ways, Dudley:** Crew List, National Archives, Queen v. Dudley and Stephens File, DPP 4/17, pp. 25–26; Simpson, *Cannibalism and the Common Law*, 21–23; "The Charge of

Murder and Cannibalism," *Daily Gazette for Middlesbrough*, September 11, 1884.

8 **Dudley did not cut:** Letter of Philippa Dudley to Ellis Lever, February 19, 1885, A36934, National Archives; "The Horrible Straits of the 'Mignonette,'" *Cornishman* (Penzance, England), September 11, 1884.

8 **There was one more quality:** "Survivors of the Mignonette."

9 **But Dudley wanted the job:** Letter of Philippa Dudley to Ellis Lever, February 19, 1885, A36934, National Archives; Simpson, *Cannibalism and the Common Law*, 25–26; "The Terrible Tale of the Sea," *Sunderland Daily Echo and Shipping Gazette*, September 10, 1884.

9 **The sailing life was especially brutal:** Foulke, "Life in the Dying World of Sail," 134–36; Carter, "From Sail to Steam," 12–13; Milne, "Steamship and the Making of a Globalized World," 6; Brassey, *British Seamen*, 326.

9 **In fact, Dudley had tried:** "The Terrible Tale of the Sea: Message from the Captain," *Sunderland Daily Echo and Shipping Gazette*, September 10, 1884; Simpson, *Cannibalism and the Common Law*, 28; "The Tale of the Sea," *Daily Gazette for Middlesbrough*, September 9, 1884.

10 **There was another consideration:** Simpson, *Cannibalism and the Common Law*, 27–28; Letter of Philippa Dudley to Ellis Lever, February 19, 1885, A36934, National Archives.

10 **Australia was in the midst:** Eric Richards, "How Did Poor People Emigrate from the British Isles to Australia in the Nineteenth Century?," *Journal of British Studies* 32, no. 3 (July 1993): 256; Paul Smyth, "The British Social Policy Legacy in Australia," in *Colonialism and Welfare: Social Policy and the British Imperial Legacy* (Cheltenham, UK: Edward Elgar, 2011), 176.

10 **Dudley got his wish:** Queen v. Dudley and Stephens OR, National Archives DPP 4/17, p. 13 (Dudley, "Account of

Foundering 'Mignonette'"); "Cannibalism for Life's Sake," *Cornishman* (Penzance, England), September 11, 1884.

11 **As the day of departure drew near:** Monique Layton, *Life at Sea: From Caravels to Cruise Ships* (Victoria, BC: FriesenPress, 2017), 203, 206; Lincoln Paine, *The Sea and Civilization: A Maritime History of the World* (New York: Vintage Books, 2013), 475.

11 **Disaster always loomed:** Layton, *Life at Sea*, 206; John Flavel, "Navigation Spiritualized," in *The Whole Works of John Flavel: Late Minister of the Gospel at Dartmouth, Devon* (London: W. Baynes and Son, 1820), 5:206; Monique Layton, *Voices from the Lower Deck: Folklore and Folkways of the Sea* (Victoria, BC: FriesenPress, 2019).

12 **For a captain seeking a crew:** Layton, *Life at Sea*, 205; Mark Strecker, *Shanghaiing Sailors: A Maritime History of Forced Labor, 1849–1915* (Jefferson, NC: McFarland, 2014); Judith Fingard, "Masters and Friends, Crimps and Abstainers: Agents of Control in 19th Century Sailortown," *Acadiensis* 8, no. 1 (Autumn 1978): 22–23.

12 **In early May, Dudley packed:** Letter of Philippa Dudley to Ellis Lever, February 19, 1885, A36934, National Archives.

13 **On May 3, Dudley left home:** Queen v. Dudley and Stephens OR, National Archives DPP 4/17, p. 13 (Dudley, "Account of Foundering 'Mignonette'"); "Narratives by Brooks and Stephens," *Cornishman* (Penzance, England), September 18, 1884; Simpson, *Cannibalism and the Common Law*, 28.

13 **While he was in Tollesbury:** "Alleged Murder & Cannibalism by Essex Sailors," *Essex Standard* (Colchester, England), September 13, 1884; Simpson, *Cannibalism and the Common Law*, 28–29.

13 **The voyage got off to a rocky start:** Queen v. Dudley and Stephens OR, National Archives DPP 4/17, p. 13 (Dudley, "Account

of Foundering 'Mignonette'"); "Cannibalism for Life's Sake"; Simpson, *Cannibalism and the Common Law*, 28–29.

14 **There were also problems:** "Narratives by Brooks and Stephens"; Crew List, National Archives, Queen v. Dudley and Stephens File, DPP 4/17, pp. 25–26; Queen v. Dudley and Stephens OR, National Archives DPP 4/17, p. 13 (Dudley, "Account of Foundering 'Mignonette'"); Queen v. Dudley and Stephens OR, National Archives DPP 4/17, p. 21 (Account of Changes in the Crew of Foreign Going Ship Before Final Departure from the United Kingdom).

14 **That same day:** "Narratives by Brooks and Stephens"; Crew List, National Archives, Queen v. Dudley and Stephens File, DPP 4/17.

14 **Brooks had some concerns:** "Account of Changes in the Crew of Foreign Going Ship Before Final Departure," National Archive DPP/17, pp. 20–22; "The Horrible Straits of the Men of the Mignonette," *Cornishman* (Penzance, England), September 25, 1884; "Thrilling Narrative of Shipwreck"; "Narratives by Brooks and Stephens."

15 **Dudley now had his crew:** Crew List, National Archives, Queen v. Dudley and Stephens File, DPP 4/17, pp. 25–26; "Survivors of the Mignonette"; Simpson, *Cannibalism and the Common Law*, 30–32.

15 **Stephens was born:** "Survivors of the Mignonette"; Simpson, *Cannibalism and the Common Law*, 31–34.

15 **That is when he suffered:** "The Wreck of the Mail Steamer European," *Daily News* (London), December 10, 1877; Simpson, *Cannibalism and the Common Law*, 32–34.

16 **But Stephens was drawn:** Crew List, National Archives, Queen v. Dudley and Stephens File, DPP 4/17, pp. 25–26; "The Charge of Cannibalism," *Standard* (London), September 11, 1884.

16 **There was one more position:** Crew List, National Archives, Queen v. Dudley and Stephens File, DPP 4/17, pp. 25–26; Simpson, *Cannibalism and the Common Law*, 36–39; "The Terrible Tale of the Sea," *Liverpool Mercury*, September 16, 1884.

17 **Parker had endured:** "Terrible Tale of the Sea," *Liverpool Mercury*, September 16, 1884; Letter of Philippa Dudley to Ellis Lever, February 19, 1885, A36934, National Archives.

17 **Parker's life had improved:** "Survivors of the Mignonette"; "Charge of Murder and Cannibalism"; "The Mignonette Cannibalism Case," *Daily News* (London), November 7, 1884.

18 **For a seventeen-year-old:** "Charge of Murder and Cannibalism."

18 **Parker learned:** "The Cannibalism by English Sailors," *Western Mail* (Cardiff, Wales), September 16, 1884.

18 **When Parker met with Dudley:** Crew List, National Archives, Queen v. Dudley and Stephens File, DPP 4/17, pp. 25–26; "Terrible Tale of the Sea," *Liverpool Mercury*, September 16, 1884; Simpson, *Cannibalism and the Common Law*, 30, 38; Letter of Philippa Dudley to Ellis Lever, February 19, 1885, A36934, National Archives.

19 **What won Parker over:** "Cannibalism by English Sailors."

19 **Parker went to the Southampton Custom House:** Queen v. Dudley and Stephens OR, National Archives DPP 4/17, p. 26 (Agreement and Account of Crew).

19 **Parker's brother Daniel:** "Cannibalism by English Sailors."

19 **As "master" of the *Mignonette:*** Queen v. Dudley and Stephens OR, National Archives DPP 4/17, pp. 21–25 (Account of Changes in the Crew of Foreign Going Ship Before Final Departure from the United Kingdom); "More Than a List of Crew," Maritime History Archive, https://mha.mun.ca/mha/mlc/toolkit/history/; Simpson, *Cannibalism and the Common Law*, 21, 40; "What Was the Clipper Route?," World

Atlas, https://www.worldatlas.com/articles/what-was-the-clipper-route.html.

20 Dudley chose: "Narratives by Brooks and Stephens"; Simpson, *Cannibalism and the Common Law*, 41.

20 Dudley had chosen: Andrew Hassam, *Sailing to Australia: Shipboard Diaries by Nineteenth Century British Emigrants* (Manchester: Manchester University Press, 1994), 8; "The Wreck of the Arniston," *Untold Lives* blog, British Library, May 25, 2023, https://blogs.bl.uk/untoldlives/2023/05/the-wreck-of-the-arniston.html.

20 Nevertheless, yachts: Simpson, *Cannibalism and the Common Law*, 42.

21 There was one more matter: Queen v. Dudley and Stephens OR, National Archives DPP 4/17, p. 24 (Agreement and Account of Crew); Simpson, *Cannibalism and the Common Law*, 30; Letter of Philippa Dudley to Ellis Lever, February 19, 1885, A36934, National Archives; "More Than a List of Crew."

12 On May 19: "Narratives by Brooks and Stephens"; Simpson, *Cannibalism and the Common Law*, 39.

22 Parker did not give: Queen v. Dudley and Stephens OR, National Archives DPP 4/17, p. 14 (Dudley, "Account of Foundering 'Mignonette'"); "Cannibalism by English Sailors."

2. The Wreck of the Mignonette

23 Late in the afternoon: Queen v. Dudley and Stephens (Murder on the High Seas) Official Record (Bound Volume), National Archives DPP 4/17, p. 14 (Dudley, "Account of Foundering 'Mignonette'") (hereafter cited as Queen v. Dudley and Stephens OR); "Narratives by Brooks and Stephens," *Cornishman* (Penzance, England), September 18, 1884.

23 On the morning of May 21: Queen v. Dudley and Stephens OR, National Archives DPP 4/17, p. 13 (Dudley, "Account of

Foundering 'Mignonette'"); A. W. Brian Simpson, *Cannibalism and the Common Law: The Story of the Tragic Last Voyage of the Mignonette and the Strange Legal Proceedings to Which It Gave Rise* (Chicago: University of Chicago Press, 1984), 43; Herman Melville, *Moby-Dick*, chap. 14; "Cannibalism for Life's Sake," *Cornishman* (Penzance, England), September 11, 1884.

24 At midnight: "Cannibalism for Life's Sake"; Jason W. Moore, "Madeira, Sugar, and the Conquest of Nature in the 'First' Sixteenth Century, Part I," *Review* (Fernand Braudel Center) 32, no. 4 (2009): 345, 358.

24 The *Mignonette* sailed: "The Horrible Straits of the 'Mignonette,'" *Cornishman* (Penzance, England), September 25, 1884; "Narratives by Brooks and Stephens"; Queen v. Dudley and Stephens OR, National Archives DPP 4/17, p. 14 (Dudley, "Account of Foundering 'Mignonette'").

25 As the *Mignonette* continued: Queen v. Dudley and Stephens OR, National Archives DPP 4/17, p. 13 (Dudley, "Account of Foundering 'Mignonette'"); "Cannibalism for Life's Sake."

25 There were seafaring traditions: Layton, *Life at Sea*, 149, 157–59, 165.

25 There does not seem to have been a ceremony: Queen v. Dudley and Stephens OR, National Archives DPP 4/17, p. 14 (Dudley, "Account of Foundering 'Mignonette'"); "Horrible Tale of the Sea," *Reynolds's Newspaper* (London), September 14, 1884.

26 The real trouble began: Queen v. Dudley and Stephens OR, National Archives DPP 4/17, p. 15 (Dudley, "Account of Foundering 'Mignonette'"); Carly Cassella, "This Is a 'Cross Sea.' You Do Not Want to Get Caught in One," ScienceAlert, June 1, 2019; Howard Patterson, *Patterson's Illustrated Nautical Encyclopedia* (Cleveland: Marine Review Publishing, 1901), 90.

26 **As the *Mignonette* rocked:** Queen v. Dudley and Stephens OR, National Archives DPP 4/17, p. 15 (Dudley, "Account of Foundering 'Mignonette'"); "Thrilling Narrative of Shipwreck," *Belfast News-Letter*, September 8, 1884; Simpson, *Cannibalism and the Common Law*, 46.

26 **Then, as suddenly:** Queen v. Dudley and Stephens OR, National Archives DPP 4/17, p. 15 (Dudley, "Account of Foundering 'Mignonette'"); "Thrilling Narrative of Shipwreck"; "Narratives by Brooks and Stephens."

27 **Dudley and the crew:** "The Cannibal Yachtsmen," *Bristol Mercury*, September 19, 1884; "Narratives by Brooks and Stephens"; Simpson, *Cannibalism and the Common Law*, 46.

27 **Being in a boat:** Stephen Crane, "The Open Boat," in *Classic American Short Stories*, ed. Paul Moliken (Clayton, DE: Prestwick House, 2006), 84.

27 **With danger looming:** Queen v. Dudley and Stephens OR, National Archives DPP 4/17, p. 13 (Dudley, "Account of Foundering 'Mignonette'"); Queen v. Dudley and Stephens OR, National Archives DPP 4/17, p. 9 (Examination of Dudley); "Narratives by Brooks and Stephens"; Simpson, *Cannibalism and the Common Law*, 46.

28 **Just after Parker reemerged:** "The Cannibalism at Sea," *Royal Cornwall Gazette* (Truro, England), September 19, 1884; Queen v. Dudley and Stephens OR, National Archives DPP 4/17, p. 13 (Dudley, "Account of Foundering 'Mignonette'"); Queen v. Dudley and Stephens OR, National Archives DPP 4/17, p. 9 (Examination of Dudley); "Narratives by Brooks and Stephens."

28 **Brooks had come up:** Queen v. Dudley and Stephens OR, National Archives DPP 4/17, p. 9 (Examination of Dudley); "Narratives by Brooks and Stephens."

28 The force of the ocean: "Narratives by Brooks and Stephens"; "Cannibal Yachtsmen"; Queen v. Dudley and Stephens OR, National Archives DPP 4/17, p. 13 (Dudley, "Account of Foundering 'Mignonette'").

29 The men looked on in horror: Queen v. Dudley and Stephens OR, National Archives DPP 4/17, p. 11 (Examination of Stephens); Queen v. Dudley and Stephens OR, National Archives DPP 4/17, p. 9 (Examination of Dudley).

29 For the next five minutes: "The Wreck of the Mignonette," *Liverpool Mercury*, September 11, 1884; "Narratives by Brooks and Stephens"; Queen v. Dudley and Stephens OR, National Archives DPP 4/17, p. 84 (Testimony of Edmund Brooks).

29 Since there were no provisions: "The Cannibalism at Sea," *Grantham Journal*, September 20, 1884; Queen v. Dudley and Stephens OR, National Archives DPP 4/17, p. 13 (Dudley, "Account of Foundering 'Mignonette'"); "Thrilling Narrative of Shipwreck"; Simpson, *Cannibalism and the Common Law*, 47.

29 First, he went on his own: Queen v. Dudley and Stephens OR, National Archives DPP 4/17, p. 16 (Dudley, "Account of Foundering 'Mignonette'"); Queen v. Dudley and Stephens OR, National Archives DPP 4/17, p. 9 (Examination of Dudley); "Cannibalism at Sea," *Royal Cornwall Gazette*, September 19, 1884; "The Mignonette Cannibalism Case," *Daily News* (London), September 19, 1884; Simpson, *Cannibalism and the Common Law*, 47.

30 Brooks steadied the lifeboat: Queen v. Dudley and Stephens OR, National Archives DPP 4/17, p. 16 (Dudley, "Account of Foundering 'Mignonette'"); "The Terrible Tale of the Sea," *Daily Gazette for Middlesbrough* (Middlesbrough, England), September 8, 1884.

30 **Water was pouring into the *Mignonette*:** Queen v. Dudley and Stephens OR, National Archives DPP 4/17, p. 86 (Testimony of Edmund Brooks); "Cannibalism at Sea," *Royal Cornwall Gazette*, September 19, 1884; "Narratives by Brooks and Stephens"; Simpson, *Cannibalism and the Common Law*, 48; Queen v. Dudley and Stephens OR, National Archives DPP 4/17, p. 9 (Examination of Dudley).

30 **The men had escaped:** Queen v. Dudley and Stephens OR, National Archives DPP 4/17, pp. 16–17 (Dudley, "Account of Foundering 'Mignonette'"); Queen v. Dudley and Stephens OR, National Archives DPP 4/17, p. 9 (Examination of Dudley); "The Case of Cannibalism," *Manchester Times* (Manchester, England), September 20, 1884.

31 **There is no way of knowing:** "Thrilling Narrative of Shipwreck"; Simpson, *Cannibalism and the Common Law*, 50–53.

31 **The men had not been pulled down:** "Narratives by Brooks and Stephens"; Simpson, *Cannibalism and the Common Law*, 19; Queen v. Dudley and Stephens OR, National Archives DPP 4/17, p. 8 (Examination of Dudley).

31 **The men's immediate concern:** Queen v. Dudley and Stephens OR, National Archives DPP 4/17, p. 17 (Dudley, "Account of Foundering 'Mignonette'"); "Cannibalism at Sea," *Lloyd's Illustrated Newspaper* (London), September 14, 1884; "Thrilling Narrative of Shipwreck"; Simpson, *Cannibalism and the Common Law*, 47.

32 **Brooks stopped up the hole:** Letter of Philippa Dudley to Ellis Lever, February 26, 1885, Doc. A 36934/25, National Archives, Regina v. Dudley and Stephens File; "Narratives by Brooks and Stephens"; "The Cannibalism at Sea," *Standard* (London), September 13, 1884; Simpson, *Cannibalism and the Common Law*, 48–49.

32 Fragile and drenched: Queen v. Dudley and Stephens OR, National Archives DPP 4/17, p. 9 (Examination of Dudley); Queen v. Dudley and Stephens OR, National Archives DPP 4/17, p. 13 (Dudley, "Account of Foundering 'Mignonette'"); "The Terrible Tale of the Sea," *Penny Illustrated Paper* (London), September 20, 1884.

32 Even if they managed: "The Mignonette Cannibalism Case: The Trial for Murder," *Reynolds's Newspaper* (London), November 9, 1884.

32 But the greatest threat of all: Queen v. Dudley and Stephens OR, National Archives DPP 4/17, p. 86 (Testimony of Edmund Brooks); Queen v. Dudley and Stephens OR, National Archives DPP 4/17, p. 9 (Examination of Dudley); "Cannibalism at Sea," *Royal Cornwall Gazette*, September 19, 1884; "The Terrible Story of the Sea," *North Devon Journal* (Barnstaple, England), September 25, 1884.

33 As the excitement: "The Mignonette Tragedy," *Cornishman* (Penzance, England), September 18, 1884; Queen v. Dudley and Stephens OR, National Archives DPP 4/17, p. 17 (Dudley, "Account of Foundering 'Mignonette'"); Nikki Wither, "How Far Away Is the Horizon?," BBC Science Focus, https://www.sciencefocus.com/planet-earth/how-far-away-is-the-horizon.

33 The castaways did not know: "The Survivors of the Mignonette," *Western Mail* (Cardiff, Wales), September 11, 1884; Simpson, *Cannibalism and the Common Law*, 49.

33 It was not only the continents: "Narratives by Brooks and Stephens"; Simpson, *Cannibalism and the Common Law*, 48–49; Queen v. Dudley and Stephens OR, National Archives DPP 4/17, p. 88 (Testimony of Edmund Brooks).

34 Making matters worse: W. H. Smith, "The Duty to Render Assistance at Sea: Is It Effective or Adrift?," *California*

Western International Law Journal 2, no. 1 (1971): 146–63; Irini Papanicolopulu, "The Historical Origins of the Duty to Save Life at Sea in International Law," *Journal of the History of International Law* 24 (2022): 149, 179; Steven F. Friedell, "Compensation and Reward for Saving Life at Sea," *Michigan Law Review* 77 (May 1979): 1218, 1226–29, 1231; Jason Parent, "No Duty to Save Lives, No Reward for Rescue: Is that Truly the Current State of International Salvage Law," *Annual Survey of International & Comparative Law* 12 (2006): 87, 90.

35 **The first night in the dinghy:** Queen v. Dudley and Stephens OR, National Archives DPP 4/17, p. 17 (Dudley, "Account of Foundering 'Mignonette'"); "Cannibalism at Sea," *Royal Cornwall Gazette*, September 19, 1884; Simpson, *Cannibalism and the Common Law*, 48–49.

35 **As soon as the shark was gone:** Henry Coleman Folkard, *Sailing Boats from Around the World: The Classic 1906 Treatise* (Mineola, NY: Dover, 2000), 156; Simpson, *Cannibalism and the Common Law*, 55.

35 **The men made it through:** "Mignonette Cannibalism Case"; "Narratives by Brooks and Stephens"; Simpson, *Cannibalism and the Common Law*, 56.

36 **Somehow, the men:** "Narratives by Brooks and Stephens"; Michael G. Mallin, "In Warm Blood: Some Historical and Procedural Aspects of *Regina v. Dudley and Stephens*," *University of Chicago Law Review* 34, no. 2 (Winter 1967).

36 **The day after the *Mignonette* sank:** Simpson, *Cannibalism and the Common Law*, 48–49; Mallin, "In Warm Blood," 387, 388; "The Cannibalism at Sea," *Standard* (London), September 12, 1884.

37 **As the men settled:** "The Case of Cannibalism at Sea," *Morning Post* (London), September 19, 1884; Copy Record

of Indictment, Trial and Verdict, Queen v. Dudley and Stephens, National Archives, Queen v. Dudley and Stephens File, DPP 4/17, p. 35.

37 **The men's instincts:** Alan Lieberson, "How Long Can a Person Survive Without Food," *Scientific American*, November 8, 2004; W. K. Stewart and Laura W. Fleming, "Features of a Successful Therapeutic Fast of 382 Days' Duration," *Postgraduate Medical Journal*, March 1973; Anne Connor, "Where on Earth Did Life Originate?," The Wire Science, July 25, 2020; Abigail Beall, "How Long Can You Survive Without Water," BBC, October 19, 2020; "Report Sets Dietary Intake Levels for Water, Salt, and Potassium to Maintain Health and Reduce Chronic Disease Risk," National Academies of Sciences, Engineering and Medicine, February 11, 2004.

37 **The men could live:** "Report Sets Dietary Intake Levels"; "How Much Water You Should Drink Daily?," Cleveland Clinic, October 4, 2024, available at https://health.clevelandclinic.org/how-much-water-do-you-need-daily; Beall, "How Long Can You Survive."

38 **There was no way to know:** "How Long Can the Average Person Survive Without Water," *Scientific American*, December 9, 2002; A. C. Ivy et al., "A Tablet Emergency Ration for Lifeboat and Rafts," *United States Naval Medical Bulletin* 42, no. 1 (1944): 841.

38 **On a boat adrift in the ocean:** "Survivors of the Mignonette"; Petition to Queen Victoria, National Archives, A36934.

38 **The men also lacked:** Queen v. Dudley and Stephens OR, National Archives DPP 4/17, pp. 88–89 (Testimony of Edmund Brooks); Petition of Dudley and Stephens to Secretary of State William Harcourt, December 4, 1884, National Archives, Doc. A35934/7; "Survivors of the Mignonette";

Examination on Oath of Edwin Stephens, National Archives, Queen v. Dudley and Stephens File, DPP 4/17.

39 **There was another source:** Frances and Michal Howorth, *The Grab Bag Book: Your Ultimate Guide to Liferaft Survival* (London: Adlard Coles Nautical, 2002), 71; *Poems of Coleridge*, ed. Arthur Symons (London: Methuen, 1905), 6.

39 **Maritime folk wisdom:** Frances Dipper, *The Marine World: A Natural History of Ocean Life* (Plympton, UK: Wild Nature Press, 2016), 20; "The Dangers of Drinking Sea Water by Shipwrecked Mariners," *Proceedings of the Merchant Marine Council* 17, no. 4 (April 1960): 60–63.

40 **And often it *is* fatal:** Rose George, *Ninety Percent of Everything: Inside Shipping, the Invisible Industry That Puts Clothes on Your Back, Gas in Your Car, and Food on Your Place* (New York: Metropolitan Books, 2013), 232; "Dangers of Drinking Sea Water," 62.

40 **Dudley, Stephens, and Brooks:** "Cannibalism at Sea," *Royal Cornwall Gazette*, September 19, 1884; "Narratives by Brooks and Stephens."

40 **There was one small source:** "Horrible Tale of the Sea."

40 **On the third or fourth day:** "Mignonette Tragedy."

3. The Captain's Proposal

42 **On July 10:** Queen v. Dudley and Stephens (Murder on the High Seas) Official Record (Bound Volume), National Archives DPP 4/17, pp. 86–87 (Testimony of Edmund Brooks) (hereafter cited as Queen v. Dudley and Stephens OR); Queen v. Dudley and Stephens OR, National Archives DPP 4/17, p. 9 (Examination of Dudley); "Narratives by Brooks and Stephens," *Cornishman* (Penzance, England), September 18, 1884.

42 The capture of the sea turtle: Queen v. Dudley and Stephens OR, National Archives DPP 4/17, p. 17 (Dudley, "Account of Foundering 'Mignonette'").

42 It was a remarkable windfall: "Dying of Thirst? Try Turtle Blood," *Ocean Navigator*, January 1, 2003, https://oceannavigator.com/dying-of-thirst-try-turtle-blood/; Frank Golden and Michael Tipton, *Essentials of Sea Survival* (Champaign, IL: Human Kinetics, 2002) 157; "The Mignonette Cannibalism Case," *Daily News* (London), September 19, 1884; Queen v. Dudley and Stephens OR, National Archives DPP 4/17, p. 17 (Dudley, "Account of Foundering 'Mignonette'").

43 Once their thirst was quenched: Queen v. Dudley and Stephens OR, National Archives DPP 4/17, p. 17 (Dudley, "Account of Foundering 'Mignonette'"); "The Cannibalism at Sea," *Royal Cornwall Gazette* (Truro, England), September 19, 1884.

43 The relief from the turtle blood: Queen v. Dudley and Stephens OR, National Archives DPP 4/17, p. 99 (Testimony of Edmund Brooks); "Are There Health Benefits to Drinking Urine," WebMD, October 22, 2020; Richard Schwartz et al., *Tactical Emergency Medicine* (Philadelphia: Lippincott, Williams & Wilkins, 2008), 58; A. W. Brian Simpson, *Cannibalism and the Common Law: The Story of the Tragic Last Voyage of the Mignonette and the Strange Legal Proceedings to Which It Gave Rise* (Chicago: University of Chicago Press, 1984), 58.

44 The men improvised: "The Alleged Murder and Cannibalism," *Essex Standard* (Colchester, England), September 20, 1884.

44 On the eleventh day: "Cannibalism at Sea," *Royal Cornwall Gazette*, September 19, 1884; "Alleged Murder and

Cannibalism"; Queen v. Dudley and Stephens OR, National Archives DPP 4/17, p. 100 (Testimony of Edmund Brooks); Petition of Thomas Dudley to William Vernon Harcourt, National Archives, A36934/14.

45 The men were back: "The Mignonette Cannibalism Case: The Trial for Murder," *Reynolds's Newspaper* (London), November 9, 1884; "Cannibalism at Sea," *Royal Cornwall Gazette*, September 19, 1884; Petition of Thomas Dudley to William Vernon Harcourt, National Archives, A36934/14; Queen v. Dudley and Stephens OR, National Archives DPP 4/17, pp. 99–100 (Testimony of Edmund Brooks); "A Terrible Story of Cannibalism," *Cheshire Observer*, September 13, 1884.

45 No time of day: "The Wreck of the Mignonette," *Liverpool Mercury*, September 11, 1884; Queen v. Dudley and Stephens OR, National Archives DPP 4/17, p. 98 (Testimony of Edmund Brooks); Queen v. Dudley and Stephens OR, National Archives DPP 4/17, p. 17 (Dudley, "Account of Foundering 'Mignonette'").

45 There was no indication: Queen v. Dudley and Stephens OR, National Archives DPP 4/17, p. 88 (Testimony of Edmund Brooks); "Cannibalism at Sea," *Royal Cornwall Gazette*, September 19, 1884; Simpson, *Cannibalism and the Common Law*, 61.

46 Dudley was invoking: Neil Hanson, *The Custom of the Sea: A Shocking True Tale of Shipwreck, Murder, and the Last Taboo* (New York: Open Road Media, 2024).

46 Stephens, Brooks, and Parker: Paul Cowdell, "Cannibal Ballads: Not Just a Question of Taste," *Folk Music Journal* 9, no. 5 (2010): 731.

46 Even many people: Lord Byron, *Don Juan*, Canto II, Verse 73; Anthony Brandt, *The Tragic History of the Sea: Shipwrecks from the Bible to the Titanic* (Washington, DC: National Geographic Society, 2006), 243.

47 **The captain was proposing:** Exodus 20:13; Matthew 19:18.

47 **For some sailors:** Proverbs 16:33; Matthew 27:35 (New American Standard Bible).

48 **The fact that the sailing world:** "Alleged Murder and Cannibalism"; Queen v. Dudley and Stephens OR, National Archives DPP 4/17, p. 24 (Form Number 19 MRVS).

50 **After Dudley's proposal:** "Terrible Sufferings at Sea," *Newcastle Courant*, September 12, 1884.

50 **Around the time:** "Narratives by Brooks and Stephens."

50 **Parker now appeared:** "Cannibalism at Sea," *Royal Cornwall Gazette*, September 19, 1884; "The Case of Cannibalism at Sea," *Morning Post* (London), September 13, 1884; "Narratives by Brooks and Stephens."

51 **When Parker became sick:** "Alleged Murder and Cannibalism"; Queen v. Dudley and Stephens OR, National Archives DPP 4/17, p. 90 (Testimony of Edmund Brooks).

52 **It is often said:** Thomas Hobbes, *Leviathan* (Mineola, NY: Dover, 2011) 70.

52 **Brooks's refusal:** "Cannibalism at Sea," *Essex Newsman* (Chelmsford, England), September 20, 1884.

52 **As the men went back:** "Narratives by Brooks and Stephens"; "Cannibalism at Sea," *Manchester Courier and Lancashire General Advertiser* (Manchester, England), September 19, 1884; Queen v. Dudley and Stephens OR, National Archives DPP 4/17, p. 104 (Testimony of Edmund Brooks).

53 **It seemed to Dudley:** "Narratives by Brooks and Stephens."

53 **But he did not seem:** "Narratives by Brooks and Stephens"; "The Terrible Tale of the Sea," *Northampton Mercury*, September 20, 1884.

53 **On July 23:** "The Survivors of the Mignonette," *Western Mail* (Cardiff, Wales), September 11, 1884; Queen v. Dudley and Stephens OR, National Archives DPP 4/17, p. 33

(Examination of Edmund Brooks); "Narratives by Brooks and Stephens."

54 **Their most dire need:** "The Terrible Tale of the Sea," *Manchester Courier and Lancashire General Advertiser* (Manchester, England), September 15, 1884; Simpson, *Cannibalism and the Common Law*, 64.

54 **There were still no passing ships:** Queen v. Dudley and Stephens OR, National Archives DPP 4/17, pp. 91–92 (Testimony of Edmund Brooks); Simpson, *Cannibalism and the Common Law*, 62.

54 **Dudley finally gave up:** "The Cannibalism at Sea," *Standard* (London), September 12, 1884; Queen v. Dudley and Stephens OR, National Archives DPP 4/17, p. 33 (Examination of Edmund Brooks); Simpson, *Cannibalism and the Common Law*, 62.

55 **"I have three and a wife":** Queen v. Dudley and Stephens OR, National Archives DPP 4/17, pp. 5–6 (Examination of Cheesman); "Cannibalism at Sea," *Standard*, September 13, 1884.

55 **Dudley did not discuss wives:** Queen v. Dudley and Stephens OR, National Archives DPP 4/17, p. 19 (Dudley, "Account of Foundering 'Mignonette'"); Simpson, *Cannibalism and the Common Law*, 64; "The Mignonette Tragedy: Committal for Murder," *Birmingham Daily Post*, September 19, 1884.

56 **Even with the appeal:** "Cannibalism at Sea," *Royal Cornwall Gazette*, September 19, 1884; "Cannibalism at Sea," *Manchester Courier and Lancashire General Advertiser*, September 19, 1884.

56 **Parker, who had been left out:** "Cannibalism at Sea," *Royal Cornwall Gazette*, September 19, 1884; "Mignonette Cannibalism Case"; "Narratives by Brooks and Stephens."

56 When morning broke: "Terrible Tale of the Sea," *Illustrated Police News* (London), September 20, 1884; "Alleged Murder and Cannibalism."

57 Dudley and his mate: "Cannibalism at Sea," *Standard*, September 13, 1884.

57 Whatever the explanation: Queen v. Dudley and Stephens OR, National Archives DPP 4/17, p. 18 (Dudley, "Account of Foundering 'Mignonette'"); "Cannibalism at Sea," *Standard*, September 13, 1884.

58 Dudley began by moving Brooks: "Narratives by Brooks and Stephens"; "Mignonette Cannibalism Case"; Queen v. Dudley and Stephens OR, National Archives DPP 4/17, p. 34 (Examination of Edmund Brooks); Simpson, *Cannibalism and the Common Law*, 63.

58 "Hold his feet": Queen v. Dudley and Stephens OR, National Archives DPP 4/17, p. 18 (Dudley, "Account of Foundering 'Mignonette'"); "Narratives by Brooks and Stephens"; "The Mignonette Case," *Standard* (London), November 7, 1884; Queen v. Dudley and Stephens OR, National Archives DPP 4/17, p. 9 (Examination of Dudley).

59 "What, me, Sir?": Queen v. Dudley and Stephens OR, National Archives DPP 4/17, p. 18 (Dudley, "Account of Foundering 'Mignonette'").

59 "Yes, my boy," Dudley replied: "The Wreck of the Mignonette," *Southampton Herald*, September 20, 1884.

59 Dudley pointed his penknife: "Narratives by Brooks and Stephens"; "Wreck of the Mignonette"; Queen v. Dudley and Stephens OR, National Archives DPP 4/17, p. 94 (Testimony of Edmund Brooks); Queen v. Dudley and Stephens OR, National Archives DPP 4/17, p. 34 (Examination of Edmund Brooks); Queen v. Dudley and Stephens OR, National Archives DPP 4/17, p. 18 (Dudley, "Account of Foundering 'Mignonette'").

59 **Brooks had not wanted:** "The Case of Cannibalism," *Manchester Times* (Manchester, England), September 20, 1884; Queen v. Dudley and Stephens OR, National Archives DPP 4/17, p. 34 (Examination of Edmund Brooks); Queen v. Dudley and Stephens OR, National Archives DPP 4/17, pp. 94–95 (Testimony of Edmund Brooks).

60 **Dudley and Stephens stripped:** Queen v. Dudley and Stephens OR, National Archives DPP 4/17, p. 18 (Dudley, "Account of Foundering 'Mignonette'"); "Alleged Murder and Cannibalism"; Queen v. Dudley and Stephens OR, National Archives DPP 4/17, pp. 95–96 (Testimony of Edmund Brooks); Simpson, *Cannibalism and the Common Law*, 68.

60 **The men dug into their meal:** "Cannibalism at Sea," *Royal Cornwall Gazette*, September 19, 1884.

60 **It was the most:** "Terrible Tale of the Sea," *Manchester Courier and Lancashire General Advertiser* (Manchester, England), September 15, 1884.

4. The Cannibalism Taboo

61 **The natural history of cannibalism:** Julian Baggini, "Eating Humans," *Times Literary Supplement*, April 13, 2017; Bill Schutt, "In Many Species, a Family Dinner Means Something Else," *New York Times*, January 30, 2017; Elizabeth Gamillo, "Male Mantises Wrestle to Escape Cannibalistic Females," *Smithsonian Magazine*, January 25, 2021.

61 **In the human evolutionary line:** "Controversial Signs of Mass Cannibalism," *Wired*, December 4, 2009; Laura Geggel, "Nom Nom Nom: Prehistoric Human Bones Show Signs of Cannibalism," *Live Science*, March 24, 2017; Nicola Davis, "Prehistoric Cannibalism Not Just Driven by Hunger, Study Reveals," *Guardian*, April 6, 2017; Mindy Weisberger, "Prehistoric Cannibal Victim Found in Death Cave ID'ed as a

Young Girl," *Live Science*, April 16, 2021; "Humans' Evolutionary Relatives Butchered One Another 1.45 Million Years Ago," *Smithsonian*, June 26, 2023.

62 **Many archaeologists:** Lewis Petrinovich, *The Cannibal Within* (New York: Routledge, 2000), 94–96; Daniel Diehl and Mark P. Donnelly, *Eat Thy Neighbor: A History of Cannibalism* (Gloucester, UK: Sutton, 2008), 21, 136; Herbert Burhenn, "Understanding Aztec Cannibalism," *Archive for the Psychology of Religion* 26 (2004): 1–3.

62 **While Western discussions:** Henry S. Lucas, "The Great European Famine of 1315, 1316, and 1317," *Speculum: A Journal of Mediaeval Studies* (1930): 355–56; Reay Tannahill, *Flesh & Blood: A History of the Cannibal Complex* (New York: Little Brown, 1996), 87; Richard Sugg, "Corpse Medicine: Mummies, Cannibals, and Vampires," *Lancet* 371, no. 9630 (June 2008); Holly Tucker, "Blood Lust: The Early History of Transfusion," *Scientific American*, July 12, 2011; Bess Lovejoy, "A Brief History of Medical Cannibalism," *Lapham's Quarterly*, November 7, 2016; Bill Schutt, *Cannibalism: A Perfectly Natural History* (Chapel Hill: Algonquin Books, 2017), 242–63; Shirley Lindenbaum, "Thinking About Cannibalism," *Annual Review of Anthropology* 24 (2004): 475–78.

63 **Famously, there were also:** Mathew Beresford, *The White Devil: The Werewolf in European Culture* (London: Reaktion, 2013), 148–58.

63 **In its own shorter history:** Paula Neely, "Jamestown Colonists Resorted to Cannibalism," *National Geographic News*, May 3, 2013; Petrinovich, *Cannibal Within*, 22–28; Hans Askenasy, *Cannibalism: From Sacrifice to Survival* (Amherst, NY: Prometheus Books, 1994), 92; George Stewart, *Ordeal by Hunger: The Story of the Donner Party* (London: Jonathan Cape, 1936), 149.

64 There were many more: Askenasy, *Cannibalism*, 96–98; "Alferd Packer," Colorado Encyclopedia, https://coloradoencyclopedia.org/article/alferd-packer; Diehl and Donnelly, *Eat Thy Neighbor*, 81, 84–90; "Just How Many Democrats Did Al Packer Eat? GW Professor Digs into the Legend," *Washington Post*, June 7, 1989.

64 The history of cannibalism: Claude Rawson, "Unspeakable Rites: Cultural Reticence and the Cannibal Question," *Food: Nature and Culture* 66, no. 1 (Spring 1999); Claude Rawson, "Eating People," *London Review of Books*, January 24, 1985; Sigmund Freud, *The Future of an Illusion* (London: Horace Liveright, 1928), 17.

64 Freud's observation: Deuteronomy 28:15, 53.

65 If the stories: Megan A. Norcia, "The Imperial Food Chain: Eating as an Interface of Power in Women Writers' Geographical Primers," *Victorian Literature and Culture* 33, no. 1 (March 2005): 253, 258.

65 Victorian literature: David Gill, "The Fascination of the Abomination: Conrad and Cannibalism," *The Conradian* 24, no. 2 (Autumn 1999): 1; Lindenbaum, "Thinking About Cannibalism," 486.

66 One major distinction: Michael Harner, "The Ecological Basis for Aztec Sacrifice," *American Ethnologist* 4, no. 1 (February 1977): 128.

66 Cultural cannibalism: Geoffrey Sanborn, *The Sign of the Cannibal: Melville and the Making of the Postcolonial Reader* (Durham: Duke University Press, 1998), 64; R. G. Latham, *The Natural History Department of the Crystal Palace Described* (London: Bradbury & Evans, 1854), 12–13.

67 Most notoriously: Beresford, *White Devil*, 158; Michael Newton, *The Encyclopedia of Serial Killers* (New York: Facts on File, 2006), 370; James Barron and Mary B. W. Tabor, "17

Killed, and a Life Is Searched for Clues," *New York Times*, August 4, 1991.

67 There is even tenderhearted cannibalism: Beth Conklin, *Consuming Grief: Compassionate Cannibalism in an Amazonian Society* (Austin: University of Texas Press, 2001), xv.

67 In medieval China: Maria Franca, "Filiality, Cannibalism, Sanctity: Fleshing Out *Gegu* in a Late Ming Tale of a Filial Girl," *Chinese Literature: Essays, Articles, Reviews* 40 (December 2018): 51; Chong quoted in Bill Schutt, *Cannibalism*, 204.

68 The cannibalism of Dudley, Stephens, and Brooks: Petrinovich, *Cannibal Within*, 6.

68 Survival cannibalism: Petrinovich, *Cannibal Within*, 47; A. W. Brian Simpson, *Cannibalism and the Common Law: The Story of the Tragic Last Voyage of the Mignonette and the Strange Legal Proceedings to Which It Gave Rise* (Chicago: University of Chicago Press, 1984), 120.

69 The most fundamental: Anna Reid, *Leningrad: The Epic Siege of World War II, 1941–1944* (New York: Bloomsbury, 2011), 288.

69 There are obvious moral and legal differences: Charles Krause, "After the Andes," *Washington Post*, November 4, 1978.

69 Many people regard corpse-eating: "The Andes Survivors: The Detailed Story," Alpine Expeditions, https://web.archive.org/web/20210303020953/https://www.alpineexpeditions.net/as-the-return-to-uruguay.html.

70 When the shipmates: Petrinovich, *Cannibal Within*, 50–51; Evan Balkan, *Shipwrecked! Deadly Adventures and Disasters at Sea* (Birmingham, AL: Menasha Ridge Press, 2008), 34–43; Andrew Vietze and Stephen Erickson, *Boon Island: A True Story of Mutiny, Shipwreck, and Cannibalism* (Guilford,

CT: Globe Pequot Press, 2012) 3, 28, 31, 35–36, 38–39, 65–66; Edward Leslie, *Desperate Journeys, Abandoned Souls* (Boston: Houghton, Mifflin, 1988), 194–95.

71 **The *Francis Mary:*** Leslie, *Desperate Journeys*, 225–27; Simpson, *Cannibalism and the Common Law*, 126–27.

71 **Perhaps the earliest:** Simpson, *Cannibalism and the Common Law*, 122–23.

72 **Another British ship:** Howard Malchow, *Gothic Images of Race in Nineteenth-Century England* (Palo Alto: Stanford University Press, 1996), 102; Petrinovich, *Cannibal Within*, 52.

72 **Six years later:** Leslie, *Desperate Journeys*, 209–14; Petrinovich, *Cannibal Within*, 51–52.

72 **One of the most famous:** Petrinovich, *Cannibal Within*, 54–55; Nathaniel Philbrick, *The Heart of the Sea: The Tragedy of the Whaleship Essex* (New York: Penguin Books, 2000).

37 **Finally, a particularly dramatic:** Leslie, *Desperate Journeys*, 231; "The Wreck of the Francis Spaight," *Times* (London), June 22, 1836.

73 **The lots were drawn:** Leslie, *Desperate Journeys*, 231–32; Simpson, *Cannibalism and the Common Law*, 130–32; "Wreck of the Francis Spaight."

74 **Clearly, there was much room:** Simpson, *Cannibalism and the Common Law*, 139; "How the Crew of the Schooner Sallie M. Steelman Kept from Starvation—Butchering, Cooking, and Eating a Negro Sailor Who Was Shot While Insane—the Case to Be Investigated," *New York Times*, February 13, 1878.

75 **All these declared:** Simpson, *Cannibalism and the Common Law*, 124; Balkan, *Shipwrecked!*, 6; Petrinovich, *Cannibal Within*, 52; "Narratives by Brooks and Stephens," *Cornishman* (Penzance, England), September 18, 1884.

75 No less an authority: "The Court of Queen's Bench Passed Sentence," *Times* (London), December 10, 1884.

75 It is not surprising: Jihwan Chae, "In-Group Favoritism Overrides Fairness When Resources Are Limited," *Scientific Reports*, March 2022; Petrinovich, *Cannibal Within*, 36.

76 Another explanation: Leslie, *Desperate Journeys*, 233.

77 When cannibalism at sea: J. R. Spencer, review of *Cannibalism and the Common Law*, by A. W. Brian Simpson, *University of Chicago Law Review* 51 (1984): 1265; Simpson, *Cannibalism and the Common Law*, 105–6; Francis Hildyard, *The Principles of the Law of Marine Insurances* (London: William, 1845), 80; Simon Daniels, *Responsibility and Accountability in Maritime Law* (London: Routledge, 2024); Becky Little, "7 Brutal Ways Sailors Were Punished at Sea," History.com, June 11, 2021.

78 The seven English sailors: "How the Crew of the Schooner Sallie M. Steelman"; Petrinovich, *Cannibal Within*, 54–55; Simpson, *Cannibalism and the Common Law*, 132–33.

5. A Difficult Homecoming

80 While Dudley, Stephens, and Brooks: Queen v. Dudley and Stephens (Murder on the High Seas) Official Record (Bound Volume), National Archives DPP 4/17, pp. 9–10 (Examination of Dudley) (hereafter cited as Queen v. Dudley and Stephens OR).

80 Brooks was more disturbed: "The Cannibalism at Sea," *Grantham Journal*, September 20, 1884; "Narratives by Brooks and Stephens," *Cornishman* (Penzance, England), September 18, 1884.

81 The men tore into their new supply: A. W. Brian Simpson, *Cannibalism and the Common Law: The Story of the Tragic Last Voyage of the Mignonette and the Strange Legal*

Proceedings to Which It Gave Rise (Chicago: University of Chicago Press, 1984), 139; "How the Crew of the Schooner Sallie M. Steelman Kept from Starvation," *New York Times*, February 13, 1878; "The Cannibalism at Sea: Narrative by the Survivors of the Mignonette," *Royal Cornwall Gazette* (Truro, England), September 19, 1884; "The Horrible Straits of the Men of the Mignonette," *Cornishman* (Penzance, England), September 25, 1884; Martin Robbins, "What Does Human Meat Taste Like?," *Guardian*, September 8, 2010; Peter Vronsky, *American Serial Killers: The Epidemic Years 1950–2000* (New York: Berkley, 2020), 22.

81 **The men in the lifeboat:** "Cannibalism at Sea," *Royal Cornwall Gazette*, September 19, 1884; Queen v. Dudley and Stephens OR, National Archives DPP 4/17, pp. 18–19 (Dudley, "Account of Foundering 'Mignonette'"); "Narratives by Brooks and Stephens"; "Horrible Straits."

82 **The day after Parker was killed:** Queen v. Dudley and Stephens OR, National Archives DPP 4/17, p. 18 (Dudley, "Account of Foundering 'Mignonette'"); Simpson, *Cannibalism and the Common Law*, 68.

82 **On July 29:** "Narratives by Brooks and Stephens"; "Cannibalism at Sea," *Royal Cornwall Gazette*, September 19, 1884; Queen v. Dudley and Stephens OR, National Archives DPP 4/17, p. 19 (Dudley, "Account of Foundering 'Mignonette'").

82 **"Sail, oh!" Brooks cried out:** "Narratives by Brooks and Stephens"; "Cannibalism at Sea," *Royal Cornwall Gazette*, September 19, 1884.

82 **Dudley and Stephens stopped eating:** "Narratives by Brooks and Stephens"; "The Alleged Murder and Cannibalism," *Essex Standard* (Colchester, England), September 20, 1884; Queen v. Dudley and Stephens OR, National Archives DPP 4/17, p. 19 (Dudley, "Account of Foundering 'Mignonette'").

83 When it was clear: "Narratives by Brooks and Stephens"; "Cannibalism at Sea," *Royal Cornwall Gazette*, September 19, 1884.

83 The ship coming toward them: Queen v. Dudley and Stephens OR, National Archives DPP 4/17, p. 10 (Examination of Dudley); "Thrilling Narrative of Shipwreck," *Belfast News-Letter*, September 8, 1884; Simpson, *Cannibalism and the Common Law*, 2, 70.

83 An hour and a half after: "Narratives by Brooks and Stephens"; Queen v. Dudley and Stephens OR, National Archives DPP 4/17, p. 28 (Examination of Erich Martin Wiese).

84 Maneuvering from the small lifeboat: Queen v. Dudley and Stephens OR, National Archives DPP 4/17, pp. 8–12 (Examination of Erich Martin Wiese); "Cannibalism at Sea," *Manchester Courier and Lancashire General Advertiser* (Manchester, England), September 19, 1884.

84 The survivors told: "The Case of Cannibalism," *Manchester Times* (Manchester, England), September 20, 1884.

84 There is no way of knowing: Letter of Philippa Dudley to Ellis Lever, February 19, 1885, A36934, National Archives.

85 Dudley made a request: "Case of Cannibalism"; Copy Record of Indictment, Trial and Verdict, Queen v. Dudley and Stephens, National Archives, Queen v. Dudley and Stephens File, DPP 4/17, p. 35; Simpson, *Cannibalism and the Common Law*, 2, 70–71.

85 The *Moctezuma* had picked the men up: "The Survivors of the Mignonette," *Western Mail* (Cardiff, Wales), September 11, 1884; "The Terrible Tale of the Sea," *Birmingham Daily Post*, September 11, 1884; Simpson, *Cannibalism and the Common Law*, 70–71; Queen v. Dudley and Stephens OR, National Archives DPP 4/17, p. 29 (Examination of Erich Martin Wiese); Queen v. Dudley and Stephens OR, National

Archives DPP 4/17, p. 19 (Dudley, "Account of Foundering 'Mignonette'").

86 **With three very unwell Englishmen:** "Terrible Tale of the Sea," *Birmingham Daily Post*, September 11, 1884; Simpson, *Cannibalism and the Common Law*, 71; Queen v. Dudley and Stephens OR, National Archives DPP 4/17, p. 19 (Dudley, "Account of Foundering 'Mignonette'").

86 **His deviations from the truth:** Queen v. Dudley and Stephens OR, National Archives DPP 4/17, p. 18 (Dudley, "Account of Foundering 'Mignonette'"); Simpson, *Cannibalism and the Common Law*, 64–65, 71.

87 **Dudley's claim:** Queen v. Dudley and Stephens OR, National Archives DPP 4/17, p. 19 (Dudley, "Account of Foundering 'Mignonette'"); "Cannibalism at Sea," *Royal Cornwall Gazette*, September 19, 1884; "Narratives by Brooks and Stephens"; "The Mignonette Cannibalism Case," *Daily News* (London), September 19, 1884.

87 **Dudley was not lying:** Queen v. Dudley and Stephens OR, National Archives DPP 4/17, p. 19 (Dudley, "Account of Foundering 'Mignonette'").

88 **When Dudley, Stephens, and Brooks arrived:** Queen v. Dudley and Stephens OR, National Archives DPP 4/17, p. 31 (Examination of Gustavus Lowry Collins); "The Terrible Story of the Sea," *Leeds Times*, September 13, 1884; Simpson, *Cannibalism and the Common Law*, 2–4; "Horrible Straits."

88 **Shortly after they landed:** Letter of Philippa Dudley to Ellis Lever, February 19, 1885, A36934, National Archives; "The Terrible Tale of the Sea," *Sunderland Daily Echo and Shipping Gazette* (Sunderland, England), September 10, 1884.

88 **The first stop:** Queen v. Dudley and Stephens OR, National Archives DPP 4/17, p. 5 (Examination of Cheesman); Queen v. Dudley and Stephens OR, National Archives DPP 4/17, p. 36

(Examination of Edmund Brooks); Queen v. Dudley and Stephens OR, National Archives DPP 4/17, p. 2 (Examination of Laverty); "Terrible Tale of the Sea," *Sunderland Daily Echo and Shipping Gazette*, September 10, 1884; "The Cannibal Yachtsmen," *Bristol Mercury*, September 18, 1884.

89 **Cheesman had his clerk:** Queen v. Dudley and Stephens OR, National Archives DPP 4/17, pp. 9–10 (Examination of Dudley); Queen v. Dudley and Stephens OR, National Archives DPP 4/17, p. 27 (Examination of Samuel Tresidder); Queen v. Dudley and Stephens OR, National Archives DPP 4/17, p. 5 (Examination of Cheesman); Simpson, *Cannibalism and the Common Law*, 5–6; "The Mignonette Tragedy: Committal for Murder," *Birmingham Daily Post*, September 19, 1884.

89 **Dudley stuck closer:** Queen v. Dudley and Stephens OR, National Archives DPP 4/17, pp. 9–10 (Examination of Dudley); Queen v. Dudley and Stephens OR, National Archives DPP 4/17, p. 19 (Dudley, "Account of Foundering 'Mignonette'").

89 **Dudley was now hewing:** Queen v. Dudley and Stephens OR, National Archives DPP 4/17, p. 9 (Examination of Dudley).

90 **In his own statement:** Queen v. Dudley and Stephens OR, National Archives DPP 4/17, pp. 11–12 (Examination of Stephens).

90 **Brooks's statement:** Simpson, *Cannibalism and the Common Law*, 7.

90 **When they were finished:** "The Mignonette Tragedy," *Leeds Mercury*, September 19, 1884; Board of Trade Document, September 6, 1884, National Archives, A36934; Simpson, *Cannibalism and the Common Law*, 5–7.

90 **After Dudley finished:** Queen v. Dudley and Stephens OR, National Archives DPP 4/17, pp. 5–6 (Examination of Cheesman); Queen v. Dudley and Stephens OR, National Archives

DPP 4/17, pp. 2–4 (Examination of James Laverty); "Horrible Straits"; "Mignonette Cannibalism Case."

91 **While Cheesman listened:** Queen v. Dudley and Stephens OR, National Archives DPP 4/17, pp. 2–4 (Examination of James Laverty); Queen v. Dudley and Stephens OR, National Archives DPP 4/17, pp. 5–6 (Examination of Cheesman); "Mignonette Cannibalism Case."

91 **Finally, Dudley provided Cheesman:** Queen v. Dudley and Stephens OR, National Archives DPP 4/17, pp. 2–4 (Examination of James Laverty); Queen v. Dudley and Stephens OR, National Archives DPP 4/17, pp. 5–6 (Examination of Cheesman); "Mignonette Cannibalism Case."

91 **While the two men talked:** Queen v. Dudley and Stephens OR, National Archives DPP 4/17, pp. 2–4 (Examination of James Laverty); Queen v. Dudley and Stephens OR, National Archives DPP 4/17, pp. 5–6 (Examination of Cheesman); "Mignonette Cannibalism Case."

92 **But Dudley was not thinking:** "The Terrible Tale of the Sea: Message from the Captain," *Sunderland Daily Echo and Shipping Gazette* (Sunderland, England), September 10, 1884.

92 **The change was being driven:** *The Merchant Shipping Act, 1854 with Observations on Part III and an Index* (London: Longman and, 1855), lii, 184–85; Simpson, *Cannibalism and the Common Law*, 8.

93 **But the Falmouth authorities were:** Simpson, *Cannibalism and the Common Law*, 8–9.

94 **Sergeant Laverty:** Queen v. Dudley and Stephens OR, National Archives DPP 4/17, pp. 2–4 (Examination of James Laverty); Simpson, *Cannibalism and the Common Law*, 7–9.

94 **In ordering the arrests:** Queen v. Dudley and Stephens OR, National Archives DPP 4/17, pp. 2–4 (Examination of James

Laverty); Simpson, *Cannibalism and the Common Law*, 9–10.

94 Dudley, Stephens, and Brooks were shocked: "Cannibalism at Sea," *Royal Cornwall Gazette* (Truro, England), September 19, 1884.

95 Suddenly, everything had changed: "The Terrible Tale of the Sea," *Daily Gazette for Middlesbrough* (Middlesbrough, England), September 10, 1884.

6. A Bad Time to Be a Cannibal

96 The defense's main argument: Glanville Williams, *The Sanctity of Life and the Criminal Law* (Cambridge: Cambridge University Press, 1957), 198; Edward B. Arnolds and Norman F. Garland, "The Defense of Necessity in Criminal Law: The Right to Choose the Lesser Evil," *Journal of Criminal Law and Criminology* 65 (1974): 289, 291; J. Budziszewski, *Commentary on Thomas Aquinas's Treatise on Law* (Cambridge: Cambridge University Press, 2014), 414.

97 But for the men: Arnolds and Garland, "Defense of Necessity," 291; United States v. Holmes, 1 Wall. Jr. 1 (1842).

97 *Holmes* arose out of the wreck: United States v. Holmes, 1 Wall. Jr. 1 (1842); Edward Leslie, *Desperate Journeys, Abandoned Souls* (Boston: Houghton, Mifflin, 1988), 233–34; A. W. Brian Simpson, *Cannibalism and the Common Law: The Story of the Tragic Last Voyage of the Mignonette and the Strange Legal Proceedings to Which It Gave Rise* (Chicago: University of Chicago Press, 1984), 162–65; Leo Katz, *Bad Acts and Guilty Minds: Conundrums of the Criminal Law* (Chicago: University of Chicago Press, 1987), 17.

98 It began to rain: Leslie, *Desperate Journeys*, 233–34; Simpson, *Cannibalism and the Common Law*, 162–65; United States v. Holmes, 1 Wall. Jr. 1 (1842)

98 A few hours after: Simpson, *Cannibalism and the Common Law*, 170–71; United States v. Holmes, 1 Wall. Jr. 1 (1842); Leslie, *Desperate Journeys*, 239; *Public Ledger of Philadelphia* quoted in Katz, *Bad Acts and Guilty Minds*, 20.

99 The Philadelphia district attorney: "Riding the Circuit," Supreme Court Historical Society, https://civics.supremecourthistory.org/article/riding-the-circuit/#:~:text=At%20the%20turn%20of%20the,practice%20known%20as%20circuit%20riding; Holmes, 26 F. Cas. at 363–64; Simpson, *Cannibalism and the Common Law*, 173–74; Leslie, *Desperate Journeys*, 239; Katz, *Bad Acts and Guilty Minds*, 20.

99 Holmes put forth: The William Gray, 1 Paine 16 (U.S. Circuit Court for the District of New York, 1810); Katz, *Bad Acts and Guilty Minds*, 12.

99 In the *William Brown* case: The William Gray, 29 F. Cas. 1300 (U.S. Circuit Court for the District of New York, 1810); Katz, *Bad Acts and Guilty Minds*, 12; Holmes, 26 F. Cas. at 366.

100 Justice Baldwin: United States v. Holmes, 1 Wall. Jr. 1 (1842); Simpson, *Cannibalism and the Common Law*, 175.

100 The other condition: United States v. Holmes, 1 Wall. Jr. 1 (1842); Simpson, *Cannibalism and the Common Law*, 175.

100 Justice Baldwin was clearly pushing: United States v. Holmes, 1 Wall. Jr. 1 (1842); Simpson, *Cannibalism and the Common Law*, 175; Arnolds and Garland, "Defense of Necessity," 295.

101 Although the defense lawyers: Francis Bacon, *The Works of Francis Bacon* (London: Shedding, Ellis & Heath eds. 1859), 343; W. H. Hitchler, "Necessity as a Defense in Criminal Cases," *Dickinson Law Review* 33 (1929): 138, 141–42; Claire Oakes Finkelstein, "Two Men on a Plank," *All Faculty Scholarship* (2001): 280, https://scholarship.law.upenn

.edu/cgi/viewcontent.cgi?article=2001&context=faculty_scholarship.

102 William Blackstone: William Blackstone, *The Laws of England*, Book IV, 185; Hitchler, "Necessity as a Defense," 142.

102 As respected: Royal Commission on Indictable Offenses (1879), 43; Simpson, *Cannibalism and the Common Law*, 235.

102 There were other influential commentators: Hale quoted in Richard Tuck, *Natural Rights Theories: Their Origins and Development* (Cambridge: Cambridge University Press, 1979), 167; P. R. Glazebrook, "The Necessity Plea in English Criminal Law," *Cambridge Law Journal* 30, no. 1 (April 1972): 87, 111–12.

103 As the Industrial Revolution: Tim Stanley, "When Britain Still Believed in God," *History Today*, May 5, 2011; Paul Puccio, "Victorian Sexuality," *Dickens Quarterly* 14, no. 3 (September 1997): 178–79; "How Did the Victorians Become a Reference Point for Joyless Prudery?," *History Today* 72, no. 4 (April 2022); Richard Gibson and Timothy Larsen, "Evangelism," Oxford Biographies, https://www.oxfordbibliographies.com/view/document/obo-9780199799558/obo-9780199799558-0071.xml; "1885 Labouchere Amendment," UK Parliament, https://www.parliament.uk/about/living-heritage/transformingsociety/private-lives/relationships/collections1/sexual-offences-act-1967/1885-labouchere-amendment/.

104 The Victorians were on a mission: Thomas Babington Macaulay, *The History of England from the Accession of James II* (Philadelphia: E. H. Butler, 1849), 14; Stephan Coote, *The Penguin Short History of English Literature* (New York: Penguin Books, 1994), 440, 444.

104 A major theme: Charles Dickens, *A Christmas Carol* (London: Bradbury & Evans, 1858), 20; Coote, *Penguin Short*

History, 457–58, 534; Charles Kingsley, *The Water-Babies* (Oxford: Oxford University Press, 2013), xxiv.

105 Crusading nonfiction: Anthony S. Wohl, "*The Bitter Cry of Outcast London*," *International Review of Social History* 13, no. 2 (1968): 189–245; Deborah Gorman, "The 'Maiden Tribute of Modern Babylon' Re-Examined: Child Prostitution and the Idea of Childhood in Late-Victorian England," *Victorian Studies* 21 (Spring 1978): 353–54.

105 There were also people: "History of the Salvation Army," Salvation Army USA, https://www.salvationarmyusa.org/usn/history-of-the-salvation-army/; Richard N. Price, "The Working Men's Club Movement and Victorian Social Reform Ideology," *Victorian Studies* 15, no. 2 (December 1971): 120–25.

106 Meanwhile, reformers in Parliament: L. C. B. Seaman, *Victorian England: Aspects of English and Imperial History, 1837–1901* (London: Methuen, 1973), 63; "Women Get the Vote," UK Parliament, "Living Heritage," https://www.parliament.uk/about/living-heritage/transformingsociety/electionsvoting/womenvote/overview/thevote/.

106 Many of the new laws: Monica Flegel, "'Facts and Their Meaning': Child Protection, Intervention, and the National Society for the Prevention of Cruelty to Children in Late Nineteenth-Century England," *Victorian Review* 33, no. 1 (2007): 87.

107 This Victorian impulse: Michelle Allen, "From Cesspool to Sewer: Sanitary Reform and the Rhetoric of Resistance, 1848–1880," *Victorian Literature and Culture* 30, no. 2 (2002): 383–84; Schülting quoted in Marjolein Platjee, "Dirt in Victorian Literature and Culture: Writing Materiality," *The Wilkie Collins Journal* 14, no. 70 (2017).

107 This reform ethos: Brad Beaven, "The Resilience of Sailortown Culture in English Naval Ports, c. 1820–1900," *Urban*

History 43, no. 1 (February 2016): 74; Herman Melville, *Redburn: His First Voyage, Being the Sailor-Boy Confessions and Reminiscences of the Son of a Gentleman in the Merchant Service* (London: Constable, 1922), 175; Alston Kennerley, "Joseph Conrad at the London Sailors' Home," *The Conradian* 33, no. 1 (Spring 2008): 73–75; Judith Fingard, "Masters and Friends, Crimps and Abstainers: Agents of Control in 19th Century Sailortown," *Acadiensis* 8, no. 1 (Autumn 1978): 22–23.

107 In the waning days of sail: *The Merchant Shipping Act, 1854*, lii, 184–85; Simon Daniels, *Responsibility and Accountability in Maritime Law* (London: Routledge, 2024); Simpson, *Cannibalism and the Common Law*, 101–9; Lars Scholl, "Introduction," *Merchants and Mariners: Selected Maritime Writings of David M. Williams*, compiled by Lars U. Scholl (St. Johns, Newfoundland: International Maritime Economic History Association, 2000), xvi; Geoffrey Marston, "Crimes by British Passengers on Board Foreign Ships on the High Seas: The Historical Background to Section 686 (1) of the Merchant Shipping Act," *Cambridge Law Journal* 58, no. 1 (1999): 172.

108 These laws also: Simpson, *Cannibalism and the Common Law*, 5, 8, 104–9; Marston, "Crimes by British Passengers," 172; *The Merchant Shipping Act of 1854 & 1855 (17 & 18 Vict. Cc. 104, 120, and 18 & 19 Vict. C. 91) with a Readable Abridgement of the Former Act and an Explanation of the Law Relating to It* (London: V. & R. Stevens & G. S. Norton, H. Sweet, and W. Maxwell, 1856).

109 There were other changes afoot: Michael Eisner, "Long-Term Historical Trends in Violent Crime," *Crime and Justice: A Review of Research* 30 (2003); Cruelty to Animals Act 1835, 5 & 6 Will. 4, c. 59; Randall McGowen, "Civilizing

Punishment: The End of the Public Execution in England," *Journal of British Studies* 33, no. 3 (July 1994): 257, 265.

109 **This growing discomfort:** Shaun Nichols, *Sentimental Rules: On the Natural Foundations of Moral Judgment* (Oxford: Oxford University Press, 2004); Andrew Linklater and Stephen Mennell, "Norbert Elias, the Civilizing Process: Sociogenetic and Psychogenetic Investigations—an Overview and Assessment," *History and Theory* 49, no. 3 (October 2010): 399.

110 **Dudley's choice of victim:** Ben Moore, "Childhood in Victorian Literature," Oxford Biographies, https://www.oxfordbibliographies.com/display/document/obo-9780199799558/obo-9780199799558-0144.xml; Margaret Higonnet, review of *Artful Dodgers: Reconceiving the Golden Age of Children's Literature* by Marah Gubar, *Victorian Studies* (Autumn 2009): 143; John Ramsland, "Mary Carpenter and the Child-Saving Movement," *Australian Social Work* 33 (1980); Thom Gehring and Fredalene Bowers, "Mary Carpenter: 19th Century English Correctional Education Hero," *Journal of Correctional Education*, September 2003, 116, 118; Rev. Benjamin Waugh, *Some Conditions of Child Life in England* (London: National Society for the Prevention of Cruelty to Children, 1889).

110 **The year before:** Patrick Brantlinger, *Rule of Darkness: British Literature and Imperialism 1830–1914* (Ithaca: Cornell University Press, 1988), 81.

111 **Seeley's declaration:** Rudyard Kipling, "The White Man's Burden: The United States & Philippine Islands, 1899," in *Rudyard Kipling's Verse: Definitive Edition* (Garden City, NY: Doubleday, 1929).

111 **All this arguably made 1884:** Shirley Lindenbaum, "Thinking About Cannibalism," *Annual Review of Anthropology* 24

(2004): 488; Patrick Brantlinger, *Taming Cannibals: Race and the Victorians* (Ithaca: Cornell University Press, 2011), 2–3.

111 The Victorian view: Herbert Ward, *Five Years with the Congo Cannibals* (London: Chatto & Windus, 1890); Hammond and Jablow quoted in Brantlinger, *Rule of Darkness*, 185.

112 Cannibalism dispatches: Richard B. Moore, "Carib 'Cannibalism': A Study in Anthropological Stereotyping," *Caribbean Studies* 13, no. 3 (October 1973): 117–35; Simpson, *Cannibalism and the Common Law*, 112; Sarah Everts, "Europe's Hypocritical History of Cannibalism," *Smithsonian*, April 24, 2013; "The Loss of the William Brown," *Times* (London), May 20, 1841; Lindenbaum, "Thinking About Cannibalism," 477; Dennis Griffiths, ed., *The Encyclopedia of the British Press, 1422–1992* (London: Macmillan, 1992), 562.

113 In fact, there were already indications: Lewis Petrinovich, *The Cannibal Within* (New York: Routledge, 2000), 59; Simpson, *Cannibalism and the Common Law*, 176–81.

113 The *Euxine*: Petrinovich, *Cannibal Within*, 59–60; Simpson, *Cannibalism and the Common Law*, 176–81; "The Malay Peninsula," *Times* (London), December 22, 1874; Leslie, *Desperate Journeys*, 204.

113 One of the sailors: Petrinovich, *Cannibal Within*, 59–60; Simpson, *Cannibalism and the Common Law*, 176–82; "Malay Peninsula"; Leslie, *Desperate Journeys*, 204–5; "Cannibalism on Board a Tyne-Laden Ship," *Derby Mercury*, January 13, 1875; G. H. Harrington, letter, *Singapore Daily Times*, November 13, 1874, quoted in A. W. B. Simpson, "*Regina v. Archer and Muller* (1875): The Leading Case That Never Was," *Oxford Journal of Legal Studies* 2, no. 2 (Summer 1982): 186.

114 After the British: Simpson, *Cannibalism and the Common Law*, 183–90; Michael G. Mallin, "In Warm Blood: Some Historical and Procedural Aspects of *Regina v. Dudley and*

Stephens," University of Chicago Law Review 34, no. 2 (Winter 1967): 387–407.

114 In the end: "Fearful Sufferings and Cannibalism at Sea," *York Herald*, December 17, 1874; "The Waif from the British Ship Euxine," *Bristol Mercury*, January 9, 1875.

114 In the ten years: Simpson, *Cannibalism and the Common Law*, 187–92; G. H. Harrington, letter, *Singapore Daily Times*, November 13, 1874, quoted in Simpson, "*Regina v. Archer and Muller* (1875)," 186.

7. From Sailors to Criminal Defendants

115 While they sat in jail: "Terrible Sufferings at Sea," *Derby Daily Telegraph*, September 8, 1884; "Terrible Tale of the Sea," *Edinburgh Evening News*, September 8, 1884; "Frightful Privations at Sea," *Daily News* (London), September 8, 1884; "The Terrible Tale of the Sea," *Daily Gazette for Middlesbrough* (Middlesbrough, England), September 10, 1884.

115 It was big news: "Cannibalism at Sea," *New York Sun*, September 7, 1884; "Horrible Tale of the Sea," *Sydney Evening News*, September 8, 1884.

116 It was little wonder: Christopher Casey, "Common Misperceptions: The Press and Victorian Views of Crime," *Journal of Interdisciplinary History* 41, no. 3 (Winter 2011): 367, 376; Judith Flanders, *The Invention of Murder: How the Victorians Revelled in Death and Detection and Created Modern Crime* (New York: St. Martin's Press, 2011) 3–5, 112; Hellen McAlpin, "Did Crime Literature Inspire Murder in Victorian England," *Washington Post*, March 22, 2019; Pauline Chapman, *Madame Tussaud's Chamber of Horror* (London: Constable, 1984), 66, 90.

116 As reports of their exploits: "Narratives by Brooks and Stephens: The Mignonette Tragedy: The Mate's Account of the

Tragic Affair," *Cornishman* (Penzance, England), September 18, 1884.

117 One citizen expressed: "The Mignonette Tragedy: The Mate's Account of the Tragic Affair," *Cornishman* (Penzance, England), September 18, 1884; "The Cannibalism at Sea," *Standard* (London), September 12, 1884.

117 While Dudley, Stephens, and Brooks waited: Queen v. Dudley and Stephens (Murder on the High Seas) Official Record (Bound Volume), National Archives DPP 4/17, p. 29 (Examination of Richard Hodge) (hereafter cited as Queen v. Dudley and Stephens OR); Queen v. Dudley and Stephens OR, National Archives DPP 4/17, pp. 2–4 (Examination of James Laverty); Statement of Richard Hodge, Mignonette, National Archives, Queen v. Dudley and Stephens File; "Narratives by Brooks and Stephens"; A. W. Brian Simpson, *Cannibalism and the Common Law: The Story of the Tragic Last Voyage of the Mignonette and the Strange Legal Proceedings to Which It Gave Rise* (Chicago: University of Chicago Press, 1984), 74.

118 Hodge delivered: Queen v. Dudley and Stephens OR, National Archives DPP 4/17, p. 29 (Examination of Richard Hodge); Queen v. Dudley and Stephens OR, National Archives DPP 4/17, pp. 2–4 (Examination of James Laverty); Statement of Richard Hodge, Mignonette, National Archives, Queen v. Dudley and Stephens File; "The Case of Cannibalism," *Manchester Times*, September 20, 1884; "The Wreck of the Mignonette," *Liverpool Mercury*, September 12, 1884; Simpson, *Cannibalism and the Common Law*, 74–75.

118 The authorities eventually decided: Advertisement for "Burton's Royal Old Curiosity Shop," *Antiquarian Magazine Advertiser*, March 1884, p. viii; "The Old Curiosity Shop," *Cornishman* (Penzance, England), May 5, 1881; Queen v. Dudley and Stephens OR, National Archives DPP 4/17, pp. 2–4 (Examination of James Laverty); Simpson, *Cannibalism and the Common Law*, 74–75; Extract from "Midsummer Society," Midsummer Number, 1881, in National Archives, Queen v. Dudley and Stephens file A36934/14.

118 **After the authorities:** "The Charge of Murder and Cannibalism," *Nottingham Evening Post*, September 11, 1884; "Narratives by Brooks and Stephens"; "Horrible Tale of the Sea," *Reynolds's Newspaper* (London), September 14, 1884; Simpson, *Cannibalism and the Common Law*, 73, 79–80; "The Survivors of the 'Mignonette,'" *Lake's Falmouth Packet and Cornwall Advertiser* (Falmouth, England), September 13, 1884.

119 **Supporters of the men:** "Editorial," *Exeter and Plymouth Gazette* (Exeter, England), October 31, 1884; "Terrible Sufferings at Sea," *Newcastle Courant*, September 12, 1884; "The Survivors of the Mignonette," *Belfast News-Letter*, September 11, 1884; *Falmouth News Slip*, quoted in Simpson, *Cannibalism and the Common Law*, 80.

119 **On Monday morning:** "Survivors of the 'Mignonette,'" *Lake's Falmouth Packet*, September 13, 1884; "The Tragedy at Sea," *Freeman's Journal* (Dublin), September 9, 1884; "Horrible Tragedy at Sea," September 8, 1884; "Cannibalism for Life's Sake," *Cornishman* (Penzance, England), September 11, 1884.

120 **The magistrates had no real choice:** Herbert Stephen, "Homicide by Necessity," *Law Quarterly Review*, January 1885, 51–53; Leon Radzinowicz and Roger Hood, *The Emergence of Penal Policy in Victorian and Edwardian England* (Oxford: Clarendon Press, 1990), 663–67.

120 **The main evidence:** Queen v. Dudley and Stephens OR, National Archives DPP 4/17, pp. 2–4 (Examination of James

Laverty); "The Mignonette Tragedy," *Cornishman* (Penzance, England), September 18, 1884; Simpson, *Cannibalism and the Common Law*, 73–74, 83.

120 There was little: Robert Popper, "History and Development of the Accused's Right to Testify," *Washington University Law Quarterly* 1962, no. 4 (1962): 454, 456.

121 The prisoners: Simpson, *Cannibalism and the Common Law*, 65.

121 Dudley, Stephens, and Brooks: "Cannibalism for Life's Sake."

121 The magistrates heard testimony: Queen v. Dudley and Stephens OR, National Archives DPP 4/17, pp. 2–4 (Examination of James Laverty); "The Wreck of the Mignonette," *Liverpool Mercury*, September 9, 1884.

121 On cross-examination: "Wreck of the Mignonette," *Liverpool Mercury*, September 9, 1884.

122 When he was done: Simpson, *Cannibalism and the Common Law*, 76; "The Dreadful Story of the Sea," *Dundee Courier* (Scotland), September 9, 1884.

122 To spectators: Pendleton Howard, "Criminal Prosecution in England II, Public Prosecutions," *Columbia Law Review* 30, no. 1 (January 1930): 12, 16–17; Simpson, *Cannibalism and the Common Law*, 76.

122 The magistrates agreed: "The Wreck of the Mignonette," *Belfast News-Letter*, September 9, 1884.

123 The mayor asked: "Wreck of the Mignonette," *Belfast News-Letter*, September 9, 1884; "Cannibalism for Life's Sake."

123 The magistrates talked: "Wreck of the Mignonette," *Belfast News-Letter*, September 9, 1884; "The Survivors of the Mignonette," *Belfast News-Letter*, September 11, 1884.

123 The following night: "Cannibalism by English Sailors."

123 When he arrived in Falmouth: "Cannibalism by English Sailors."

123 Daniel presented himself to Dudley: "Cannibalism by English Sailors."

123 On the same day: "Terrible Tale of the Sea," *Daily Gazette for Middlesbrough*, September 10, 1884.

124 As bad as things looked: "Cannibalism at Sea," *Lloyd's Illustrated Newspaper* (London), September 14, 1884; "The Terrible Tale of the Sea: Message from the Captain," *Sunderland Daily Echo and Shipping Gazette*, September 10, 1884.

124 Philippa Dudley: "The Terrible Tale of the Sea," *Daily Gazette for Middlesbrough*, September 10, 1884.

124 Mrs. Dudley: "Terrible Tale of the Sea," *Daily Gazette for Middlesbrough*, September 10, 1884.

124 Stephens's wife, Ann: "Cannibalism at Sea," *Standard*, September 12, 1884; Simpson, *Cannibalism and the Common Law*, 34; "The Charge of Murder and Cannibalism," *Daily Gazette for Middlesbrough* (Middlesbrough, England), September 11, 1884.

125 While Falmouth authorities: Introduction to *Office-Holders in Modern Britain, Vol. 5, Home Office Officials 1782–1870* (London: University of London, 1975), available at British History Online, https://www.british-history.ac.uk/office-holders/vol5/pp1-10.

125 When the first reports: Lewis Harcourt journal, 2 June–11 September (September 10), box 359, Archive of Sir William and Lewis Harcourt, 1st Viscount Harcourt, Bodleian Libraries, University of Oxford.

125 Far from the bustling: David Cannadine, *Victorious Century: The United Kingdom, 1800–1906* (New York: Viking, 2017), 294–95, 385; George W. E. Russell, "Sir William Harcourt," *North American Review* 179, no. 576 (1904) 706–8; A. G. Gardiner, *The Life of Sir William Harcourt* (London: Constable, 1923), 1:33–34; Patrick Jackson, *Harcourt and*

Son: A Political Biography of Sir William Harcourt, 1827–1904 (Madison, NJ: Fairleigh Dickinson University Press, 2004), 15–16; L. C. B. Seaman, *Victorian England: Aspects of English and Imperial History, 1837–1901* (London: Methuen, 1973), 294–95.

126 Harcourt was elected: Jackson, *Harcourt and Son*, 17–20, 33; Russell, "Sir William Harcourt," 704–7.

126 Harcourt married a woman: Jackson, *Harcourt and Son*, 24; Russell, "Sir William Harcourt," 707–8.

126 In Parliament: Jackson, *Harcourt and Son*, 78–80; Gardiner, *Life of Sir William Harcourt*, 1:80; Keith Laybourn, *British Political Leaders: A Biographical Dictionary* (Santa Barbara, CA: ABC-CLIO, Inc. 2001) 154–56.

126 As home secretary: Gardiner, *Life of Sir William Harcourt*, 1:391, 394; Laybourn, *British Political Leaders*, 154–56.

127 Harcourt had a special concern: Gardiner, *Life of Sir William Harcourt*, 1:394–95.

127 Harcourt's concern for the disadvantaged: Gardiner, *Life of Sir William Harcourt*, 607–8.

128 When the urgent request: Board of Trade Document, September 6, 1884, National Archives, A36934; Memo of Home Office, September 8, 1884, National Archives, A36934; Simpson, *Cannibalism and the Common Law*, 246; Letter of James to Harcourt, n.d., Letters of Lord James of Hereford, 1873–1904, box 86, Archive of Sir William and Lewis Harcourt, 1st Viscount Harcourt, Bodleian Libraries, University of Oxford.

129 Harcourt's own reaction: Memo of Home Office, September 8/10, 1884, National Archives, A36934/2.

129 Harcourt said: Memo of Home Office, September 8, 1884, National Archives, A36934/2; Simpson, *Cannibalism and the Common Law*, 77.

129 When the instructions from London: "Cannibalism at Sea," *Standard*, September 12, 1884.

129 Dudley, Stephens, and Brooks again: "Cannibalism at Sea," *Standard*, September 12, 1884.

130 Tilly told the magistrates: "Cannibalism at Sea," *Standard*, September 12, 1884.

130 The court clerk reported: "The Alleged Murder on the High Seas," *Leeds Mercury*, September 12, 1884; "The Cannibal Yachtsmen," *Bristol Mercury*, September 12, 1884.

130 The bail decision: Simpson, *Cannibalism and the Common Law*, 79; A. K. Bottomley, "The Granting of Bail: Principles and Practice," *Modern Law Review* 31, no. 1 (January 1968): 49–51.

131 Low as the bail was: "Mignonette Tragedy," *Cornishman*, September 18, 1884; "The Cannibalism at Sea," *Belfast News-Letter*, September 12, 1884; "Cannibalism by English Sailors"; Simpson, *Cannibalism and the Common Law*, 79–80.

131 When the hearing ended: "The Survivors of the Mignonette," *Western Mail* (Cardiff, Wales), September 13, 1884; "Narratives by Brooks and Stephens."

131 Stephens and Brooks returned: "Narratives by Brooks and Stephens."

131 Stephens and Brooks left town: "Cannibalism at Sea," *Standard*, September 13, 1884.

132 When Brooks: "Narratives by Brooks and Stephens."

132 Dudley, who was headed home: "Narratives by Brooks and Stephens"; "The Cannibalism at Sea: Narrative by the Survivors of the Mignonette," *Royal Cornwall Gazette* (Truro, England), September 19, 1884.

132 The Dudleys traveled: "The Case of Cannibalism at Sea," *Daily News* (London), September 13, 1884.

132 Dudley had brought his wife: "Case of Cannibalism at Sea."

133 Reporters continued to descend: "The Loss of the Yacht Mignonette," *Southampton Herald* (England), September 17, 1884; "Case of Cannibalism at Sea"; "Cannibalism at Sea," *Standard*, September 13, 1884.

134 Brooks was not doing much better: "Loss of the Yacht Mignonette"; "Alleged Murder & Cannibalism by Essex Sailors," *Essex Standard* (Colchester, England), September 13, 1884.

134 When they were not worrying: "The Cannibalism at Sea," *Royal Cornwall Gazette* (Truro, England), September 19, 1884.

134 Donations were still coming in: "Cannibalism at Sea," *Standard*, September 15, 1884; Simpson, *Cannibalism and the Common Law*, 86.

134 The maritime community: Paul Cowdell, "Cannibal Ballads: Not Just a Question of Taste," *Folk Music Journal* 9, no. 5 (2010): 732.

135 Some of the men's supporters: Letter to William Harcourt, September 10, 1884, National Archives, A36934.

135 The men were grateful: "Narratives by Brooks and Stephens," *Cornishman* (Penzance, England), September 18, 1884.

136 On September 18: "The Cannibal Yachtsmen," *Bristol Mercury*, September 19, 1884.

136 A large crowd: "The Alleged Murder and Cannibalism," *Essex Standard* (Colchester, England), September 20, 1884; "The Charge of Cannibalism Against a Shipwrecked Crew," *Royal Cornwall Gazette* (Truro, England), September 19, 1884.

136 William Danckwerts: "The Cannibal Yachtsmen," *Bristol Mercury*, September 19, 1884; Simpson, *Cannibalism and the Common Law*, 89.

137 The formal charge: Queen v. Dudley and Stephens OR, National Archives DPP 4/17, p. 1; "Horrible Story of Cannibalism at Sea," *Bath Chronicle and Weekly Gazette* (Bath, England), September 11, 1884.

137 **In deference to the sympathies:** "The Mignonette Case," *Glasgow Herald*, September 19, 1884.

137 **The killing of Parker:** "The Horrible Straits of the Men of the Mignonette," *Cornishman* (Penzance, England), September 25, 1884.

137 **Then Danckwerts did something:** "Horrible Straits"; "The Mignonette Cannibalism Case," *Daily News* (London), September 19, 1884.

138 **The prosecution's first witness:** "Horrible Straits."

139 **Next was Cheesman:** "Horrible Straits."

139 **There was a moment of drama:** "Horrible Straits."

139 **The interjection was shocking:** "Horrible Straits."

139 **Danckwerts said:** "Mignonette Cannibalism Case"; "The Wreck of the Mignonette," *Southampton Herald*, September 20, 1884.

140 **On cross-examination:** "Mignonette Cannibalism Case."

140 **Next, the prosecution:** "Wreck of the Mignonette," *Southampton Herald*, September 20, 1884.

140 **The prosecution's final witness:** "Cannibalism at Sea," *Manchester Courier and Lancashire General Advertiser* (Manchester, England), September 19, 1884.

141 **As if that were not enough:** "Cannibalism at Sea," *Manchester Courier and Lancashire General Advertiser*, September 19, 1884.

141 **Brooks's testimony began:** Queen v. Dudley and Stephens OR, National Archives DPP 4/17, pp. 32–37 (Examination of Brooks); "The Mignonette Tragedy," *Birmingham Daily Post*, September 19, 1884.

141 **It was clear from his account:** "Mignonette Cannibalism Case."

142 **Finally, Brooks gave up:** Queen v. Dudley and Stephens OR, National Archives DPP 4/17, pp. 32–37 (Examination of Brooks).

142 **He told the magistrates:** Queen v. Dudley and Stephens OR, National Archives DPP 4/17, pp. 32–37 (Examination of Brooks).

142 **Brooks did not seem eager:** "Horrible Straits"; Queen v. Dudley and Stephens OR, National Archives DPP 4/17, pp. 32–37 (Examination of Brooks).

142 **Tilly tried to show:** "Mignonette Tragedy," *Birmingham Daily Post*, September 19, 1884; Queen v. Dudley and Stephens OR, National Archives DPP 4/17, p. 36 (Examination of Edmund Brooks).

143 **Tilly questioned Brooks:** Queen v. Dudley and Stephens OR, National Archives DPP 4/17, pp. 32–37 (Examination of Brooks); "The Mignonette Tragedy: Committal for Murder," *Birmingham Daily Post*, September 19, 1884; Queen v. Dudley and Stephens OR, National Archives DPP 4/17, p. 36 (Examination of Edmund Brooks).

143 **Tilly also wanted Brooks:** Queen v. Dudley and Stephens OR, National Archives DPP 4/17, p. 36 (Examination of Edmund Brooks).

143 **On redirect questioning:** Queen v. Dudley and Stephens OR, National Archives DPP 4/17, pp. 32–37 (Examination of Brooks).

144 **When Brooks's testimony ended:** "Horrible Straits"; "Mignonette Tragedy," *Birmingham Daily Post*, September 19, 1884.

144 **The mayor declared:** "Mignonette Tragedy," *Cornishman*, September 19, 1884; "Horrible Straits"; "Wreck of the Mignonette," *Southampton Herald*, September 20, 1884.

144 **The defendants had displayed:** "Mignonette Tragedy," *Birmingham Daily Post*, September 19, 1884; "Horrible Straits."

145 Dudley and Brooks left town: Simpson, *Cannibalism and the Common Law*, 93.

8. The Grand Jury Weighs In

146 As that day of reckoning drew near: "The Alleged Murder and Cannibalism," *Essex Standard* (Colchester, England), September 20, 1884; "The *Mignonette* Cannibalism Case," *Daily News* (London), September 19, 1884; "The Charge of Cannibalism Against a Shipwrecked Crew," *Royal Cornwall Gazette* (Truro, England), September 19, 1884.

146 By now, everyone knew: "Horrible Tragedy at Sea," *Freeman's Journal* (Dublin); "Terrible Sufferings at Sea," *Derby Daily Telegraph*, September 8, 1884.

147 As the proceedings in Exeter: "The Loss of the Yacht Mignonette," *Southampton Herald* (England), September 17, 1884.

147 News stories: "The Charge of Murder and Cannibalism," *Nottingham Evening Post*, September 11, 1884.

147 That was an overstatement: "Alleged Murder & Cannibalism by Essex Sailors," *Essex Standard* (Colchester, England), September 11, 1884; "Cannibalism for Life's Sake," *Cornishman* (Penzance, England), September 11, 1884.

148 Parker's hometown: "The Terrible Tale of the Sea," *Liverpool Mercury*, September 16, 1884.

148 Mrs. Mathews did not share: "Terrible Tale of the Sea."

148 John Mathews's nephew: "The Cannibalism at Sea," *Standard* (London), September 15, 1884; "Terrible Tale of the Sea."

149 This perspective began: "The Spectator," in *The Encyclopedia of the British Press* (New York: Macmillan, 1992), 525–26; "The Apologists for Cannibalism," *Spectator* (London), September 13, 1884; "The Mignonette Murder," *Reynolds's Newspaper* (London), December 14, 1884.

150 An anonymous barrister: Another Barrister [pseud.], "Terrible Tale of the Sea," *Daily Telegraph* (London), September 12, 1884.

150 The most unexpected letters: Thomas Dudley, letter to the editor, *Standard* (London), September 22, 1884; Thomas Dudley, letter to the editor, *Times* (London), September 22, 1884; Thomas Dudley, letter to the editor, *Western Daily Mercury* (Devon, England), quoted in "The Cannibalism at Sea," *Derby Daily Telegraph*, September 22, 1884.

150 Newspapers generally did not: Jack Smith-Hughes, *Unfair Comment: Upon Some Victorian Murder Trials* (London: Cassell, 1951) 304.

151 The prosecution: "The Assizes," UK Parliament, https://www.parliament.uk/about/living-heritage/transformingsociety/laworder/court/overview/assizes/; "The Mignonette Cannibalism Case," *Daily News* (London), November 4, 1884; A. W. Brian Simpson, *Cannibalism and the Common Law: The Story of the Tragic Last Voyage of the Mignonette and the Strange Legal Proceedings to Which It Gave Rise* (Chicago: University of Chicago Press, 1984), 197, 200.

151 The Exeter Assize: Simpson, *Cannibalism and the Common Law*, 198.

151 The assize system: Simpson, *Cannibalism and the Common Law*, 198–99.

152 The presiding judge: Simpson, *Cannibalism and the Common Law*, 197; "Mignonette Cannibalism Case," *Daily News*, November 4, 1884; Michael G. Mallin, "In Warm Blood: Some Historical and Procedural Aspects of *Regina v. Dudley and Stephens*," *University of Chicago Law Review* 34, no. 2 (Winter 1967): 392.

152 Baron Huddleston was known: *Eminent Persons: Biographies Reprinted from the Times, 1887–1890* (London:

Macmillan, 1893), 4:308; Curtis Wright Jr., "Instructions to the Jury: Summary Without Comment," *Washington University Law Quarterly* 1954, no. 2 (April 1954): 177, 178.

152 The Dudley and Stephens prosecution: *Eminent Persons*, 4:304; Simpson, *Cannibalism and the Common Law*, 197.

153 At the grand jury: "The Mignonette Case at Exeter Assizes," *Southampton Herald*, November 5, 1884; Simpson, *Cannibalism and the Common Law*, 93, 198.

153 Baron Huddleston began: "Mignonette Case at Exeter Assizes."

154 The St. Kitts case: "The Mignonette Case at Exeter Assizes."

154 Baron Huddleston went further: "The Mignonette Case," *Standard* (London), November 4, 1884.

154 Having rejected: "Mignonette Cannibalism Case," *Daily News*, November 4, 1884.

155 In his remarks: "Mignonette Cannibalism Case," *Daily News*, November 4, 1884.

155 Another broad: "The Mignonette Case," *Standard* (London), November 4, 1884.

155 Having covered both: "Mignonette Case," *Standard*, November 4, 1884.

156 Finally, the judge: "The Mignonette Case," *Essex Standard* (Colchester, England), November 8, 1884; "The Devon and Cornwall Winter Assize," *Western Times* (Exeter, England), November 4, 1884.

156 In Victorian England: Jennifer Schweppe, "Pardon Me: The Contemporary Application of the Prerogative of Mercy," *Irish Jurist* 211 (2013): 212–13; Rob Turrell, "'It's a Mystery': The Royal Prerogative of Mercy in England, Canada and South Africa," *Crime, Histoire & Sociétés / Crime, History & Societies* 4, no. 1 (2000): 83–101.

157 Sovereigns could use: Schweppe, "Pardon Me," 213; Sir Sidney Lee, *Queen Victoria: A Biography* (London: Smith, Elder & Co., 1903), 57–58.

157 As the de facto decision-maker: Patrick Jackson, *Harcourt and Son: A Political Biography of Sir William Harcourt, 1827–1904* (Madison, NJ: Fairleigh Dickinson University Press, 2004), 89.

158 If the Victorian reformers: Thackeray quoted in Randall McGowen, "Civilizing Punishment: The End of the Public Execution in England," *Journal of British Studies* 33, no. 3 (July 1994): 257; Randall McGowen, "History, Culture and the Death Penalty: The British Debates, 1840–70," *Historical Reflections* 29, no. 2 (Summer 2003): 229–30, 247; Victor Bailey, "The Shadow of the Gallows: The Death Penalty and the British Labour Government, 1945-51," *Law and History Review* 18, no. 2 (Summer 2000): 305, 307; Leon Radzinowicz and Roger Hood, *The Emergence of Penal Policy in Victorian and Edwardian England* (Oxford: Clarendon Press, 1990), 664.

158 The abolitionists pushed: Randall McGowen, "Interpreting the Death Penalty: Spectacles and Debates," *Historical Reflections*, Summer 2003, 229–30.

158 The Victorian reformers also failed: Bailey, "Shadow of the Gallows," 307; Radzinowicz and Hood, *Emergence of Penal Policy*, 663–67.

159 All this put the grand jurors: McGowen, "History, Culture and the Death Penalty," 236.

159 Baron Huddleston started: Simpson, *Cannibalism and the Common Law*, 203.

159 The judge's way of proceeding: Simpson, *Cannibalism and the Common Law*, 203.

160 In the end, the grand jurors did: "Mignonette Cannibalism Case," *Daily News*, November 4, 1884.

160 The day after: Petition of Thomas Dudley to William Vernon Harcourt, National Archives, A36934/14; Simpson, *Cannibalism and the Common Law*, 204.

160 The visitor was aware: Petition of Thomas Dudley to William Vernon Harcourt, National Archives, A36934/14; Simpson, *Cannibalism and the Common Law*, 204.

9. A Special Verdict

162 On Thursday, November 4: "The Mignonette Cannibalism Case," *Daily News* (London), November 7, 1884.

162 The crowd: "The Mignonette Cannibalism Case," *Daily News* (London), November 7, 1884.

162 The audience was "spellbound": "The Mignonette Case," *Gloucester Citizen*, November 7, 1884; "The Mignonette Cannibalism Case," *Daily News* (London), November 7, 1884.

163 The differences between: Petition of Thomas Dudley to William Vernon Harcourt, National Archives, A36934/14.

163 The trial began: "Mignonette Cannibalism Case," *Daily News*, November 7, 1884.

163 The case would be argued: "The Mignonette Case," *Aberdeen Journal*, November 7, 1884; A. W. Brian Simpson, *Cannibalism and the Common Law: The Story of the Tragic Last Voyage of the Mignonette and the Strange Legal Proceedings to Which It Gave Rise* (Chicago: University of Chicago Press, 1984), 205.

164 The counsel for both sides: "The Mignonette Case," *Standard* (London), November 7, 1884.

164 Speaking softly: Queen v. Dudley and Stephens OR, National Archives DPP 4/17, p. 48 (Trial Before the Petit Jury, Exeter Assize) and pp. 56, 62–63 (Queen v. Dudley and Stephens, trial transcript) (hereafter cited as Queen v. Dudley and Stephens OR); Queen v. Dudley and Stephens OR, National Archives DPP 4/17, p. 48 and pp. 56, 62–63 (Queen v. Dudley and Stephens, trial transcript).

164 Charles said that much: Queen v. Dudley and Stephens OR, National Archives DPP 4/17, pp. 62–63 (Trial Before the Petit Jury, Exeter Assize); Queen v. Dudley and Stephens OR, National Archives DPP 4/17, pp. 62–63 (Queen v. Dudley and Stephens, trial transcript); "The Mignonette Case," *Aberdeen Journal*, November 7, 1884.

165 As for the other element: Queen v. Dudley and Stephens OR, National Archives DPP 4/17, p. 48 (Trial Before the Petit Jury, Exeter Assize) and pp. 62–63 (Queen v. Dudley and Stephens, trial transcript).

165 Charles then argued: Queen v. Dudley and Stephens OR, National Archives DPP 4/17, pp. 64–65 (Queen v. Dudley and Stephens, trial transcript); "The Mignonette Case," *Aberdeen Journal*, November 7, 1884; "The Mignonette Case," *Belfast News-Letter*, November 7, 1884; "Devon & Cornwall Winter Assize," *Exeter and Plymouth Gazette* (Exeter, England), November 7, 1884; Blackstone, *Commentaries on the Laws of England, Book the Fourth, Public Wrongs* (New York: Collins and Hannay, 1832), 42.

166 In the defendants' opening statement: Queen v. Dudley and Stephens OR, National Archives DPP 4/17, p. 76 (Trial Before the Petit Jury, Exeter Assize, and Regina v. Dudley and Stephens, trial transcript).

166 But Collins still refused: Queen v. Dudley and Stephens OR, National Archives DPP 4/17, p. 81 (Trial Before the Petit Jury, Exeter Assize); Francois Gorphe, "Reform of the Jury System in European Countries: England," *Journal of Criminal Law and Criminology*, May–June 1936, 26; Queen v. Dudley and Stephens OR, National Archives DPP 4/17, p. 81 (Queen v. Dudley and Stephens, trial transcript); "Devon & Cornwall Winter Assize," *Exeter and Plymouth Gazette* (Exeter, England), November 7, 1884; Simpson, *Cannibalism and the Common Law*, 207.

166 In this exchange: Queen v. Dudley and Stephens OR, National Archives DPP 4/17, p. 77 (Queen v. Dudley and Stephens, trial transcript); "Devon & Cornwall Winter Assize," *Exeter and Plymouth Gazette* (Exeter, England), November 7, 1884.

167 Baron Huddleston then did something: Queen v. Dudley and Stephens OR, National Archives DPP 4/17, p. 77 (Queen v. Dudley and Stephens, trial transcript); "Devon & Cornwall Winter Assize," *Exeter and Plymouth Gazette* (Exeter, England), November 7, 1884; Michael G. Mallin, "In Warm Blood: Some Historical and Procedural Aspects of *Regina v. Dudley and Stephens*," *University of Chicago Law Review* 34, no. 2 (Winter 1967): 392; "Mignonette Cannibalism Case," *Daily News* (London), November 7, 1884.

167 There were likely two reasons: Simpson, *Cannibalism and the Common Law*, 208–9; Alan Scheflin and Jon Van Dyke, "Jury Nullification: The Contours of a Controversy," *Law and Contemporary Problems* 43, no. 4 (Autumn 1980): 56–57; Hannah Forsyth, "Can a Jury Ignore the Law? Perverse Verdicts in Protest Cases," Exchange Chambers, February 24, 2022, https://www.exchangechambers.co.uk/can-a-jury-ignore-the-law/.

168 Baron Huddleston had good reason: "Mignonette Cannibalism Case," *Daily News* (London), November 7, 1884; Simpson, *Cannibalism and the Common Law*, 199.

168 The jurors' potential hesitation: Randall McGowen, "History, Culture and the Death Penalty: The British Debates, 1840–70," *Historical Reflections / Réflexions Historiques* 29, no. 2 (Summer 2003): 236; Leon Radzinowicz and Roger Hood, *The Emergence of Penal Policy in Victorian and Edwardian England* (Oxford: Clarendon Press, 1990), 667.

168 The second reason: Simpson, *Cannibalism and the Common Law*, 208–9.

170 These advantages notwithstanding: Lester Orfield, "History of Criminal Appeal in England," *Missouri Law Review* 11, no. 1 (1936): 326, 327.

171 Troubling though the use: Orfield, "History of Criminal Appeal," 327.

172 By using this: John Baldwin and Michael McConville, "Criminal Juries," *Crime and Justice* (Chicago: University of Chicago Press, 1980), 2:270–72; Gerald Torres and Donald P. Brewster, "Judges and Juries: Separate Moments in the Same Phenomenon," *Law and Inequality* 4, no. 1 (1986); Edmund M. Morgan, "A Brief History of Special Verdicts and Special Interrogatories," *Yale Law Journal* 32, no. 6 (April 1923): 575, 582.

173 Baron Huddleston was satisfied: Queen v. Dudley and Stephens OR, National Archives DPP 4/17, p. 79 (Trial Before the Petit Jury, Exeter Assize.).

173 The prosecution could also: Queen v. Dudley and Stephens OR, National Archives DPP 4/17, p. 82.

173 The Crown could now start: Queen v. Dudley and Stephens OR, National Archives DPP 4/17, pp. 79, 91–92 (Trial Before the Petit Jury, Exeter Assize); "The Mignonette Cannibalism Case," *Daily News* (London), November 7, 1884; Simpson, *Cannibalism and the Common Law*, 210.

173 Brooks was the first: "The Mignonette Case," *Aberdeen Journal*, November 7, 1884; "Special Telegram," Letter, Belfast, Ireland, November 7, 1884.

174 Charles, the prosecutor: Queen v. Dudley and Stephens OR, National Archives DPP 4/17, pp. 95–96 (Testimony of

Edmund Brooks); "The Mignonette Case," *Belfast News-Letter*, November 7, 1884.

174 **With this, Brooks once again:** Queen v. Dudley and Stephens OR, National Archives DPP 4/17, p. 109 (Trial Before the Petit Jury, Exeter Assize) and p. 109 (Testimony of Edmund Brooks); "Mignonette Case," *Standard*, November 7, 1884.

174 **In his cross-examination:** Queen v. Dudley and Stephens OR, National Archives DPP 4/17, p. 107 (Trial Before the Petit Jury, Exeter Assize and Testimony of Edmund Brooks); "The Mignonette Cannibalism Case: Trial for Murder: Special Verdict," *Daily News* (London), November 7, 1884.

175 **"Yes, no doubt," Brooks said:** Queen v. Dudley and Stephens OR, National Archives DPP 4/17, p. 107 (Testimony of Edmund Brooks).

175 **Brooks testified that the lifeboat:** "The Mignonette Cannibalism Case," *Daily News* (London), November 7, 1884.

175 **Collins was using Brooks:** Queen v. Dudley and Stephens OR, National Archives DPP 4/17, p. 110 (Trial Before the Petit Jury, Exeter Assize); Simpson, *Cannibalism and the Common Law*, 211; Queen v. Dudley and Stephens OR, National Archives DPP 4/17, p. 107 (Testimony of Edmund Brooks).

176 **The remaining witnesses stuck:** Queen v. Dudley and Stephens OR, National Archives DPP 4/17, pp. 119–23, 127–39; "Mignonette Cannibalism Case," *Daily News* (London), November 7, 1884; Queen v. Dudley and Stephens OR, National Archives DPP 4/17, pp. 112–17 (Trial Before the Petit Jury, Exeter Assize), 112 (Testimony of Julius Wiese), and 112–15 (Testimony of Gustavus Collins); "The Terrible Story of the Sea," *Burrows Worcester Journal*, November 8, 1884.

176 **The prosecutors entered:** "The Mignonette Cannibalism Case: Trial for Murder: Special Verdict," *Daily News*

(London), November 7, 1884; Queen v. Dudley and Stephens OR, National Archives DPP 4/17, pp. 127–43.

176 Dudley's knife: Queen v. Dudley and Stephens OR, National Archives DPP 4/17, p. 144; "Mignonette Cannibalism Case," *Daily News* (London), November 7, 1884.

177 The defense did not present: Queen v. Dudley and Stephens OR, National Archives DPP 4/17, p. 144 (Trial Before the Petit Jury, Exeter Assize); Simpson, *Cannibalism and the Common Law*, 211.

177 But the defense: Queen v. Dudley and Stephens OR, National Archives DPP 4/17, p. 144 (Trial Before the Petit Jury, Exeter Assize); "Mignonette Cannibalism Case," *Daily News* (London), November 7, 1884; Geoffrey Marston, "Crimes by British Passengers on Board Foreign Ships on the High Seas: The Historical Background to Section 686 (1) of the Merchant Shipping Act," *Cambridge Law Journal* 58, no. 1 (1999): 172; Simpson, *Cannibalism and the Common Law*, 211.

177 Baron Huddleston asked: Simpson, *Cannibalism and the Common Law*, 211.

177 Collins may have had a point: Queen v. Dudley and Stephens OR, National Archives DPP 4/17, pp. 144–45 (Trial Before the Petit Jury, Exeter Assize); "The Charge of Cannibalism at Sea," *Morning Post* (London), November 7, 1884.

178 Baron Huddleston was in no mood: Queen v. Dudley and Stephens OR, National Archives DPP 4/17, pp. 144–49; "Mignonette Cannibalism Case," *Daily News* (London), November 7, 1884.

178 After a short dispute: Queen v. Dudley and Stephens OR, National Archives DPP 4/17, p. 164 (Trial Before the Petit Jury, Exeter Assize).

178 Collins was asking the jurors: Queen v. Dudley and Stephens OR, National Archives DPP 4/17, p. 164 (Trial Before the Petit Jury, Exeter Assize); "Devon & Cornwall Winter Assize," *Exeter and Plymouth Gazette* (Exeter, England), November 7, 1884.

178 **Collins, however:** Queen v. Dudley and Stephens OR, National Archives DPP 4/17, p. 175; "Mignonette Cannibalism Case," *Daily News* (London), November 7, 1884.

179 **He was, in effect:** Gregory Claeys, "The 'Survival of the Fittest' and the Origins of Social Darwinism," *Journal of the History of Ideas* 61, no. 2 (April 2000): 230.

179 **Collins's social Darwinist reasoning:** James Allen Rogers, "Darwinism and Social Darwinism," *Journal of the History of Ideas* 33, no. 2 (April–June 1972): 266; Queen v. Dudley and Stephens OR, National Archives DPP 4/17, p. 175.

180 **Collins then switched:** Mark Dimmock and Andrew Fisher, *Ethics for A-Level* (Open Book Publishers, 2017) 15.

180 **Collins contended:** Queen v. Dudley and Stephens OR, National Archives DPP 4/17, p. 176; "Devon & Cornwall Winter Assize," *Exeter and Plymouth Gazette* (Exeter, England), November 7, 1884.

181 **Before he ended:** Queen v. Dudley and Stephens OR, National Archives DPP 4/17, p. 165; "Devon & Cornwall Winter Assize," *Exeter and Plymouth Gazette* (Exeter, England), November 7, 1884.

181 **Charles began:** Queen v. Dudley and Stephens OR, National Archives DPP 4/17, p. 184 (Trial Before the Petit Jury, Exeter Assize).

181 **For Charles, the case was straightforward:** Queen v. Dudley and Stephens OR, National Archives DPP 4/17, p. 186.

181 **Baron Huddleston gave:** Queen v. Dudley and Stephens OR, National Archives DPP 4/17, pp. 186–89 (Trial Before the Petit Jury, Exeter Assize); "Mignonette Cannibalism Case," *Daily News* (London), November 7, 1884.

182 Under the rules: Queen v. Dudley and Stephens OR, National Archives DPP 4/17, pp. 191–92, 195; "Devon & Cornwall Winter Assize," *Exeter and Plymouth Gazette* (Exeter, England), November 7, 1884.

182 Baron Huddleston rebuked: Queen v. Dudley and Stephens OR, National Archives DPP 4/17, pp. 191–92, 195; "Devon & Cornwall Winter Assize," *Exeter and Plymouth Gazette* (Exeter, England), November 7, 1884.

182 The jurors accepted: Queen v. Dudley and Stephens OR, National Archives DPP 4/17, p. 186 (Trial Before the Petit Jury, Exeter Assize); "Devon & Cornwall Winter Assize," *Exeter and Plymouth Gazette* (Exeter, England), November 7, 1884.

183 Baron Huddleston produced: Queen v. Dudley and Stephens OR, National Archives DPP 4/17, p. 206 (Trial Before the Petit Jury, Exeter Assize); "The Mignonette Cannibalism Case: Trial for Murder: Special Verdict," *Daily News* (London), November 7, 1884.

183 From this point on: Queen v. Dudley and Stephens OR, National Archives DPP 4/17, pp. 206–15; "Mignonette Cannibalism Case," *Daily News* (London), November 7, 1884; Simpson, *Cannibalism and the Common Law*, 213.

183 The document remained: Queen v. Dudley and Stephens OR, National Archives DPP 4/17, pp. 213–17 (Trial Before the Petit Jury, Exeter Assize); Simpson, *Cannibalism and the Common Law*, 214.

184 It is possible: Queen v. Dudley and Stephens OR, National Archives DPP 4/17, pp. 213–17 (Trial Before the Petit Jury, Exeter Assize); Simpson, *Cannibalism and the Common Law*, 214.

185 Another sentence in the draft: Queen v. Dudley and Stephens OR, National Archives DPP 4/17, p. 217 (Trial Before the Petit Jury, Exeter Assize); Simpson, *Cannibalism and the Common Law*, 215.

185 In addition to undermining: Simpson, *Cannibalism and the Common Law*, 215; Queen v. Dudley and Stephens OR, National Archives DPP 4/17, pp. 216–17.

185 The jury agreed: Queen v. Dudley and Stephens OR, National Archives DPP 4/17, p. 217; Simpson, *Cannibalism and the Common Law*, 214–15.

186 After Baron Huddleston finished: Queen v. Dudley and Stephens OR, National Archives DPP 4/17, pp. 217–18 (Trial Before the Petit Jury, Exeter Assize); Simpson, *Cannibalism and the Common Law*, 215; "Mignonette Cannibalism Case," *Daily News* (London), November 7, 1884.

186 "Yes, my Lord": Queen v. Dudley and Stephens OR, National Archives DPP 4/17, p. 218 (Trial Before the Petit Jury, Exeter Assize); "The Captain and Mate Technically Guilty of Murder, but Released on Bail," *Cornishman* (Penzance, England), November 13, 1884.

186 Baron Huddleston assured: Queen v. Dudley and Stephens OR, National Archives DPP 4/17, p. 218 (Trial Before the Petit Jury, Exeter Assize); Mallin, "In Warm Blood," 396.

186 Baron Huddleston released: Queen v. Dudley and Stephens OR, National Archives DPP 4/17, p. 218 (Trial Before the Petit Jury, Exeter Assize); "Mignonette Cannibalism Case," *Daily News* (London), November 7, 1884.

187 The members of the public: "Mignonette Cannibalism Case," *Daily News* (London), November 7, 1884; "The Mignonette Case—Trial and Verdict," *Manchester Times*, November 8, 1884.

187 The jurors seemed just: "Mignonette Cannibalism Case," *Daily News* (London), November 7, 1884.

187 The press gave: "A Very Remarkable Case, Unique in the History of English Criminal Law," *Times* (London), November 7, 1884.

188 *The Times* also praised: "Very Remarkable Case."

10. The Lord Chief Justice Rules

189 For the first time: Queen v. Dudley and Stephens (Murder on the High Seas) Official Record (Bound Volume), National Archives DPP 4/17, pp. 221–30 (hereafter cited as Queen v. Dudley and Stephens OR); "Mignonette Case," *Daily News* (London), November 26, 1884.

189 On November 25: Letter of James to Harcourt, n.d., Letters of Lord James of Hereford, 1873–1904, box 86, Archive of Sir William and Lewis Harcourt, 1st Viscount Harcourt, Bodleian Libraries, University of Oxford; Queen v. Dudley and Stephens OR, National Archives DPP 4/17, pp. 221–30; "The Mignonette Case," *Essex Standard* (Colchester, England), November 29, 1884.

189 The attorney general acknowledged: Queen v. Dudley and Stephens OR, National Archives DPP 4/17, pp. 221–30; "Mignonette Case," *Daily News*, November 26, 1884; A. W. Brian Simpson, *Cannibalism and the Common Law: The Story of the Tragic Last Voyage of the Mignonette and the Strange Legal Proceedings to Which It Gave Rise* (Chicago: University of Chicago Press, 1984), 219–20.

190 The lawyers started discussing: Queen v. Dudley and Stephens OR, National Archives DPP 4/17, pp. 216–17, 230; "Mignonette Case," *Daily News*, November 26, 1884.

190 On December 4: Queen v. Dudley and Stephens OR, National Archives DPP 4/17, p. 239; "Mignonette Case," *Daily News*, December 5, 1884; "A Very Remarkable Case, Unique in the History of English Criminal Law," *Times* (London), November 7, 1884.

190 If Baron Huddleston: "Reminiscences of Lord Chief Justice Coleridge," *Irish Monthly*, January 1901, 31–32.

191 Like Baron Huddleston: "Reminiscences," 31–32; Ernest Hartley Coleridge, *Life & Correspondence of John Duke Lord*

Coleridge Lord Chief Justice of England (New York: D. Appleton and Co., 1904), 2:288–89; "House of Commons—Yesterday," *Freeman's Journal* (Dublin), March 22, 1866; "Very Remarkable Case."

192 **The attorney general, James:** Queen v. Dudley and Stephens OR, National Archives DPP 4/17, p. 240; "The Mignonette Murder: Sentence by the Judges," *Standard* (London), December 10, 1884; "The Mignonette Case," *Morning Post* (London), December 5, 1884; Simpson, *Cannibalism and the Common Law*, 225; "Mignonette Case," *Daily News*, December 5, 1884.

192 **Two people:** Queen v. Dudley and Stephens OR, National Archives DPP 4/17, pp. 216–17; Queen v. Dudley and Stephens, QBD, December 4, 1884, p. 240, in National Archives, Regina v. Dudley and Stephens File; "Mignonette Case," *Daily News*, December 5, 1884; "The Mignonette Cannibalism Case: Trial for Murder: Special Verdict," *Daily News* (London), November 7, 1884.

192 **Collins did not appear:** Queen v. Dudley and Stephens OR, National Archives DPP 4/17, p. 240; Queen v. Dudley and Stephens, QBD, December 4, 1884, p. 240, in National Archives, Regina v. Dudley and Stephens File; "Mignonette Case," *Daily News*, December 5, 1884.

192 **Ten minutes later:** "Mignonette Case," *Daily News*, December 5, 1884.

193 **The attorney general suggested:** Queen v. Dudley and Stephens OR, National Archives DPP 4/17, p. 241; Queen v. Dudley and Stephens, QBD, December 4, 1884, pp. 240–41, in National Archives, Regina v. Dudley and Stephens File; "Mignonette Case," *Daily News*, December 5, 1884.

193 **After the reading:** Queen v. Dudley and Stephens OR, National Archives DPP 4/17, pp. 240–42; "The 'Mignonette'

Case," *Exeter and Plymouth Gazette* (Exeter, England), December 5, 1884; Simpson, *Cannibalism and the Common Law*, 226.

194 **Collins argued:** Queen v. Dudley and Stephens, QBD, December 4, 1884, pp. 240–42, in National Archives, Regina v. Dudley and Stephens File, 242–44.

194 **The lord chief justice ordered:** Queen v. Dudley and Stephens, QBD, December 4, 1884, pp. 240, 245, 267 in National Archives, Regina v. Dudley and Stephens File; "Mignonette Case," *Morning Post*, December 5, 1884.

194 **The attorney general told:** Queen v. Dudley and Stephens, QBD, December 4, 1884, pp. 240, 267–69 in National Archives, Regina v. Dudley and Stephens File; "Mignonette Case," *Morning Post*, December 5, 1884.

195 **Turning to the legal issues:** Queen v. Dudley and Stephens, QBD, December 4, 1884, p. 270, in National Archives, Regina v. Dudley and Stephens File; "Mignonette Case," *Morning Post*, December 5, 1884.

195 **Lord Coleridge interjected:** Queen v. Dudley and Stephens, QBD, December 4, 1884, p. 270, in National Archives, Regina v. Dudley and Stephens File; "Mignonette Case," *Daily News*, December 5, 1884.

195 **Once it was established:** Queen v. Dudley and Stephens, QBD, December 4, 1884, pp. 275–76, in National Archives, Regina v. Dudley and Stephens File; "Mignonette Case," *Morning Post*, December 5, 1884.

195 **"Great writers on criminal law":** Queen v. Dudley and Stephens, QBD, December 4, 1884, p. 277, in National Archives, Regina v. Dudley and Stephens File; "Mignonette Case," *Morning Post*, December 5, 1884.

196 **Nevertheless, before concluding:** Queen v. Dudley and Stephens, QBD, December 4, 1884, pp. 278–81, in National

Archives, Regina v. Dudley and Stephens File; "Mignonette Case," *Daily News*, December 5, 1884.

196 **The lord chief justice then asked:** Queen v. Dudley and Stephens, QBD, December 4, 1884, p. 287.

196 **Collins began by invoking:** Queen v. Dudley and Stephens, QBD, December 4, 1884, pp. 283, 294–95, 316, in National Archives, Regina v. Dudley and Stephens File; "The Mignonette Case," *Essex Standard* (Colchester, England), December 5, 1884.

197 **"That is for the jury":** Queen v. Dudley and Stephens, QBD, December 4, 1884, in National Archives, Regina v. Dudley and Stephens File, 316.

197 **The lord chief justice asked Collins:** Queen v. Dudley and Stephens, QBD, December 4, 1884, in National Archives, Regina v. Dudley and Stephens File, 333.

197 **"I should have thought":** Queen v. Dudley and Stephens, QBD, December 4, 1884, in National Archives, Regina v. Dudley and Stephens File, 323–24, 333.

197 **This "great instinct":** Queen v. Dudley and Stephens, QBD, December 4, 1884, pp. 328–29 in National Archives, Regina v. Dudley and Stephens File; "Mignonette Case," *Daily News*, December 5, 1884.

198 **With the central legal argument:** Queen v. Dudley and Stephens, QBD, December 4, 1884, p. 343 in National Archives, Regina v. Dudley and Stephens File; "Mignonette Case," *Daily News*, December 5, 1884.

198 **"Does it make any difference?":** Queen v. Dudley and Stephens, QBD, December 4, 1884, p. 343 in National Archives, Regina v. Dudley and Stephens File.

198 **Baron Pollock insisted:** Queen v. Dudley and Stephens, QBD, December 4, 1884, pp. 366–67 in National Archives, Regina v. Dudley and Stephens File; "Mignonette Case," *Daily News*, December 5, 1884.

198 After the break: "The Mignonette Case," *Standard* (London), December 5, 1884; Simpson, *Cannibalism and the Common Law*, 236.

199 But right now: Queen v. Dudley and Stephens, QBD, December 4, 1884, pp. 367, 388 in National Archives, Regina v. Dudley and Stephens File; "Cannibalism at Sea the Legal Argument," *Derby Daily Telegraph* December 4, 1884.

199 The importance of the moment: Queen v. Dudley and Stephens, QBD, December 4, 1884, p. 389 in National Archives, Regina v. Dudley and Stephens File.

199 Collins still hoped: "Cannibalism at Sea the Legal Argument."

199 The lord chief justice denied: Queen v. Dudley and Stephens, QBD, December 4, 1884, p. 389 in National Archives, Regina v. Dudley and Stephens File; "Mignonette Case," *Essex Standard*, December 6, 1884.

200 Even so, the men might have found: Queen v. Dudley and Stephens, QBD, December 4, 1884, p. 390 in National Archives, Regina v. Dudley and Stephens File; "The Mignonette Case," *Leeds Mercury*, December 5, 1884.

200 When they settled in: "The Mignonette Case," *Western Mail* (Cardiff, Wales), December 10, 1884.

200 Asked about his wife: "Mignonette Case," *Western Mail*, December 10, 1884.

102 "If I could have": "Mignonette Case," *Western Mail*, December 10, 1884.

201 The lord chief justice and the home secretary: Lewis Harcourt journal, 27 November–31 December, p. 26 (December 5), box 362, Archive of Sir William and Lewis Harcourt, 1st Viscount Harcourt, Bodleian Libraries, University of Oxford.

201 Lewis Harcourt: Leon Radzinowicz and Roger Hood, *The Emergence of Penal Policy in Victorian and Edwardian*

England (Oxford: Clarendon Press, 1990), 677; Lewis Harcourt journal, 27 November–31 December, p. 26 (December 5), box 362, Archive of Sir William and Lewis Harcourt, 1st Viscount Harcourt, Bodleian Libraries, University of Oxford.

202 **There was no formula:** Simpson, *Cannibalism and the Common Law*, 242–43; Rob Turrell, "'It's a Mystery': The Royal Prerogative of Mercy in England, Canada and South Africa," *Crime, Histoire & Sociétés / Crime, History & Societies* 4, no. 1 (2000): 83–101; Radzinowicz and Hood, *Emergence of Penal Policy*, 678–80; Ann Lousin, book review, "Cannibalism and the Common Law," *John Marshall Law Review* 19 (1986): 821, 827–28.

202 **In the end:** A. G. Gardiner, *The Life of Sir William Harcourt* (London: Constable, 1923), 1:397; Lousin, book review, "Cannibalism and the Common Law," 827–28; Turrell, "'It's a Mystery,'" 83–101; Simpson, *Cannibalism and the Common Law*, 243–44; Patrick Jackson, *Harcourt and Son: A Political Biography of Sir William Harcourt, 1827–1904* (Madison, NJ: Fairleigh Dickinson University Press, 2004), 89.

202 **When Harcourt considered:** Simpson, *Cannibalism and the Common Law*, 243–44; Jackson, *Harcourt and Son*, 89.

203 **The decision was not Harcourt's:** Gardiner, *Life of Sir William Harcourt*, 1:397–98; Julia Baird, *Victoria the Queen: An Intimate Biography of the Woman Who Ruled an Empire* (New York: Random House, 2014), 204.

203 **Dudley and Stephens's mercy request:** Letter of Irvine Hodges to William Harcourt, December 5, 1884, National Archives, A36934/7; Simpson, *Cannibalism and the Common Law*, 240; Petition of Dudley and Stephens to Secretary of State William Harcourt, December 5, 1884, National Archives, Doc. A35934/7.

204 In the appeal: Petition of Dudley and Stephens to Secretary of State William Harcourt, December 4, 1884, National Archives, Doc. A35934/7.

204 Meanwhile, Dudley and Stephens's supporters: "Derby, December 5, 1884," *Derby Daily Telegraph*, December 5, 1884.

204 Harcourt was also receiving: Letter of James to Harcourt, n.d., Letters of Lord James of Hereford, 1873–1904, box 86, Archive of Sir William and Lewis Harcourt, 1st Viscount Harcourt, Bodleian Libraries, University of Oxford; Letter of James to Harcourt, December 5, Letters of Lord James of Hereford, 1873–1904, box 86, Archive of Sir William and Lewis Harcourt, 1st Viscount Harcourt, Bodleian Libraries, University of Oxford.

204 Now the attorney general: Letter of James to Harcourt, December 5, Letters of Lord James of Hereford, 1873–1904, box 86, Archive of Sir William and Lewis Harcourt, 1st Viscount Harcourt, Bodleian Libraries, University of Oxford.

205 In his response: Letter of Harcourt to James, December 6, Letters of Lord James of Hereford, 1873–1904, box 86, Archive of Sir William and Lewis Harcourt, 1st Viscount Harcourt, Bodleian Libraries, University of Oxford.

206 Harcourt's response: Lewis Harcourt journal, 27 November–31 December, p. 27 (December 5), box 362, Archive of Sir William and Lewis Harcourt, 1st Viscount Harcourt, Bodleian Libraries, University of Oxford.

206 Lewis was, like the attorney general: Lewis Harcourt journal, 27 November—31 December, p. 27 (December 5), box 362, Archive of Sir William and Lewis Harcourt, 1st Viscount Harcourt, Bodleian Libraries, University of Oxford; Lewis Harcourt journal, 27 November–31 December, p. 50 (December 8), box 362, Archive of Sir William and Lewis Harcourt, 1st Viscount Harcourt, Bodleian Libraries,

University of Oxford; Simpson, *Cannibalism and the Common Law*, 247.

206 On Tuesday, December 9: "Mignonette Case," *Daily News*, December 10, 1884; "Cannibalism at Sea," *Cambridge Independent Press*, December 13, 1884.

207 Dudley once again: "Mignonette Case," *Essex Standard*, December 13, 1884; "An Interview with Stephens," *Essex Standard*, December 13, 1884.

207 At 10:40 a.m.: "The Mignonette Murder Case," *Morning Post* (London), December 10, 1884; "Cannibalism at Sea," *Cambridge Independent Press*, December 13, 1884.

207 A court officer announced: "Cannibalism at Sea," *Cambridge Independent Press*, December 13, 1884; "Our London Letter," *Belfast News-Letter*, December 10, 1884.

207 The lord chief justice started: Queen v. Dudley and Stephens OR, National Archives DPP 4/17, pp. 396–97 (Transcript of December 9 Proceeding); Queen v. Dudley and Stephens, (1884) 14 QBD 273; "Mignonette Case," *Daily News*, December 10, 1884.

208 Lord Coleridge then pivoted: Queen v. Dudley and Stephens OR, National Archives DPP 4/17, pp. 396–97 (Transcript of December 9 Proceeding); Queen v. Dudley and Stephens, (1884) 14 QBD 273; "Mignonette Case," *Daily News*, December 10, 1884.

208 The justices did not see this: Queen v. Dudley and Stephens OR, National Archives DPP 4/17, pp. 402–3 (Transcript of December 9 Proceeding); Queen v. Dudley and Stephens, (1884) 14 QBD 273; "Mignonette Murder," *Standard*, December 10, 1884.

208 Lord Coleridge had more to say: "Mignonette Murder Case"; Queen v. Dudley and Stephens OR, National Archives DPP 4/17, p. 413 (Transcript of December 9 Proceeding).

209 Lord Coleridge supported: Queen v. Dudley and Stephens, (1884) 14 QBD 273; "Cannibalism at Sea," *Cambridge Independent Press*, December 13, 1884; Ben Johnson, "Women and Children First," Historic UK, https://www.historic-uk.com/CultureUK/Women-Children-First; Rudyard Kipling, "Soldier an' Sailor Too," Kipling Society, https://www.kiplingsociety.co.uk/poem/poems_soldiersailor.htm.

210 Directly contrary: Queen v. Dudley and Stephens, (1884) 14 QBD 273; "Mignonette Case," *Essex Standard*, December 13, 1884; Queen v. Dudley and Stephens OR, National Archives DPP 4/17, p. 419 (Transcript of December 9 Proceeding).

210 Lord Coleridge did not: Queen v. Dudley and Stephens OR, National Archives DPP 4/17, p. 420 (Transcript of December 9 Proceeding); Queen v. Dudley and Stephens, (1884) 14 QBD 273; "Mignonette Murder Case."

211 The lord chief justice was: Queen v. Dudley and Stephens, (1884) 14 QBD 273; Queen v. Dudley and Stephens OR, National Archives DPP 4/17, p. 420 (Transcript of December 9 Proceeding); "Mignonette Murder Case."

211 The lord chief justice insisted: "Mignonette Murder Case"; Queen v. Dudley and Stephens OR, National Archives DPP 4/17, p. 421 (Transcript of December 9 Proceeding); Queen v. Dudley and Stephens, (1884) 14 QBD 273.

212 The defense's arguments: Queen v. Dudley and Stephens OR, National Archives DPP 4/17, p. 421 (Transcript of December 9 Proceeding); Queen v. Dudley and Stephens, (1884) 14 QBD 273; "Mignonette Murder Case."

212 Lord Coleridge was now ready: Queen v. Dudley and Stephens OR, National Archives DPP 4/17, pp. 422–23 (Transcript of December 9 Proceeding); Queen v. Dudley and Stephens, (1884) 14 QBD 273; "Mignonette Murder Case";

"The Mignonette Case," *North Devon Journal* (Barnstaple, England), December 11, 1884.

212 **A half hour after:** Queen v. Dudley and Stephens OR, National Archives DPP 4/17, p. 423 (Transcript of December 9 Proceeding).

212 **"My lord, it is my duty":** Queen v. Dudley and Stephens OR, National Archives DPP 4/17, p. 423 (Transcript of December 9 Proceeding).

212 **Dudley and Stephens were ordered:** Queen v. Dudley and Stephens OR, National Archives DPP 4/17, p. 423 (Transcript of December 9 Proceeding); "Mignonette Murder: Sentence by the Judges."

213 **Dudley, speaking so softly:** Queen v. Dudley and Stephens OR, National Archives DPP 4/17, p. 423 (Transcript of December 9 Proceeding); "Mignonette Murder: Sentence by the Judges."

213 **Lord Coleridge allowed:** Queen v. Dudley and Stephens OR, National Archives DPP 4/17, pp. 423–24 (Transcript of December 9 Proceeding); "Mignonette Murder: Sentence by the Judges."

213 **But having endorsed:** Queen v. Dudley and Stephens OR, National Archives DPP 4/17, pp. 423–24 (Transcript of December 9 Proceeding); "'Mignonette' Case," *Exeter and Plymouth Gazette*, December 12, 1884.

214 **It was a foreboding recitation:** "Mignonette Case," *Essex Standard*, December 13, 1884.

214 **Dudley had been tormented:** Petition of Thomas Dudley to William Vernon Harcourt, National Archives, A36934/14.

214 **With their duties:** "The Mignonette Murder," *Gloucester Citizen* (Gloucester, England), December 10, 1884; "The Mignonette Murder," *Manchester Courier and Lancashire General Advertiser*, December 10, 1884.

215 If there was any consolation: Memorandum of William Harcourt, December 9, 1884, National Archives, A36934/8; Memorandum of Governor of Holloway Prison, December 9, 1884, National Archives, A36934/8.

216 Although the ruling was occasioned: "Mignonette Murder Case."

216 The opinion was largely: "The Court of Queen's Bench Passed Sentence," *Times* (London), December 10, 1884.

217 In a similar vein: Queen v. Dudley and Stephens, (1884) 14 QBD 273.

217 In championing the weak: Queen v. Dudley and Stephens OR, National Archives DPP 4/17, p. 184 (Trial Before the Petit Jury, Exeter Assize).

218 Lord Coleridge's message: Queen v. Dudley and Stephens, (1884) 14 QBD 273.

11. Fading Away

220 The news of Dudley's and Stephens's death sentences: "The Mignonette Cannibals," *The Wheeling Daily Intelligencer*, December 12, 1884; "The Queen's Bench," *Times*, December 20, 1884; "The Mignonette Affair," *Sydney Morning Herald*, December 11, 1884; "The Mignonette Cannibals," *New York Times*, December 10, 1884.

220 With the dire sentences: "Our London Letter," *Northern Echo* (Darlington, England), December 10, 1884; "Our London Letter," *Belfast News-Letter*, December 10, 1884.

221 It was certainly possible: "Sentence of Death Was Yesterday Formally Pronounced," *Daily Telegraph* (London), December 10, 1884; "The Mignonette Case," *Essex Standard* (Colchester, England), December 13, 1884 (quoting London's *Daily News*).

221 But there remained: "The Court of Queen's Bench Passed Sentence," *Times* (London), December 10, 1884.

222 The radical *Reynolds's Newspaper*: "The Mignonette Murder," *Reynolds's Newspaper* (London), December 14, 1884.

222 Some newspapers did sympathize: "Sentence of Death."

223 Dudley and Stephens were now back: "The Mignonette Case," *Royal Cornwall Gazette* (Truro, England), December 19, 1884.

223 The newspapers were reporting plans: "The Mignonette Case," *Southampton Herald*, December 13, 1884; A. W. Brian Simpson, *Cannibalism and the Common Law: The Story of the Tragic Last Voyage of the Mignonette and the Strange Legal Proceedings to Which It Gave Rise* (Chicago: University of Chicago Press, 1984), photo opposite p. 131.

223 The second quotation: "The Mignonette Case," newspaper clipping, no newspaper name, no date, National Archives, A36934/15; Simpson, *Cannibalism and the Common Law*, 241–42.

224 On Friday, December 12: "The Mignonette Trage[d]y," *Western Times* (Exeter, England), December 15, 1884; Simpson, *Cannibalism and the Common Law*, 247.

225 The next morning: "The Mignonette Case," *Edinburgh Evening News*, December 16, 1884.

225 On December 15: Simpson, *Cannibalism and the Common Law*, 245; Conditional Pardon, National Archives, KB 33/46.

225 The Home Office prepared: Simpson, *Cannibalism and the Common Law*, 245–47; Conditional Pardon, National Archives, KB 33/46.

226 The order reducing: "The Mignonette Case," *Daily News* (London), December 15, 1884.

226 The changes happened quickly: "The Mignonette Case," *Sheffield Independent* (Sheffield, England), December 18,

1884; "The Mignonette Prisoners," *Western Times* (Exeter, England), December 25, 1884; "The Mignonette Murder," *Star* (Saint Peter Port, Guernsey, UK), December 16, 1884.

226 **While he was confined:** "The Mignonette Prisoners," *Leeds Mercury*, December 24, 1884; "Mignonette Prisoners," *Northern Echo* (Darlington, England), December 25, 1884; "The Mignonette Prisoners," *Western Daily Mercury* (Plymouth, England), December 17, 1884.

227 **Far less was known:** "The Mignonette Case," *Nottingham Evening Post*, December 16, 1884; "The Mignonette Tragedy Decision of the Home Secretary," *Gloucester Citizen*, December 15, 1884; "Mignonette Prisoners," *Western Times*, December 24, 1884.

227 **While Dudley was locked up:** "Gridiron Gossip," *Sunday Times* (London), December 28, 1884; Classified Ads, *Standard* (London), January 13, 1885; Pauline Chapman, *Madame Tussaud's Chamber of Horror* (London: Constable, 1984), 87, 90; Howard Malchow, *Gothic Images of Race in Nineteenth-Century England* (Palo Alto: Stanford University Press, 1996), 87; Simpson, *Cannibalism and the Common Law*, 248; Madame Tussaud & Sons' Catalog (1886) 39–44; "Madame Tussaud & Sons" advertisement, *The Era Almanack and Annual* (1885), https://www.google.com/books/edition/The_Era_Almanack_Dramatic_Musical/hDs5AAAAIAAJ?hl=en&gbpv=1&dq=%22madame+tussaud%22+%22captain+dudley%22&pg=RA1-PA4&printsec=frontcover.

227 **While the public gawked:** Petition of Thomas Dudley to William Vernon Harcourt, National Archives, A36934/14.

228 **In this personal appeal:** Petition of Thomas Dudley to William Vernon Harcourt, National Archives, A36934/14.

228 **Stephens wrote a petition:** Petition of Edwin Stephens, National Archives, A36934/23; Letter of J. B. Garvey to

William Harcourt, January 20, 1884, National Archives, A36934/5; "The Mignonette Cannibalism Case," *Evening Telegraph* (Dundee, Scotland), January 14, 1885; "Penzance, or Other, Gossip," *Cornishman* (Penzance, England), January 15, 1885.

229 **There was only one place:** Letter of Alice Lever to William Harcourt, December 24, 1884, National Archives, A36931/1; Simpson, *Cannibalism and the Common Law*, 286.

229 **The home secretary did not appreciate:** Simpson, *Cannibalism and the Common Law*, 286.

229 **Ellis Lever, who supported:** Ellis Lever Letter to Queen Victoria, National Archives, A36934.

230 **Lever's appeal to the queen:** Ellis Lever Letter to Queen Victoria, National Archives, A36934.

230 **Lever also informed the queen:** Ellis Lever Letter to Queen Victoria, National Archives, A36934; Frank Lewis, "The Cost of Convict Transportation from Britain to Australia, 1796–1810," *Economic History Review* 41, no. 4 (1988).

230 **The heart of Lever's appeal:** Letter of Philippa Dudley to Ellis Lever, February 19, 1885, A36934, National Archives.

231 **In Philippa Dudley's telling:** Letter of Philippa Dudley to Ellis Lever, February 19, 1885, A36934, National Archives.

231 **Dudley's honesty:** Letter of Philippa Dudley to Ellis Lever, February 19, 1885, A36934, National Archives.

232 **This was another inaccurate framing:** Letter of Philippa Dudley to Ellis Lever, February 19, 1885, A36934, National Archives.

232 **Mrs. Dudley included:** Letter of Philippa Dudley to Ellis Lever, February 19, 1885, A36934, National Archives.

232 **The home secretary received:** Letter from Windsor Castle. March 8, 1885, National Archives, A 36934; Simpson, *Cannibalism and the Common Law*, 287.

233 On May 20, 1885: "The Mignonette Case," *Daily Gazette for Middlesbrough*, May 20, 1885; Simpson, *Cannibalism and the Common Law*, 287–88.

233 It was not long: Simpson, *Cannibalism and the Common Law*, 283; Letter of Philippa Dudley to Ellis Lever, February 19, 1885, A36934, National Archives.

234 Although he had considered: Simpson, *Cannibalism and the Common Law*, 288–89.

234 Brooks was said to have carried: Simpson, *Cannibalism and the Common Law*, 283.

234 After Stephens was released: Simpson, *Cannibalism and the Common Law*, 289–90.

234 Dudley had the shortest: Simpson, *Cannibalism and the Common Law*, 290–94; Letter of Philippa Dudley to Ellis Lever, February 19, 1885, A36934, National Archives.

235 But the good times did not last: Barry R. Catchlove, "Plague Sydney 1900," *Hektoen International: A Journal of Medical Humanities* 2, no. 2 (Spring 2010); "The Bubonic Plague: Another Case in Sydney," *Adelaide Evening Journal*, February 26, 1900; "Australia: Plague in Sydney," *Public Health Reports* 15, no. 17 (April 1900), entry for April 27, 1900, pp. 1000–1001; Carol Benedict, "Bubonic Plague in Nineteenth-Century China," *Modern China* 14, no. 2 (April 1988): 107–8.

235 Dudley's shop: Catchlove, "Plague Sydney 1900"; Simpson, *Cannibalism and the Common Law*, 295–96; "Bubonic Plague: Another Case."

235 Dudley's was the first: "Bubonic Plague Epidemic of 1900," *The Dictionary of Sydney*, https://dictionaryofsydney.org/event/bubonic_plague_epidemic_1900; Julie Power, "Plague's Ground Zero: When the Black Death Hit Sydney," *Stuff*, February 9, 2019; Simpson, *Cannibalism and* *the Common Law*, 291, 296–98; Catchlove, "Plague Sydney 1900"; "Bubonic Plague: Another Case."

236 **As the city's first:** Simpson, *Cannibalism and the Common Law*, 296.

Afterword

237 **In *Life of Pi*:** "Yann Martel on Tigers, Cannibals and Edgar Allan Poe," *Canongate*, May 14, 2002.

237 **Other people see:** "Cabin Boy Cutlets," *Times Literary Supplement*, July 27, 1984.

238 **For literary people:** "The Mysterious Power of Chance," *Sunday Times*, May 5, 1974.

238 **For lawyers:** *London Borough of Southwark v. Williams* 2 All E.R. 175, 179 (1971), quoted in Mervyn E. Bennun, "Necessity—Yet Another Analysis," *Irish Jurist*, Winter 1976, 186, 200.

239 **The impact:** Oliver Wendell Holmes, *The Common Law* (Boston: Little, Brown, 1881), 47.

239 **The rule changed:** Benjamin Cardozo, *Law and Literature* (New York: Harcourt, Brace, 1931), 113; Joshua Dressler, "Reflections on *Dudley and Stephens* and Killing the Innocent: Taking a Wrong Conceptual Path," in *The Sanctity of Life and the Criminal Law: The Legacy of Glanville Williams*, ed. Dennis J. Baker and Jeremy Horder (Cambridge: Cambridge University Press, 2013), 128. Though accepted by most courts, the rule is not followed uniformly. In the Model Penal Code, a model law drafted as an example that can be followed by drafters of state laws, the provision on the "choice of evils" defense does not rule out its use in homicide cases, and some states accordingly allow it in their own statutes. Dressler, "Reflections on *Dudley and Stephens*," 128n14.

239 The reason *Dudley and Stephens* has remained: Michael Sandel, "Justice," Harvard University, lecture 2. https://scholar.harvard.edu/sandel/justice.

241 Lord Coleridge eloquently insisted: Queen v. Dudley and Stephens, (1884) 14 QBD 273.

242 Lord Coleridge was skeptical: Queen v. Dudley and Stephens (Murder on the High Seas) Official Record (Bound Volume), National Archives DPP 4/17, p. 175; "The Mignonette Cannibalism Case: Trial for Murder: Special Verdict," *Daily News* (London), November 7, 1884; Queen v. Dudley and Stephens, (1884) 14 QBD 273.

245 This ethical tension: John Harris, "Why Kill the Cabin Boy?," *Cambridge Quarterly of Healthcare Ethics* 30, no. 1 (January 2021): 4–9.

245 John Harris: Harris, "Why Kill," 1–6.

245 As Harris explained: Harris, "Why Kill," 1–6.

245 The policy: Harris, "Why Kill," 1–6.

246 There are many more: Charles Lane, "In Quebec, a Warning That More Euthanasia Means More Risk," *Washington Post*, September 13, 2023; Charles Lane, "How Many Botched Cases Would It Take to End Euthanasia of the Vulnerable," *Washington Post*, January 24, 2018.

246 Medical care: Carla Kotze and Johannes Lodewikus Roos, "Ageism, Human Rights and Ethical Aspects of End-of-Life Care for Older People with Serious Mental Illness," *Frontiers in Psychiatry*, July 28, 2022.

247 A classic debate: David Luban, "Liberalism, Torture and the Ticking Time Bomb," *Virginia Law Review* 91 (2005): 1425; Richard A. Posner, "Torture, Terrorism, and Interrogation," in *Torture: A Collection*, ed. Sanford Levinson (Oxford: Oxford University Press, 2004), 291–98.

248 Arguments like the lord chief justice's: "The 'Ticking Bomb' Problem," BBC Ethics Guide, https://www.bbc.co.uk/ethics/torture/ethics/tickingbomb_1.shtml.

248 The area in which *Dudley and Stephens:* Edd Gent, "Moral Dilemma of Self-Driving Cars: Which Lives to Save in a Crash," CBS News, June 24, 2016, https://www.cbsnews.com/news/moral-dilemma-of-self-driving-cars-which-lives-to-save-in-a-crash/.

249 Some ethicists argue: Dietmar Hübner and Lucie White, "Crash Algorithms for Autonomous Cars: How the Trolley Problem Can Move Us Beyond Harm Minimisation," *Ethical Theory and Moral Practice* 21 (2018): 685–98.

250 Those are some of the ways: Rousseau quoted in Donald Black, *The Behavior of Law* (Bingley, UK: Emerald Group, 2010), 12.

251 One thing that can be said about life: Cardozo, *Law and Literature*, 113.

251 And so it was with Parker: "Narratives by Brooks and Stephens: The Mignonette Tragedy: The Mate's Account of the Tragic Affair," *Cornishman* (Penzance, England), September 18, 1884.

ACKNOWLEDGMENTS

This is the first book I have written for which most of the primary sources were housed outside of the United States, and the British archivists I relied on to obtain them were of enormous help. The National Archives, which is the custodian of much of the Dudley and Stephens record, is a treasure—and very scholar-friendly. In addition to poring over its collection of court transcripts, administrative documents, and correspondence from *Queen v. Dudley and Stephens*, it was a thrill to be able to hold the original statements in which Thomas Dudley and Edwin Stephens described in their own words the wreck of the *Mignonette*, their struggle to survive—and their historic act of cannibalism.

The University of Oxford's Bodleian Libraries, which have the papers of William and Lewis Harcourt, were both beautiful places to work and welcoming ones. Their staff went above and beyond the call of duty (including shipping me back an iPad I left behind in my rush to get to the airport). The British Library was a valuable source of histories of the Victorian era, biographies of the important political figures in the book, and monographs on the legal and social background of the case.

For a late-in-life Anglophile like myself, it was a special pleasure to spend time in England tracking down some of the sites where the story unfolded. The people of Falmouth put up with my weak left-side-of-the-road driving skills and cheerfully answered my questions about the old Custom House, the Sailors' Home, and the site where the Falmouth police jail once stood.

Closer to home, the New York Public Library is an extraordinary resource for authors. When the COVID-19 pandemic struck, it put many of its resources online, including its databases of British newspapers, which allowed me to read contemporary accounts of the Dudley and Stephens saga during lockdown. The library's staff was of enormous help in tracking down obscure books and articles. The New York Public Library is a great force for democratizing information and for putting independent scholars on an even plane with those at resource-rich institutions.

I am indebted to the scholars who came before me. Four decades ago, A. W. Brian Simpson wrote a well-researched and influential book that told Dudley and Stephens's story in considerable detail—and presented them as the victims of the story. I am grateful for Professor Simpson's many insights about the case, even if I see the moral issues within it quite differently. I especially enjoyed reading the provocative work of some of the leading scholars of cannibalism. Shirley Lindenbaum's writings were particularly illuminating, and Beth Conklin's study of the Wari Indians' tenderhearted cannibalism left a deep impression on me.

As an undergraduate, I took Michael Sandel's legendary course "Justice," and his words about utilitarianism and individual rights, and many other subjects, have stayed with me throughout my life. I also want to thank Sarah Bilston, professor of English at Trinity College, for explaining to me—at a dinner party, of all places—the importance of the year 1883 to my story.

My greatest stroke of good fortune in writing *Captain's Dinner* was being taken up by the remarkable people at Authors Equity. It is exciting to be part of a brilliant and innovative group that is reimagining the publishing model for the modern age while also harking back to the best of the old days of the book world—real human connection (and even holiday parties). Endless thanks to the visionary Madeline McIntosh, who believed in this book from the beginning, the wonderful Nina von Moltke and Don Weisberg, and the whole fantastic team: David Georgi, Andrea Bachofen, Carly Gorga, Craig Young, Rose Edwards, Ilana Gold, JoliAmour Dubose-Morris, Deb Lewis, Sarah Christensen Fu, Katherine Myers, and Jenny Pouech.

I will forever be in debt to my extraordinary agent, Kris Dahl, who has guided and supported me since my first book. Her retirement is a great loss not only for me but for the publishing world. I am grateful to the legendary Sloan Harris for stepping into the void and picking up where Kris left off.

I was sustained, entertained, educated, and challenged throughout the writing of this book by dear family and friends: Noam Cohen, Aviva Michaelov, Kika Cohen, and Nuli Cohen; Elizabeth Taylor; Paul Engelmayer; Eileen Hershenov, Elisabeth Benjamin, Patti Galluzzi, and Amy Goodman; Professors Amy Chua and Jed Rubenfeld; Tina McGerald Smith; Caroline Arnold; Liz Glazer; the Fishing Trip gang: Jim Rosenthal, Antony Blinken, Eric Washburn, Michael Abramowitz, Peter Vigeland, Jacob Schlesinger, and Peter Mandelstam; the folks out east: Lally Weymouth, Lewis Liman and Lisa Liman, Larry Grafstein and Rebecca Grafstein, Nina Rosenwald, Ilyse Wilpon, and Greg and Judith Kelly; Dorothy Samuels; the Dunster House crew: Amy Schwartz, Laura Haight, Carol Owens, Mary Hennessey, Luis Silva, Terry Lohrenz, and John Capeci; the hikers: David Propp, Daniel Cunningham, Chris DeFilippi, and Stephen Grinspoon;

P.J. Posner and Michael Dubno; Maria Laurino; Kathy Bishop; Amy Gutman; Mike Miller and Sarah Paul; Dan Pool; Dorothy Samuels; Sandra Hoffen and Howard Hoffen; Emily Mandelstam; Rick Hornick and Susan Hornik; Kirk Swinehart; Claudia Dowling, Aisha Labi, Barbara Maddux, and Hope Hamashige; and Sally Blair.

And finally, to Richard Parker, who deserved so much better.

INDEX

ABOUT THE AUTHOR

ADAM COHEN is an author and lawyer. He was a member of the *New York Times* Editorial Board and a Lecturer in Law at Yale Law School. He is the author, most recently, of *Imbeciles: The Supreme Court, American Eugenics, and the Sterilization of Carrie Buck* and *Supreme Inequality: The Supreme Court's Fifty-Year Battle for a More Unjust America*. He is a graduate of Harvard Law School.

Want to dive deeper into the world of the *Mignonette*?

Subscribe to the official Substack for *The Captain's Dinner* for exclusive serialized chapters, behind-the-scenes insights, and immersive explorations of this gripping true tale of survival, cannibalism, and the legal precedent that changed history forever. Join Adam Cohen and Adrienne Westenfeld as they guide you through the dark waters of this Victorian-era tragedy and its lasting impact on how we think about morality, law, and the ultimate question: What would *you* do?

Scan to subscribe:

Or visit captainsdinner.substack.com.